Truants from Life

This book is dedicated by the editor,
with affection and esteem,
to Dr James Hemming

Truants from Life:

Theory and Therapy

Edited by
Ved P. Varma

David Fulton Publishers
London

David Fulton Publishers Ltd
2 Barbon Close, London WC1N 3JX

362.78
T865

First published in Great Britain by
David Fulton Publishers, 1991

British Library Cataloguing in Publication Data

Truants from life.
  I. Varma, Ved P. (ved Prakash), *1931–*
362.7

  ISBN 1-85346-156-3

Typeset by Chapterhouse, Formby L37 3PX
Printed and bound in Great Britain by
Biddles Ltd, Guildford and King's Lynn

Contents

PART THREE: **Treatment**

Contributors

Philip Barker	Professor of Child Psychiatry and Paediatrics Alberta Children's Hospital University of Calgary
Muriel Barrett	Educational Therapy Consultant
Michael J. Boulton	Department of Psychology University of Sheffield
Francis M.J. Dale	Principal Child Psychotherapist Child Guidance Clinic Torquay
Christopher Dare	Senior Lecturer Department of Psychiatry University of London Honorary Consultant Psychotherapist Bethlem Royal and Maudsley Hospital
Ann Drake	Bereavement Counsellor Bristol
Robin Higgins	Former Consultant Child and Family Psychiatrist Richmond-upon-Thames
David Jones	Department of Psychology Birkbeck College University of London
Sheila Melzak	Senior Child and Adolescent Psychotherapist London
Merkel Sender	Educational Therapist and Advisory Teacher Haringey, London

John Simmonds   Lecturer in Social Work
                       Goldsmiths College
                       University of London

Peter K. Smith   Department of Psychology
                       University of Sheffield

Ved P. Varma   Former Educational Psychologist
                       London

Introduction

Ved P. Varma

As is well known the aggressive children have, by definition, put up a fight in the face of their hurt, fear and uncertainty; the withdrawn have capitulated. However, there is no universally accepted definition of withdrawn children. In fact it is a descriptive term applied to children who do not thrive but fail to meet expectations of others in terms of interactions and social relationships. Their features are that they are usually uncomfortable, anxious, confused, puzzled, frightened, shy, quiet, guilty and angry. This can be due to constitutional, emotional, social, biological, developmental or familial reasons – that occur either alone or in combinations. Such children communicate by not communicating. Lesley Webb (1967) says that to the imperceptive adults they may be less of a problem as compared to their aggressive contemporaries but to the perceptive they are a frightening prospect. It is a truism, but one that bears repeating that it is at the withdrawn and quiet children that we must look very carefully indeed. If a teacher, for example, reads through records and finds she has written nothing about them for several weeks; if she remembers that they have never asked her a question; or chatted about their doings at home; if she cannot recall seeing them play with others – then they are in need of her special attention, observation, guidance and help.

Furthermore, withdrawn children tend to be ignored by busy teachers, indeed, being ignored is usually what they want, and the strategy is therefore 'successful' in its own terms. For teachers, however, information about helping such children could be particularly useful in the current climate because the National Curriculum and Assessment requirements mean that teachers will have to take notice of the withdrawn children, and will have to assess their abilities to cooperate with others, to ask questions and so on, for English and other Attainment Targets.

Despite this, and all the pains and sufferings they undergo, withdrawn children have received comparatively little attention but the recent highlight of children who are abused, as well as research into bullying suggest that they should not be ignored and the time is perhaps ripe for a study as this to be put before the public. Incidentally, it may be asked why the public has given so little attention to withdrawn children? It may be because it is too often assumed that withdrawn children are bad. It is not generally understood that the unhappy truants from life show evidence of an inability to achieve normal life and that they deserve compassion rather than neglect or condemnation.

Hence this sound, warm, penetrating and practical book. It is written by three child psychiatrists, three psychologists, two psychotherapists, a social worker, a bereavement counsellor and two specialist teachers. The result is an excellent, fascinating, authoritative and wide-ranging examination of such children at home, in school and society. It outlines – how well do we understand difficulties of such children? How can they be helped to have a more robust, adequate and mature life? This is why there are chapters on causes, assessments and treatments of withdrawal from life. Reliable and rich case histories illustrate themes where appropriate.

It is sincerely hoped that the book will be of great interest to helping and caring professionals and students of these disciplines. The reader might also like to read this competent book because it explains and illuminates some of her or his own truancy feelings!

The editor would like to thank the reader for taking the trouble to read the book. As regards my colleagues and contributors, it is impossible to express my deep debt in words – it is implied in working in partnership with them in this context.

Reference

Webb, L. (1967) *Children with Special Needs*. London, Colin Smythe Ltd.

PART ONE

Causes

CHAPTER 1

Escape to Starvation: Eating Disorders and the Withdrawn Child

Christopher Dare

From time to time an adolescent but sometimes a child of primary school age, stops eating. She[1] begins to opt out of her normal pattern of life, especially that with friends and family. Consternation overtakes the parents. Their daughter has anorexia nervosa.

Feeding and upbringing

The feeding of the new born baby, of the growing infant and young toddler has been an important preoccupation for all mothers and fathers. It is impossible to bring children into the world and to be unconcerned about their state of nutrition. Most infants and toddlers go through periods of feeding problems which will naturally alarm parents, grandparents and friends of the family. Huddled, worried conversations with friends and family and consultations with professionals spring from feeding worries about young children. By the age of four or five, however, such worries are usually over. The child reaches an established pattern of healthy, lusty eating or finicky picking at food and seemingly arbitrarily conservative faddism. The tendency to overeat or the faddiness may cause alarm, despair and mealtime confrontation, but the child's life will not be threatened. From time to time the parents will talk to each other about the child's physical progress:

> Is he too fat? Is he too thin? Is he healthy? Is he eating the right food? Is he being badly affected by some foods? Is he lacking certain foods? What about aspartamine? Should he have vitamin supplements?

3

And so on. Parents worry about food and diet as part of their primary task to maintain the healthy development of their children. Medical worries about the dangers of obesity or of the effect of certain sorts of dietary patterns will get into the media and will influence parents. Stories will go around about the dangers of food additives, caffeine in cola drinks, the effect of 'junk food' on children leading to inadequate vitamin intake and poor school performance, the risks of eggs, cheese, beef and so on, will cause rumours and worries. Even in the absence of dietary or nutritional worries, mealtimes are a focus for family tensions and dispute. This is true, when, in other ways, family life is going smoothly and comfortably. Children come home from school hungry and needing to lose the tensions of the demands of school and they take those tensions out on their parents, if present. When mother or father come in from work they too, may want to get away from the stress of their occupations. Food is the obvious comforter. The demand for attractive, comforting and reassuring food will be met by raiding the refrigerator or food cupboard or by demanding food of the parent seen as the provider. The adult will want to produce the food but will also feel that the request is an additional and perhaps terminal demand, the last straw, after a hard day. It is no wonder, therefore, that the evening meal can become a point at which family tensions are expressed. Even at weekends and holidays when work and school pressures are not bearing down upon family members quite so imminently, mealtimes require that each family member encounters everyone else. Family meals represent the time at which sharing, the nature of family rules, the precedence or otherwise given to adults or children and so on, will become literally face to face. And the provision of food at mealtimes is a focus for family life. It is no coincidence that the kitchen is the central meeting ground for family members in most households. A major part of the family budget goes on food and the process of shopping for food and preparing meals is a major drain on the adult members of the family, with or without the company, the support or interference of the non-adults.

Anorexia nervosa

Food, diet, cooking and family life are inextricably bound up. Hence the consternation when a child stops eating because of anorexia nervosa. Nine out of ten such children are female, girls or young women. As children starve themselves, they lose weight, become irritable, moody and they become withdrawn. Many children who starve themselves have been very successful schoolchildren. They tend to be hardworking, conscientious, 'model' pupils. Most will also have been friendly and sociable, interested in friends and the pursuits of children of their age. They will have been close to their mothers and fathers, usually, and involved in the wider family. They will have been known as conformers. Some children who develop anorexia nervosa will have had problems before the eating disorder began. They will have been obviously shy and uncertain in social relationships; may have been unsuccessful in school despite their persistence and commitment to the school work. They may have been known as moody and difficult children.

Such a withdrawn state preceding the development of eating disorder, is unusual.

This chapter, therefore, will be emphasising the occurrence of severe withdrawal in children, mostly girls, who heretofore have been socially and academically successful. Many will have even been outstanding academically or in physical pursuits, and above all in those activities such as gymnastics or dancing, which emphasise discipline, control, gracefulness and physical fitness and slimness. The transformation of a sociable, successful, hardworking attractive young woman into a moody gaunt, isolated, walking skeleton is horrifying. This is what happens in anorexia nervosa. How it comes about and how such young women can be helped is the subject matter of this chapter.

The anorexic condition

Anorexia nervosa has been well known in medical circles for one hundred years. It has been described, occasionally, by doctors in Britain, France and Japan as early as the 18th century. Scholars have suggested that some of the ecstatic religious states of starvation and the practice of religious asceticism may have been, occasionally, associated with anorexia nervosa. Likewise, it has been suggested, that there have been displays of human 'freaks' as 'living skeletons' in shows and fairgrounds in the 18th and 19th centuries. Whether or not these fairground 'freaks' and religious fanatics were sufferers from anorexia nervosa, will never be known. In the late 19th century doctors recognised something they realised was a psychological condition of self-imposed starvation in young women and, much more rarely in young men. The word *anorexia* means lacking in appetite, whilst the word *nervosa* refers to the apparent nervous origins of the disturbance. The name is unfortunate in that many people with anorexia nervosa do not have a suppression of appetite. They will freely admit, often, to being hungry all the time. And in any case they will make it clear that their struggle to starve is against the demand of appetite. They are not therefore suffering from a lack of appetite.

The ambiguity of the phrase 'nervosa' relates to an ambiguity in the mind of the medical profession as to the nature of anorexia nervosa. It carries the implication, on the one hand, of 'nerves' meaning psychological upset and, on the other hand, of 'nerves' as neuronal structures. Whether or not anorexia nervosa is mainly psychological or mainly physical or some interaction between the two remains a matter of dispute. German clinicians call anorexia nervosa *'pubertatig magersuch'*. *Pubertatig* means to do with adolescence and *magersuch* means the pursuit of thinness. This phrase emphasises the relentless pursuit of thinness which for many is the central feature of anorexia nervosa. For others the fear of fatness is seen as more important and is believed to derive from a distortion in perception of body shape. People with anorexia nervosa will often talk as though a minute meal that they have just taken has made them fat. They will point to their wrists or ankles or thighs or buttocks, but above all to their belly and say 'There, you can see that I am fat'.

By means of subtle psychological experiments, they can be proved to believe themselves to be larger than their actual dimensions. This apparent belief in their current or looming fatness is quite unshakeable by reasonable argument. Reduction or cessation of eating, the fear of fatness and the desire to lose weight result in a loss of weight. The body fat falls away relentlessly. The face becomes gaunt, the limbs become 'like broomsticks', the ribcage protrudes scrawnily as do the hipbones and limb joints. As 15 per cent, 20 per cent, 25 per cent of body weight is lost, the hands and feet tend to become rather blue and cold, the pulse rate drops, the eyes deep sunk and the face pale. Because they feel cold and also in order to hide their bodies which they know others will believe are horribly thin, they often wear bulky and baggy clothing. Their inadequate diet and slowed down metabolism, leads to constipation. They openly refuse to eat food. To get them to eat against their will is extremely difficult because of the enormous level of anxiety they feel about the risks of eating – the risk of fatness, the risk of feeling guilty, the risk of losing control. The right not to eat is defended with all their strength, with a fanaticism and ruthlessness so that a previously compliant and well behaved daughter becomes adept at lying, cheating, arguing, blackmail and tyranny. The parents feel weak in comparison with their child and defeated.

Most anorexic people become expert in the calorific content of different items of diet, choosing to eat very low calorie foods. To acquire this knowledge they read food labels and slimming articles and usually become expert in knowing which foods may contain nutrition and which do not. They defend their choice of diet by reference to the healthy nature of the food they eat. This is very often accompanied by an insistence on a vegetarian diet, which again is defended on health and ethical grounds. The fact that the diet they are taking is resulting in them desperately losing weight is brushed aside or denied.

As they lose weight other physical consequences ensue. The main one is the loss of secondary sexual function so that young women stop menstruating and young men lose any sexual drive. In a small proportion of cases, young women cease menstruating even before any weight loss has followed on from their initiating starvation diet.

Adolescents with severe weight loss commonly grow an unusual downy hair rather like that found on some newborn babies. This so-called 'lanugo' hair is often dark and downy, it may grow on the limbs and body or even the face. Because of the loss of body fat the nerves are nearer the surface of the body and can be injured by sitting down, for example, leading to sciatica or footdrop. Girls or boys who are still in the growth period of adolescence will stop gaining height and therefore the longer the anorexia nervosa continues the smaller they will become in relationship to people of the same age. The young anorexic, therefore, not only looks horribly thin, but often looks much younger than their age because of their low stature and their juvenile features.

The vitamin and trace element content of the diet of patients with anorexia nervosa is usually reasonable and so they do not commonly suffer from vitamin or other deficiencies. Occasionally this is not so and anorexics may develop any sort of vitamin depletion. The commonest seen are beri-beri with swollen limbs from fluid retention and wide spread neuritis and an acute brain impairment causing a form of encephalopathy. Anorexia nervosa, is therefore, a physically dangerous condition. In order to enhance the loss of weight, an adolescent who wants to stay thin may use other techniques. The commonest is to exercise vigorously and persistently. One of the most grotesque sights is to see a young person who is hideously thin forcing themselves to run long distances, to skip, to do aerobics, weight training and machine assisted exercises in order to lose weight. In addition some young people will take large amounts of laxatives to cause a purging diarrhoea which they hope will enhance weight loss.

The technique of great potential danger is the resort to vomiting in order to lose the nutritional value of the stomach contents. This technique is most commonly used by young women who find that they cannot resist the pangs of hunger that their starvation inevitably induces. This produces the condition now known as 'bulimia' (an expression made up from words of the classical Greek language meaning 'as hungry as an ox'). It is a natural, human physiological tendency to respond to the state of starvation by eating vast amounts of food. A person who is eating voraciously will explain, 'I'm starving!' and we will understand. Someone who is starving eats a lot of food and so this is what many anorexics find themselves doing. When they have eaten food they feel bloated and often have an enormous wave of panic and of guilt. This may lead them to make themselves vomit if they can. A common technique is to drink salt water or, and this is the most usual, they put their fingers down their throats. Soon, many anorexics learn to be able to vomit up the stomach contents apparently effortlessly. Although this is done to relieve overwhelming guilt feelings for having given into the impulse to eat, having vomited they feel guilty and disgusted, both at having eaten and at having thrown up. Many young people who use this technique of alternating binge eating, followed by vomiting and then a period of starvation, claim that they have to do it because their stomach has shrunk. This is illusory and untrue. It is true to say that the stomach of a starving person tends to empty much more slowly than the stomach of a non-starving person. The emptying, into the smaller bowel, leaves the stomach rather full and often causes the sensation of being bloated after a meal in the starving person. The answer is, of course, not to stop eating or to vomit, but to return to a normal regular diet. The frequent passage of the acid stomach contents over teeth causes severe dental caries. The vomiting habit causes swelling of the salivary glands just in front of and below the ears (the ones that also enlarge in mumps). The swelling is sometimes taken by the young woman to be further distressing proof of her fatness.

Most young women and men with anorexia nervosa are so able to resist pangs of hunger that they do not resort to excessive eating and vomiting. Young people who have many of the intense desires for the thinness that occurs in anorexia nervosa but who have not the capacity to resist eating can get into a particular pattern of eating. They take large amounts of food which they may try to discard by vomiting. They then starve themselves for a period of a few hours or a few days. The starvation provokes hunger which leads to a 'binge' which, in turn, leads once more to vomiting or purging themselves and subsequent food abstinence. If such a pattern produces weight loss, the habit can lead the person to be as thin as an anorexic patient. This condition, 'bulima nervosa' is generally more dangerous than a purely diet restricting anorexia. Often a person with a dietary pattern of binges and starvation has a more or less normal weight or she can even be overweight. This is called 'normal weight bulimia'. Social and psychological accompaniments and results of these bulimic states are different to those of anorexia nervosa and will not be extensively discussed in this chapter.

The starvation state, the pre-occupation with the food that goes with it, the relentless over-activity, the increasing tendency to concentrate on school work in private study, lead to the serious withdrawal of the anorexic young woman.

The causes of anorexia nervosa

The relationship between the overall clinical picture of anorexia nervosa and the withdrawal of the children and adolescents who suffer from it is both uncertain, complicated and important.

There are those who would argue that anorexia nervosa is 'caused' by a need to withdraw from adolescent development. Others argue in quite the opposite direction. They propose that the withdrawal of anorexia nervosa is secondary to the starvation which is induced by a primarily genetic physiological condition. The stage is thus set for a classical 'nature versus nurture' contest.

Those that advocate a psychological, developmental 'cause' suggest that anorexia nervosa comes about as a result of a fear of the consequences of the development of adult sexuality, potency and power to be independent. Thus it is suggested that anorexia nervosa is a result of a deep wish to 'truant from life'. The essentially adolescent nature of the condition is adduced as the main evidence for this suggestion. It is very clear how much the adolescent who develops anorexia sidesteps facing the usual demands that are a consequence of entering into adulthood. Anorexic patients are seen as coming from families that prize conformity, low levels of conflict and high levels of commitment to closeness and family life. Such a family style may seem to oppose the natural thrust of adolescent physical maturation. According to the psychological theories, both the anorexic adolescent and her family have a problem in moving through the adolescent phase of development and the anorexia nervosa serves to avoid that process. At the same time within such families there seems to be a 'claustrophobic' quality of life. Although the adolescent wants to conform with the family's ideals of closeness, freedom from conflict and the maintenance of a childlike relationship with the parents, she also wants her own personality and her own independence. In such claustrophobic families there is an intense battle for control. The parents want to control the children, the children want to control their own lives. In the conflict between submission to the family demand for conformity and the adolescent's wish for independence, anorexia nervosa is seen as a compromise. In refusing to eat, in insisting in controlling her own diet and body shape the adolescent is making her bid for independence. In being ill, physically immature and the focus for enormous parental worry and concern, she remains a child closed within the family.

Those who argue the biological nature of anorexia nervosa point out that the cessation of menstruation can occur before the starvation. This, it is suggested, indicates a pre-existing biological condition. The control of appetite and the control of secondary sex characteristics, such as menstruation, resides within that central portion of the brain, the hypo-thalamus and the adjacent endocrine gland, the pituitary body. People and animals with a lesion in this part of the central nervous and endocrine systems occasionally develop abnormalities of body weight, appetite and sexuality. Close examination of people who are made to starve either involuntarily in prison camps for example, or voluntarily in hunger strikes or as paid experimental subjects, shows that there are many psychological consequences of food deprivation. As people cease to eat and lose weight they become irritable, moody, food pre-occupied and fanatically interested in diet. They eat their food very slowly, taking minute mouthfuls, exactly like an anorexic patient. Those who argue for a physiological cause for anorexia nervosa point out that volunteers who starve themselves have emotional changes and interests in food and diet eating patterns so similar to an anorexic patient as to suggest that many of the phenomena of anorexia nervosa are the *consequence* of starvation not the cause of it. It is also true to say that sometimes a person who has to starve, for whatever reason, will find themselves developing an 'addiction' to starving, gaining pleasure from denying themselves food and losing weight and feeling guilty if they eat, hating the sense of being bloated and looking forward to being able to shed the weight by starvation. This condition *is* anorexia nervosa, for all intents and purposes, except that it can be made to disappear by the easy enforcement of a regular dietary pattern. The anorexia does not return in these cases.

A somewhat similar source for anorexia nervosa also occurs in children with an organic bowel disease that puts them off food by, for example, causing pain in the stomach after eating. Such children occasionally go on to develop anorexia, although in these cases, also, the anorexic state is not so persistently and ruthlessly adhered to, nor for so long.

For those that propose a physical cause for anorexia nervosa, the genetic distribution of anorexia nervosa within families is conclusive proof. It has been demonstrated that in identical twins, where one has got anorexia nervosa the chances of the other suffering likewise are between 40 per cent and 60 per cent. For non-identical twins, the likelihood of another twin having anorexia where one already suffers is in the region of 2 per cent to 3 per cent.

There are others who argue that it is inadequate to describe anorexia nervosa as caused by either psychological, family processes or physiological malfunctions. In proposing a social or cultural theory a number of facts are emphasised. First, anorexia nervosa, if it were physiological or psychological, need not be so much the perquisite of feminity. Second, anorexia nervosa should be much more uniformly spread throughout the world. In fact, it seems possible that anorexia nervosa is predominantly a disturbance of Western industrialised countries. Moreover, it has been much more common amongst middle and professional classes than amongst working class young women and men. There are suggestions that anorexia nervosa has become much more common over the last three or four decades and that in becoming more common it has spread throughout the classes in Western countries and is beginning to spread to non-Western nations, such as Japan. It is unusual in Hong Kong and Singapore, industrialised Asian nations, and is very rare in the Indian sub-continent or in mainland China.

Social cultural theorists propose that anorexia nervosa is a disturbance characteristic of societies that have certain attitudes towards femininity, women's body shape and the process of growing up. These theorists point out that anorexia nervosa seems to occur most often amongst people who are trying to get thin, either because they live in a culture within which women are expected to be slim and boyish in shape, or because they are members of training groups, especially ballet dancers, who are expected to be thin for professional reasons. It can be shown that in most Western societies, as children enter puberty the girls become pre-occupied with the fear of being too fat. They begin to think about dieting and do indeed restrict their food intake. Boys are rarely so affected. The admired physique for boys is one of a fully grown, tall, muscular perhaps even massive body. Extensive body hair, the need to shave and well developed genitals complete the image, even though the latter may not commonly be expressed. This is the image of a fully grown, mature adult with very obvious secondary sex changes. For girls and women, the admired physique is petite, slim, with only slight buttocks and thigh curves, slender waist and firm, not droopy breasts. Body hair should be confined to a small area around the genital and is largely untolerated in all the other places that seems to be normal in caucasian women, namely in the armpits, legs, around the nipples and quite often on the upper lip. The admired image is not of a grown woman but of a girl quite early during puberty. The social conditioning whereby girls try to avoid the normal growth of puberty becomes so intense that by the time children are sixteen or seventeen most girls are slimming or have just stopped slimming or intend to slim, whilst boys are no so affected except in some families that have very strong views and habits in the pursuit of healthy bodies and diet. Even in such families teenage boys are much more resistant to the family culture of healthy living, than are the girls.

There is another striking social phenomenon. It is clear that whilst the general level of nutrition has tended to increase the predicted body size and weight of both men and women the ideals of feminine shape have moved towards slimness and a striking absence of bulk in breasts, bottom and thighs. For most women the pursuit of the ideals of the fashion magazine and modelling world, required that they eat much less than their physiology might require of them. To maintain a body outline at which *for purely social and cultural reasons* they feel attractive and good about themselves, women must be conscious of what they are eating and food's possible effect on their figure, *all the time*. They must acquire a long term *dieting mentality*. Superficially it might be supposed that women live in a dieting mentality to enhance their sexual attractiveness to men, and this is in part true, but it is also obvious that the need is deep ingrained. Women report that they need to be slim to look good to their female friends and relatives but also to feel right about themselves. Time and again a woman will say:

> I feel awful. I must really lose some weight. I can't go on holiday, to my sister's wedding, to the job interview, on the course at university, to keep fit classes, looking like this! I'm pounds too heavy. When I'm like this I feel ashamed. I would hate myself if I were to gain even more weight.

Feminist writers have pointed out that there is special quality given to the power relationship between men and women if the ideal image of a woman is girlish whilst that for a man is of physical adulthood. It is not true to say, however, that in cultures where women are expected to have the full curves and body hair of physiological adulthood, that they are accorded equal social and economic parity with men. It is really quite unclear why the physical stereotypes for womanhood in modern post-industrial culture resemble biological immaturity.

Given the plausibility and yet the contradictory nature of all these observations, the best way to understand anorexia nervosa is probably to assume that there are physiological, psychological, familial, cultural and social processes taking a hand in the development of the condition. It seems likely that anorexia nervosa will only occur when people actually begin to diet and especially when they get into a dieting mentality. The dieting is usually determined by a child believing themselves to be fat and that comes from either having been told they are fat or from the fact that they live with a family or with peers who are pre-occupied with body weight and are always talking of the need to slim. For the cultural reasons outlined above, young women are likely to see themselves to be in need of losing weight. As a young woman tries to lose weight for whatever reason, she has to confront her capacity to cope with food deprivation. Some people are very good at dieting but most people are very bad. Most young women find they cannot resist their appetite. They are not able to develop anorexia nervosa. Some young women find that they have a real capacity to starve and find they lose weight. This gives them an especial kudos, initially, in the eyes of their peers, but above all in themselves. They gain an enormous sense of satisfaction and achievement from the ability to withstand the pangs of hunger. They may even get a sense of elation in their slimming achievement. This elation has been compared to the thrill that committed joggers and other exercisers gain. As the person finds that she can lose weight and gets her pleasure and sense of achievement from so doing she puts herself into a state of chronic starvation within which she finds herself thinking all the time about food. This makes her believe that she is a dangerously greedy and starving person and leads her to redouble her efforts not to eat. In the more chronic starving state, mood disturbance, irritability and a lack of social motivation develops. The periods cease. For some young women the withdrawal into a preoccupation with food and diet, the absence of sexual desire, and the low level of social motivation is a secondary benefit. It is indeed true that some young women are confused about what is expected of them because of the ambiguities in social expectations of women. There is a double demand on the one hand to be sexually pre-occupied, interested in men and to see themselves as developing with an aim to achieve the state of wifehood and motherhood. Such a patriarchally determined stereotype is opposed by other processes which say that women should be modest, virtuous, non-sexual. This is also a patriarchal imposition. In addition, there are increasing realisations that women should not accept the patriarchally derived stereotypes and should seek their own identities and pursue a line of development designed to give them a full and equal place in society and not to be identity bound to their relationship with men and the world of man. The confusion and conflict implicit in these three different ideals may make it easy for women to wish to withdraw altogether into the achievement of the chronic starvation state.

It is also true to say that any families that have functioned extremely well with the school age children may fear the impact of teenagers on family life and may feel very uncertain about coping with adolescence. The demand for autonomy, independence and resources, that adolescents make it disruptive to a pattern of family life that has been designed for the care, protection, nourishment and enhancement of younger children. Some families may not only be slow to adapt to the needs of adolescence but may positively resist the change. A family that sees itself as very 'child orientated' may be uncertain as to its future function when children have become grown-up and separate. For such a family adolescence threatens an established, comfortable and rewarding pattern of life. It highlights the question as to what will be the nature of the family life and above all of the marital relationship after the children have grown up. Many parents who have dedicated themselves to the children have, to some extent, neglected the development of their own careers, especially if they are women, and have failed to maintain a line of special relationship between the parents as man and wife.

It is arguable that such families are in a certain sense 'helped' by the withdrawal of a daughter into anorexia, because the need to be concerned with her state of mind keeps the parents in a parent-orientation rather than a spouse and self orientation. There is a widespread clinical impression that the families of an anorexic child have some distinguishing features when compared with families that have a child with another sort of psychiatric problem, such as depression, psychosis or behaviour difficulties. Those clinicians who identify consistent family traits around an anorexic patient identify four characteristics; first the families seem to be extraordinarily, emotionally bound up with each other. They are very sensitive to each others feelings and often assume that they know what each other feel. Such families often act as though there is no clear boundary between the lives of the children and those of the adult members of the family. Second, going along with this great emotional sensitivity there is said to be an overprotectiveness – of the children by the parents, of the parents by the children and also between the children. It is not clear how much protectiveness is appropriate for parents with a daughter who is starving herself nearly to death. The idea of over-protectiveness, therefore is dangerous as it implies that the parents are, in some way, to blame for their daughter's withdrawal into starvation. The protectiveness between parents is less striking and indeed there is a tendency for a parent to take sides with a child against the other parent in these families. Third, the families are described as rigid, being both unusually loyal to family traditions, about gender roles, for example, but also rigid in the application of their own rules of family life. The rigidity is thought to be implicated in the therapeutic resistiveness to change, ascribed to the families. Fourth, the families are said to show a problem of resolving conflicts. Leading them, mostly, to abjure conflict between family members.

Anorexia and withdrawal

In the clinical picture that has been built up so far it has been emphasised that the anorexic child becomes withdrawn as the eating disorder takes over her life. Acknowledgement has been made of young people for whom social interaction has been painful and difficult *before* the onset of anorexia nervosa. For many clinicians and for many afflicted families it is not at all obvious that the withdrawal derives from the eating disorder. It may seem more logical to believe that the eating problem ensues from the pre-existing personal relationship difficulties. Very often, an anxious mother or father will propose that a re-feeding programme should not be given to the daughter until 'She's sorted herself out!' This may be suggested in the hope that the family can be relieved of the distress that refeeding causes their daughter with the accompanying protests, anguish and despair in her and other family members. But it may also be based upon a belief in the primarily psychological nature of the feeding problem. The viewpoint of this chapter is that the relationship between the withdrawal and the eating problem should be seen as complicated.

Any young woman might be expected to have complicated and not necessarily entirely enthusiastic reactions to evidence in her own body and in the responses of other people to her, that indicate that she is about to become adolescent. She will be alerted by the advent of breast changes, of axillary and genital hair, by the increase in hip size and the subjective sense, however vague, of sexual arousal. The first period is the most dramatic of the signals. Other people may tell her of these things, as they happen, or may warn her, tease her, or praise her, in anticipation of these events. It is not surprising that many young women, even those who most welcome and enjoy the signs of their incipient womanhood, also have some fear of the new territory to which their biological development leads them. Any pubescent woman, therefore, may wish sometimes, to slow down or inhibit her sexual maturation. There may be less uncertainty and more unalloyed pleasure for young men making this transition as society seems to give less ambiguous messages to young men about the desirability of growing up. Independent mindedness, self-sufficiency, an apparent ability to manage the world of adults with confidence are all welcomed, as a rule, in adolescent boys. Independence of action, opinion and survivability are even in the present changing climate, more likely, in young women, to create anxiety in her family and school teachers. Just as a quite normal teenage woman may have anxieties about her pubertal changes, so might her family have some regrets not only about the loss of 'their little girl' but also about the change of relationships and roles that that change implies for the parents and their lives. There is no reason to believe that the uncertainties and reluctance to change *cause* anorexia nervosa, although it is possible that they do. It is quite possible that once anorexia begins, for whatever reason, these things may make it in some way, welcome. The withdrawal of the patient may be accompanied by a withdrawal from the next stage of life in her parents. The siblings of an anorexic woman, may sense the family anxiety about the future. They may think that leaving home is abandoning their parents to a boring life. They may have an unvoiced sense of relief that at least the parents will have Sarah, Emma or Lucy, or whatever the anorexic daughter is called, to look after and keep them from complaining of the other children's absence.

The management of anorexia nervosa

It is extremely important to keep an open mind as to the causes and nature of anorexia nervosa. There are no simple treatments for the condition. Those who propose psychological causes tend also to espouse psychological treatments, those who propose physiological causes tend to think in terms of pharmacological treatments; those who envisage familial origins might be thought to propose family treatments. So far there is very little evidence that pyschological or physiological treatments are much help in anorexia nervosa in adolescence. On the other hand, some forms of family therapy have been shown to be extremely effective. There are no clear forms of social or cultural interventions that have so far been suggested. However, the fact that family therapy has been shown to be effective whilst other forms of therapy have not, need not be taken as evidence of any family etiology for anorexia nervosa. It simply means that a family intervention is the most successful way so far identified of breaking into the cycle of factors which give rise to the chronic anorexic state. However the nature of successful family therapy is useful in considering the management of the condition by other professionals who come in contact with the young sufferers.

In order to describe the family management of anorexia nervosa a particular family will be described.

Case description

Anna was the eldest of three daughters. At the age of twelve she was hard working, not academic, but able and successful in school, full of her friends and their interests in pop music, 'Neighbours' and fashion. She shared their giggles about the dishy men of the music and television world but she did not share their excitement when a young man took notice. She could not share their thrill at being 'chatted up'. She said that she was not interested 'in that sort of thing'. She had an idea that sex was central to the break up of her parents' marriage. This had happened three years before. Her father she saw as a stout, harassed and quick tempered man. He was a Scotsman and they lived in this large and industrial home town. Nearby, lived his widowed mother and his youngest sister. Anna had become her father's favourite after the birth of her four and a half years younger sister Monica. The closeness was cemented when, two years later, Margareta was born. Anna's mother had been born to her parents in Naples, had lived there until she was ten and to this day spoke her Scots with an Italian accent. Her parents (Anna's maternal grandparents) worked, initially in a cafe, and had then tried their hand at ice cream vending. This failed and Anna's maternal grandfather had ended his working life in a factory whilst her grandmother cleaned at the cafe the two had struggled to profit from. Despite their lack of the wealth that they had hoped to find in Scotland, Anna's maternal grandparents returned to Naples to live and Anna's mother took her daughters with pride to Italy every year.

After Margareta was born, Anna realised that her mother and father were always quarrelling. He became moody, angry even with Anna, kept promising to do things with her which never happened and complained about his work as a foreman for the City Bus Company. The fun of family outgoings stopped. Monica and Margareta and mother semed to Anna to be close, giggling together in Italian. They did not seem to miss father. One day when Anna returned home from school there was a strange man in the kitchen. Margareta, just walking, was holding on to his knees. Monica was laughing at something he had just finished saying and mother was looking with a loving happy look at him. The look flashed from her face as Anna came in. Anna knew at once that the four in the kitchen were very familiar with each other. She felt angry and terrified. She ran to the bedroom she shared with Monica and her mother followed. Through her tears, without further conversation, she asked her mother what would happen to daddy. Her mother said that he stopped caring years ago. He had wanted her to get rid of Margareta. He was more with his mother than with her. Let his sister wash his dirty pants and mend his smelly socks.

That night Anna's mother and father had the noisiest and most prolonged row that she had heard. Her father packed his things and went to his mother. The next morning Anna asked her mother if she could live with her Nan and her mother said that it was up to her. But Anna had never felt close to her Nan and when she went there after school, her father was still at work and her Nan rather bluntly told her that a girl's place was with her mother. Anna had thought that that was illogical, given that her father had gone to his mother. Mother's new man, Brian, was an Englishman, a skilled computer technician on a contract from his firm in a satellite town north of London.

He did not move in with mother and the girls, but returned to the south, sold his bachelor apartment and bought a house near his firm. Mother and the girls moved there six months later. In the intervening time Anna had seen her father grow more miserable, angry and fat. She had tried to persuade him to let her live with him but it seemed that Nan had again vetoed it.

One day Anna's periods started. She was shocked. She had been intrigued and excited when in the previous year other girls had began. To her surprise she was disgusted by the blood, by having to deal with her genital and by the thought that now she could have sexual intercourse. In her mind, it seemed, menstruating, being able to make love and actually having sex happened one after the other. Brian, on a weekend visit heard her news and said 'And you've got a pretty little b.t.m. as well'. Anna was desperate. Now she was going to do what mother and Brian did and it would hurt her father just like they had hurt him. That evening she threw her helping of spaghetti into the rubbish bin. Her mother excused her on the grounds that she was upset by her period. Over the weeks and months as Anna threw more and more of her meal away, she began to lose weight 'like a greyhound training for the Derby'. Mother ran out of explanations.

Anna's first period was her last for three years. She felt both glad, virtuous and somehow faithful to her father in the loss. She became even more scornful of her friends interest in boys and even more sure that she would never have sex, would certainly not have babies. She was determined to concentrate on school work so that she could leave home and become independent as soon as possible. She took less interest in her friends who found her moody, a swat, not funny like she had been. They were initially very impressed by and envious of her ability to eat no lunch and to lose weight. At first they admired her slimness but soon they became frightened by her compulsion to slim, by her constant talk about food, calories, diets and the dangers of eating. They felt she had become a 'bit of a ween (baby)' and were mostly relieved when she moved to Brian's home counties town. There she entered the English comprehensive system, found that her Scottish education gave her an advantage over her new companions. She made few friends and told only two girls about her dieting. They promptly shared the gossip with their friends and a young teacher and Anna became furious withdrawing even more into work and food pre-occupation.

With one part of her mind she thought that she was mad. She felt it was crazy to think about food all the time, planning how long it would be before she would eat, visualising the mound of food on her plate, worrying about how many grammes she would have gained, when she next got on the biology weighing machine and planning how to lose what she had had for breakfast by jogging around the playground at lunch time. Sometimes she would decide to stop thinking about food and concentrate on work, ignoring how much she ate and how much she weighed. However much she counselled herself to stop it, in a few minutes she would find herself again obsessing about what she had eaten four hours before, wondering when she had burned it off and could have another few mouthfuls with no chance of gaining weight. She was very troubled by her dreams, always about food, of gargantuan feasts, cannibalism, animals tearing meat from a carcase, of herself as a huge fat chef in a posh restaurant. She was really upset by the rows with her mother and with Brian, although she did not mind so much making him uncomfortable. She had become even more intolerant of her mother and Brian showing physical affection. She was especially horrified when she imagined that she heard them softly talking to each other in their bedroom late at night. She had disgusted fleeting thoughts of them making love in unmentionable postures and pleasures. She was fascinated but shocked by her own interest. Every time she thought of them making love she would renew her pledge to herself to lose more weight.

She had occasional telephone conversations with her father and visited him at half term. He had promised her mother that *he* could make her eat; would not put up with her dieting nonsense. Anyway he had always been closer to her than her mother. When she was with him, and her two sisters had not come with her, she loved it but could hear herself being horrible to him, flouncing out if he wanted to talk confidingly to her of his anger with her mother and his loneliness. She had imagined that they would enjoy her holiday together but she was snappy and rude, moody and difficult and lost more weight in a week whilst with him than she had in two weeks at home. Back with her mother and Brian things went from bad to worse. She ate so little, exercised so much, devoted so much time to her school work that life was murder. At school she was now seen as an oddball. The other pupils knew something about anorexia and were in no doubt that Anna was starving herself. They were frightened and repelled, sympathetically wishing they could help her but baffled.

When she was fully established in her family's and general doctor's mind as a case of anorexia nervosa she was sent to a psychiatrist. He saw her with her mother and step-father and, later, with her father. Talking to both sets of parents about the need to wrest control of her diet back to themselves, in a loving and sympathetic way, took many sessions. Fortunately the mother and step-father were both loving and determined and, in the end succeeded. Anna herself fought her parents and the psychiatrist all the way. This was no bad thing because it enabled her to come out of her starving state with a sense of her own powerfulness and self control increased. She returned to life!

Further reading

Chernin, K. (1985) *The Hungry Self: Women, Eating and Identity*. New York, Random House.

Garfinkel, P. E. and Garner, D. M. (1982) (eds) *Anorexia Nervosa: A Multi-dimensional Perspective*. New York, Brunner/Mazel.

Sours, J. A. (1980) *Starving to Death in a Sea of Objects*. New York, Jason Aronson.

Note

[1] Nine out of ten people with anorexia nervosa are female. To avoid the clumsy use of boy/girl and his/her, the chapter will assume that the truant from life is a young woman.

CHAPTER 2

Bullying and Withdrawn Children

Michael J. Boulton and Peter K. Smith

Two of the most distressing aspects of peer relationship problems during childhood are victimisation and social withdrawal. The factors related to the causes and consequences of these difficulties have been examined in two more or less separate research traditions. In this chapter we shall look at what research has revealed about bully–victim problems, and about social withdrawal, and, using evidence from our own research and elsewhere, attempt to examine how they might be inter-related, and how armed with this knowledge we may place ourselves in a better position to help those children who are involved.

Bully–victim problems

Bullying has been defined in a variety of ways by different people. However, two of the most important points about bullying that are widely recognised are that it must occur repeatedly to some extent and that it does not necessarily have to involve physical acts. In our own recent surveys of the incidence of bullying (Ahmad *et al.*, 1991; Ahmad and Smith, 1990; Boulton *et al.*, 1991) we have used the following definition which satisfies these and other criteria:

> We say a child/young person is being bullied, or picked on, when another child/young person, or a group of children/young people, say nasty and unpleasant things to him or her. It is also bullying when a child/young person is hit, kicked, threatened, locked inside a room, sent nasty notes, when no one ever talks to them and things like that. These things can happen frequently and it is difficult for the child/young person being bullied to defend himself or herself. It is also

bullying when a child/young person is teased repeatedly in a nasty way. But it is not bullying when two children/young people of about the same strength have the odd fight or quarrel.

This definition is based on the work of Olweus (1978, 1989), with minor modifications, mainly introducing 'sent nasty notes' and 'no one ever talks to them' as additional examples of the less physical, more psychological kinds of bullying, which we have found to be more common in girls. When using the definition in questionnaire surveys, we use the term 'child' in junior/middle schools, and 'young person' in secondary schools.

Over the last decade and a half, researchers working in various countries have shown that bullying problems are extensive during middle childhood and early adolescence. Most of this work has been carried out within or about schools, probably because it is in this environment of high densities of young people that bullying is likely to occur. In a very large scale study, Olweus (1978, 1989) devised a self-report questionnaire which was administered to over 140,000 Norwegian students aged between eight and sixteen years. About 9 per cent reported being bullied, and about 7 per cent reported bullying others, 'now and then' or more frequently. Other researchers working outside of Scandinavia have employed versions of Olweus's questionnaire with equally or even more disturbing results (Smith, 1991). The lowest figures are from Scotland, where Mellor (1990) found 6 per cent of reported victims and 4 per cent of bullies in a sample of secondary school children. But in Ireland, O'Moore and Hillery (1989) found that out of nearly 800 seven- to thirteen-year-old Dublin school children, about 10 per cent reported being involved in 'serious' bullying (once a week or more frequently), either as aggressors or as victims. We have now carried out a number of surveys in England. In one study, involving six classes of eight- and nine-year-olds and six classes of eleven- and twelve-year-olds attending three middle schools, we found that about 21 per cent of the children reported being bullied and about 17 per cent reported bullying others 'sometimes' or more often in the previous school term (Boulton et al., 1991). A study of secondary schools found 22 per cent of reported victims and 12 per cent of bullies, using the 'now and then' criterion (Yates and Smith, 1989). A survey we are just completing of some 7,000 pupils in 24 junior, middle and secondary schools in South Yorkshire shows that while there are variations between schools, the figures just quoted are not unrepresentative (Ahmad et al., 1991, and in preparation).

As an alternative to a questionnaire approach, we have also asked children to nominate those classmates who were bullies and those who were victims, providing them with the definition of bullying given above. This gives a slightly different metric and perspective on the problem. In one study, we used this method in six middle school classes with children aged eight and nine years. The proportion of boys and girls that were nominated as bullies or as victims by various percentages of peers are shown in Table 2.1. Thus, whichever method of assessment we use, we can be left in no doubt that bully–victim problems are widespread.

Table 2.1 Percentage of boys and girls that were nominated as bullies and as victims

| | Percentage of peers | | | |
	25%	33%	40%	50%
Bully				
Boys (n = 83)	57.8	53.0	43.4	30.1
Girls (n = 75)	10.7	5.3	1.3	1.3
Both (n = 158)	35.4	30.4	23.4	16.5
Victim				
Boys (n = 83)	30.1	20.5	8.4	4.8
Girls (n = 75)	37.3	22.7	12.0	2.7
Both (n = 158)	33.5	21.5	10.1	3.8

A common finding from studies of bullying is that boys are more likely than girls to be perpetrators, whereas the two sexes are about equally likely to be on the receiving end (see also Table 2.1). This may be explained in several different ways, for example in terms of the relative strength of girls and boys. Boys are generally stronger than girls and so girls may have less opportunity to bully other people. Alternatively, the way boys and girls are socialised may be important – physical aggression may be tolerated to a greater extent in boys than in girls, with greater sanctions being applied to girls who perform this type of behaviour. Both of these suggestions are consistent with our finding that whereas most boys reported being bullied by male peers only, girls generally indicated that they were picked on by children of either sex.

Other evidence suggests that the actual forms of bullying experienced by the two sexes may differ. A common finding is that girls are more likely to resort to verbal and 'psychological' types of bullying, such as excluding an individual from their activities and spreading unpleasant rumours, whereas boys more often use physically aggressive acts (Lagerspetz *et al.*, 1982; Lowenstein, 1978; Perry *et al.*, 1988; Ahmad *et al.*, 1991). However these findings are of general trends; we have come across cases of girls resorting to physical bullying, as well as of boys using subtle psychological tactics.

Research has also indicated that it is important to distinguish between different types of victim. Olweus (1978) reported that whereas most victims were 'passive', a smaller sub-group could also be considered 'provocative'. The former may be anxious and insecure, but do nothing to actively 'invite' attacks. The latter on the other hand may be characterised as having a 'short fuse', and seem to deliberately do things they know will irritate and tease others, often with the apparent aim of provoking a hostile response. In our experience, many children act in this way at some time or another: for example a group of boys may disrupt a game of skipping being played by their female peers, and a group of girls may embarrass a boy in front of his friends by saying he 'fancies' one of the girls. However, for a small number of individuals, this pattern of interaction may become typical of their dealings with their peers.

It also seems that another sub-group of children exists, those who are bullies with some of their peers but victims at the hands of others (Stephenson and Smith, 1989). This type of individual may be more common than was first thought – in our recent work with middle school children we have found 'bully/victims' to be more common than either 'bullies' or 'victims' separately, when assessed by peer nominations. This may reflect the generally high level of teasing and harassment which may go on in these groups, where the children are from ethnically mixed backgrounds and somewhat disadvantaged circumstances. Thus, many children may be seen by others as being involved in both sides of bullying incidents.

Relatively few researchers have examined the stability of a child's propensity to bully peers or be bullied by them, but the available evidence suggests at least a fair degree of stability in both cases. In Norway, Olweus (1978) found that many children who were classified as bullies and victims at thirteen years could be similarly classified some three years later, even despite a change in classes, teachers and/or schools. In our study involving eight- and nine-year-olds (Boulton and Smith, 1991), we examined stability in these areas across four assessment periods that were roughly equally spaced between the beginning of one school year and the start of the next. For both children identified as bullies, and as victims, by a third or more of their peers, there was evidence for a high degree of stability. At present, we are collecting and analysing more peer nomination data on a sample of children that were first assessed for bully/victim status about two and a half years ago when they were aged eight to ten years. These seem to support the hypothesis that a child's status as a bully or as a victim is fairly stable through middle childhood and adolescence.

Being consistently victimised at school may be prognostic of longer term problems, just as being consistently involved in bullying may be (Olweus, 1989; Smith, 1991). Whereas children who bully others may later get in trouble with violent and law-breaking behaviour, children who are persistently victimised may experience later problems with self-esteem and with forming stable and trusting relationships. Whether or not the experience of being bullied is a primary cause of these difficulties, it is certainly doing nothing to help a child or young person escape from this kind of developmental pathway. In extreme cases, being persistently bullied has clearly been a major factor on some tragic cases of child suicide.

Social withdrawal

Social withdrawal is one of a number of possibly problematic aspects of peer relationships. On the whole, peer relation problems have been examined in a separate research tradition from that of the investigations on bullying we have just described. Much of the research has been done in North America, and most has focused on varieties of sociometric measurements of children's friendships; or else self-assessments (or sometimes peer or teacher ratings) of loneliness, or aggressiveness, or low self-esteem. For recent surveys, see Berndt and Ladd (1989), and Asher and Coie (1990).

Parker and Asher (1987) have reviewed what is known about the long term consequences of three types of peer relation problems: low peer acceptance, or rejection; high aggressiveness; and shyness/withdrawal. Of these, the last was represented by the fewest studies and the least conclusive results. While some individual studies found links from shyness/withdrawal to early dropping out of school, and also to indicators of adult psychopathology, sufficient other studies found null results to suggest that clear conclusions cannot yet be drawn.

Part of the uncertainty here may lie with difficulties in defining and measuring withdrawal. Those individuals who experience relatively few contacts with peers have not, until relatively recently, been the focus of systematic research and concern. Moreover, as Rubin et al. pointed out, the existing literature on social withdrawal 'presents a mixed-bag of approaches, foci, and conclusions' (Rubin et al., 1989: 238), and that 'clearly, the study of social withdrawal in childhood is fraught with conceptual confusion, methodological difficulties, and inappropriate conclusions' (1989: 240). Rubin et al. noted that many different terms – behavioural inhibition, social reticence, shyness, social isolation, sociometric neglect and sociometric rejection – have often been applied as if they were interchangeable.

In this research tradition, children have usually been distinguished by sociometric procedures which involve asking children to nominate liked most and liked least classmates (Coie et al., 1982), or more recently, to rate each classmate in terms of how much they like them. Based on the patterns of nominations (or ratings), each child is placed in one of six sociometric status groups – popular, average, rejected, neglected, controversial and other. This approach is useful because it draws attention to the fact that different types of unpopular children may exist. While both rejected and neglected groups are liked by few if any peers, the former are actively disliked by many group members whereas the latter are not.

Children identified as sociometrically neglected may overlap to a considerable extent with those who have been identified by other procedures as socially withdrawn. However, Dygdon and Conger found that the overlap was limited. They used two more direct measures of social withdrawal. One was peer nominations of 'someone to whom your classmates don't pay very much attention' (Dygdon and Conger, 1990). The other was direct observation of being alone, and inattentive to peers, in small play groups. These measures had only partial overlap with 'neglect' based on few peer nominations of either liking or disliking. Rubin et al. (1989) also question the equation of social withdrawal and neglect; some withdrawn children may be rejected, for example, with many 'dislike' nominations.

Thus, as researchers have examined social withdrawal more closely, it has become apparent that it is a complex phenomenon, and that there are different types of social withdrawal. There seems to be a distinction between withdrawn children who are ignored, and withdrawn children who are actively disliked. Rubin and Mills differentiate between two varieties of socially withdrawn children, 'the quiet passive and, yet, constructive youngster whose isolation from the peer group reflects social anxiety and negative self-perceptions of social competence and the rambunctious, immature solitary player whose isolation reflects impulsivity and aggressiveness' (Rubin and Mills, 1988: 921).

Evidence concerning the stability of social withdrawal is mixed, and appears to depend on what index is employed and what ages are examined. Rubin et al. (1989) found little evidence of stability of overall observed social withdrawal from kindergarten, and only modest stability (r = 0.37) from grade 2 (seven years), when reassessed at grades 4 and 5 (nine to ten years). When they used peer assessments, higher stability correlations were obtained for this same period (r = 0.64); however the stability of peer nominations of withdrawal prior to the third grade in the US (about eight years) remains weak in some other studies (Moskowitz et al., 1985). This mixed evidence may be because children's actual conceptualisation of social withdrawal is a developmental phenomenon, and that prior to grades 4 and 5 they may lack a cohesive mental representation of what it actually is (Younger et al., 1985).

Bullying and social withdrawal/neglect by peers

As we have seen, research is advancing our understanding of the complex problems of bullying and social withdrawal, but what do we know of the relation between these two phenomena? Unfortunately the answer must be, not very much at the present time. In considering this issue, it is necessary to keep in mind the different subgroups of victims and socially withdrawn children that we have drawn attention to above.

Popularity

Several studies have shown that bullies may enjoy at least average levels of popularity within the peer group, but that victims tend to be unpopular (Lagerspetz et al., 1982). However, given that there are different types of low peer status, notably rejection and neglect, we set out to look at the patterns of association between children's sociometric and bully/victim status. In a sample of 158 middle school children (Boulton and Smith, 1991), we found that of the six sociometric status types identified by Coie et al. (1982), rejected and neglected children received the most 'victim' nominations from peers (on average they were nominated as such by more than 25 per cent of classmates); popular children received the least (at 15 per cent; although the difference was not statistically significant). Although children identified as sociometrically rejected or neglected should not be seen as identical to those who are socially withdrawn, these two sociometric status categories together are likely to overlap with many of them.

Several interesting and potentially important findings have come out of the research on the relationship between children's popularity with peers and their participation in aggression. In particular, there is not a linear inverse relationship between these two variables, rather it appears that aggression in some circumstances is *positively* correlated with popularity. For example, aggression in response to provocations, and to aggression from peers, has been shown to be positively correlated with acceptance by peers (Coie *et al.*, 1982; Lesser, 1959).

How might this help us consider the relationship between bully/victim problems and social withdrawal? Olweus (1987) has reported that the typical response of many victims to being bullied, is crying and submission. Similarly, research by Rubin and his colleagues suggests that withdrawn children also show inappropriate/ineffective behaviour in some of their peer interactions. In kindergarten and grade 2, they found that social withdrawal was concurrently associated with submissiveness with peers (Rubin and Borwick, 1984), an inability to successfully handle interpersonal dilemmas (Rubin and Krasnor, 1986), and high levels of anxiety and fearfulness (Rubin and Clark, 1983). Children who perceive themselves as being of low status, are also less likely to use successful strategies of group entry – finding successful ways of joining a new group, such as making appropriate and helpful comments – and are more likely to hover on the edge of the group (shy, withdrawn children) or barge in or try to dominate the activity, inappropriately (provocative children) (Putallaz and Wasserman, 1990).

Such a pattern of responding (especially in boys) may be viewed negatively by other children, and it could be one reason why they avoid selecting victims as friends, and why some/many victims have rejected or neglected socio-metric status. This social isolation, if it occurs in this way, is not voluntary but is under peer control; but it could then precipitate more 'voluntary' or at least self-initiated and self-maintained social withdrawal on the part of the victim. At present, we are examining this possibility by means of presenting social vignettes to children previously identified as bullies, victims and not-involved controls. The vignettes differ in the response made by one of the target children to being bullied, such as hitting back, telling a teacher or crying, and the dependent variables are how effective our subjects think each response will be in deterring the bully then and in the future, and how much they like the victim for responding as they did. In a similar way, we are examining how much the three groups like other children who do/do not show various types of bullying behaviours.

Of course it is possible, even likely, that different children will respond in different ways to being bullied by peers, and that this may depend on many different factors, such as the individual's disposition towards behaving aggressively, and on the relatively simple fact of just who is 'available' in the peer group. The weakest/youngest children that are victims may have no one available to pick on even should they be disposed to do so, and hence social withdrawal may be a more viable course of action in response to their being bullied. However, where weaker peers are available, these may become the 'new' targets for the children who were bullied to begin with. We noted above that bully/victims may constitute an appreciable proportion of some groups of children, and this subgroup may overlap to some extent with a subgroup of aggressive/withdrawn children identified in the sociometric literature (Milich and Landau, 1984; Schwartzman *et al.*, 1985), since both groups may withdraw from some peers and yet act aggressively towards others. There may also be some overlap between provocative victims and aggressive/withdrawn children, since Lyons *et al.* (1988) noted that the latter often interrupted ongoing activities and were verbally provocative, behaviours that are, as we have seen, also characteristic of provocative victims.

Time spent alone and feelings of loneliness

Children may respond in different ways to being bullied, including withdrawing from the peer group. This withdrawal may be reflected in such measures as how often a child is alone, and how lonely they report feeling (Rubin *et al.*, 1989). Our data bear these suppositions out. More victims than non-victims reported feeling lonely at school. Fewer victims than non-victims reported never being alone on the school playground and conversely more victims than non-victims reported being alone there sometimes or even several times a week. However, it is still not clear whether this high degree of social isolation and loneliness characteristic of many victims of bullying represents withdrawal *per se* on their part, or whether they are willing to associate with their peers should those peers wish it. For some victims at least, the former may be more likely: we found that victims were reported by more of their peers to 'act shy' than were bullies and non-involved children.

Bullying and children's views of themselves

Typically, victims of bullying appear to have a low opinion of themselves, and to be anxious and insecure (Olweus, 1987); as do many socially withdrawn children (Rubin *et al.*, 1989). In our own studies, we found that victims perceived themselves as being less physically competent than did bullies and non-involved children, and that female victims perceived themselves as being less well accepted by their peers than did the other two groups. At present, it remains unclear if these and other aspects of low self-esteem exhibited by victims precede or follow a child's experiences of being bullied. What little evidence there is suggests a two-way relationship. Olweus (1987) carried out detailed interviews with the parents of victimised boys and found that these children were often cautious and sensitive to how other people behaved towards them at an early age. He suggested that these traits were partly responsible for these children being the victims of bullying in the first place, and that this type of experience was likely to have a greater impact on their self-esteem than it would have on less sensitive individuals. He also suggested that being the victim of bullying over a prolonged time span may further erode a child's self confidence and lead to an increased negative view of themselves.

In our own research programme, we are investigating this important issue further. We have initiated a series of semi-structured interviews with victims to try to assess what sort of opinion they had of themselves prior to the onset of their being bullied, and whether they thought any less of themselves since that time. In another approach, we are examining whether popularity within the peer group may mediate between being bullied and low self-esteem. Informal observations we have made suggested that those victims who showed low self-esteem, anxiety and withdrawal tended to be those who also lacked good friends, though it is not yet clear whether the latter was a cause or consequence of the former.

Developmental pathways leading to social withdrawal

What are the origins of social withdrawal, and of victimisation? Surprisingly, the two phenomena have not often been closely linked. Yet, two different approaches have been made to explaining both kinds of problem. These are, first, a social skills deficit approach; and second, an approach via attachment theory. Recently, a more complex approach in terms of developmental pathways has been put forward by Rubin et al. (1990).

One influential group of theorists (Dodge et al., 1986) see the cause of many problems in peer relationships as lying in a lack of appropriate social skills. Following an information processing model of social interaction, they hypothesise that some children may interpret social signals incorrectly, or have only a very limited range of response options available. Thus, withdrawn children may lack the social skills of group entry; victims may lack social skills of assertiveness. Also, some children may be deliberately avoided and isolated by peers as a consequence of them showing many inappropriate hostile and aggressive acts (Rubin et al., 1990). However, these latter children are probably best viewed as being rejected by the peer group rather than withdrawn from it.

Another group of theorists see problems in peer relationships as lying in family circumstances and particularly in early parent–child attachment relationships; they feel that these relationships may 'set the scene' for future peer relationships. Attachment theorists suggest that a child develops 'internal working models' of relationships (Bowlby, 1988) which may be secure or insecure. Troy and Sroufe (1987) related parent–child attachment type to bully–victim involvement in preschoolers. The theoretical argument is most thoroughly worked out by Renken et al. (1989). They suggest that children with 'avoidant–insecure' attachment relationships lack trust and expect hostility, and may thus develop aggressive patterns of interaction with peers. By contrast, children with 'ambivalent–avoidant' attachment relationships with parents are likely to be getting haphazard care and doubt their own effectiveness in influencing the caregiver. While staying somewhat dependent, they lack self-esteem and confidence in their own worth; and are thus susceptible to being victimised by peers. Renken et al. (1989) report some (limited) confirmation of these associations.

Rubin et al. (1990) take up and extend this idea. They propose a more complex model, or set of developmental pathways, linking familial circumstances, infant temperament, mother–infant attachment, child-rearing techniques, self-esteem and peer relationships. However they also postulate two main pathways, one leading to aggressive or provocative peer problems, the other leading to more passive/withdrawal problems and difficulties in initiating and maintaining relationships. The latter is linked to disposit-ional/temperamental traits in the child such as shyness, behavioural reticence or behavioural inhibition (Kagan *et al.*, 1987; Plomin and DeFries, 1985); and to insecure attachment patterns; leading to anxiety, lack of social success and further withdrawal. This is perceived by potential bullies who then select the individual as their victim. These experiences lower the individual's self-esteem, which further marks them out as an easy victim in the peer group. A vicious cycle can then be set up, reinforced by the child's reputation in the peer group.

This latter approach does not put so much emphasis on social skills, as on dispositional factors in the child, and the child's model of relationships. However, social withdrawal will in itself lead to less practice in important peer social skills; so many withdrawn children, and many victims, may indeed lack some social skills, even if this may not be a primary cause for their condition.

What can be done?

Here we can only briefly indicate some approaches. One, based on the social skills model, is to provide victims, or withdrawn children, with appropriate skills of assertiveness, joining in groups, cooperation and sharing. Furman *et al.* (1979) provided this by pairing withdrawn children with well-adjusted children who were younger and thus perhaps at a comparable level of social skill. This proved quite successful on a small scale. However the skills can also be taught directly. For a review of social skills work with victims of bullying, see Arora (1991).

Adopting a developmental pathway model such as that of Rubin *et al.* (1990) suggests many avenues of intervention, each of which might only have partial success on its own. If their model is correct, both family circumstances, and rearing practices, would be important determinants which, however, are not often open to intervention. In the school setting, nevertheless, more can be done. We are currently looking at cooperative group work techniques in the classroom as a way of improving social relationships (Smith *et al.*, 1989; Cowie and Rudduck, 1991). Here, children are helped and encouraged to work together on common tasks, sharing experiences, and dealing with difficulties and conflicts in relationships (with the help of the teacher) as they arise. So far, this looks like being a helpful technique both in integrating withdrawn children into the peer group, and reducing problems of bullying.

Finally, much work is currently in progress in the UK on ways of coping with school bullying. This work is reviewed in Smith and Thompson (1991) and Elliott (1991). If the link we are suggesting between social withdrawal and victimisation is as important as it seems, then reducing the amount of

28

bullying may in itself encourage or allow more quiet and shy children to play the more active role in the peer group that we suspect most of them would really wish to do.

References

Ahmad, Y. and Smith, P. K. (1990) Behavioural measures: bullying in schools, *Newsletter of Association for Child Psychology and Psychiatry,* **12**, 26–7.

Ahmad, Y., Whitney, I. and Smith, P. K. (1991) A survey service for schools on bully/victim problems, in P. K. Smith and D. A. Thompson (eds) *Practical Approaches to Bullying.* London, David Fulton.

Arora, C. M. J. (1991) The use of victim support groups, in P. K. Smith and D. A. Thompson (eds) *Practical Approaches to Bullying.* London, David Fulton.

Asher, S. R. and Coie, J. D. (1990) *Peer Rejection in Childhood.* Cambridge, Cambridge University Press.

Berndt, T. J. and Ladd, G. W. (1989) *Peer Relationships in Child Development.* New York and Chichester, Wiley & Sons.

Boulton, M. J. and Smith, P. K. (1991) Bully/victim problems in middle school children: stability, self-perceived competence, peer perceptions, and peer acceptance. Manuscript submitted for publication.

Boulton, M. J., Underwood, K. and Smith, P. K. (1991) Bully/victim problems among middle school children. Manuscript submitted for publication.

Bowlby, J. (1988) *A Secure Base: Clinical Applications of Attachment Theory.* London, Tavistock/Routledge.

Coie, J. D., Dodge, K. A. and Coppotelli, H. A. (1982) Dimensions and types of social status: a cross-age perspective, *Developmental Psychology,* **18**, 557–69.

Cowie, H. and Rudduck, J. (1991) *Co-operative Group Work in the Multi-ethnic Classroom. Learning Together, Working Together, Volume Four.* London, BP Educational Service.

Dodge, K. A., Pettit, G. S., McClaskey, C. L. and Brown, M. M. (1986) Social competence in children. *Monographs of the Society for Research in Child Development,* **51**, 2, 1–85.

Dygdon, J. A. and Conger, A. J. (1990) A direct nomination method for the identification of neglected members in children's peer groups, *Journal of Abnormal Child Psychology,* **18**, 55–74.

Elliott, M. (1991) (ed.) *Bullying: A Practical Guide to Coping for Schools.* Harlow, Longman.

Furman, W., Rahe, D. F. and Hartup, W. W. (1979) Rehabilitation of socially withdrawn children through mixed-aged and same-age socialization, *Child Development,* **50**, 915–22.

Kagan, J., Reznick, J. S. and Snidman, N. (1987) The physiology and psychology of behavioral inhibition in children, *Child Development,* **58**, 1459–73.

Lagerspetz, K. M. J., Bjorkqvist, K., Berts, M. and King, E. (1982) Group aggression among school children in three schools, *Scandinavian Journal of Psychology*, **23**, 45–52.

Lesser, G. S. (1959) The relationship between various forms of aggression and popularity among lower-class children, *Journal of Educational Psychology*, **50**, 20–5.

Lowenstein, L. F. (1978) Who is the bully? *Bulletin of the British Psychological Society*, **31**, 147–9.

Lyons, J., Serbin, L. A. and Marchessault, K. (1988) The social behavior of peer-identified aggressive, withdrawn, and aggressive/withdrawn children, *Journal of Abnormal Child Psychology*, **16**, 539–52.

Mellor, A. (1990) Bullying in Scottish secondary schools, *Spotlights 23*, Edinburgh, SCRE.

Milich, R. and Landau, S. (1984) A comparison of the social status and social behavior of aggressive and aggressive/withdrawn boys, *Journal of Abnormal Child Psychology*, **12**, 277–88.

Moskowitz, D., Schwartzman, A. E. and Ledingham, J. (1985) Stability and change in aggression and withdrawal in middle childhood and adolescence, *Journal of Abnormal Psychology*, **94**, 30–41.

Olweus, D. (1978) *Aggression in the Schools: Bullies and Whipping Boys.* Washington, D.C., Hemisphere.

Olweus, D. (1987) Bully/victim problems among schoolchildren in Scandinavia, in J. P. Mykelbust and R. Ommundsen (eds) *Psykogprofesjonen mot år 2000.* Oslo, Universitetsforlaget.

Olweus, D. (1989) Bully/victim problems among schoolchildren: basic facts and effects of a school based intervention program, in K. Rubin and D. Pepler (eds) *The Development and Treatment of Childhood Aggression.* Hillsdale, N.J., Erlbaum.

O'Moore, A. M. and Hillery, B. (1989) Bullying in Dublin schools, *Irish Journal of Psychology*, **10**, 426–41.

Parker, J. G. and Asher, S. R. (1987) Peer relations and later personal adjustment: are low-accepted children at risk? *Psychological Bulletin*, **102**, 357–89.

Perry, D. G., Kusel, S. J. and Perry, L. C. (1988) Victims of peer aggression, *Developmental Psychology*, **24**, 807–14.

Plomin, R. and DeFries, J. C. (1985) *Origins of Individual Differences in Infancy.* New York, Academic Press.

Putallaz, M. and Wasserman, A. (1990) Children's entry behavior, in S. R. Asher and J. D. Coie (eds) *Peer Rejection in Childhood.* Cambridge, Cambridge University Press.

Renken, B., Egeland, B., Marvinney, D., Mangelsdorf, S. and Sroufe, L. A. (1989) Early childhood antecedents of aggression and passive-withdrawal in early elementary school, *Journal of Personality*, **57**, 257–81.

Rubin, K. H. and Borwick, D. (1984) Communicative skills and sociability, in H. E. Sypher and J. L. Applegate (eds) *Communication by Children and Adults: Social Cognitive and Strategic Processes*, pp. 152–70. Beverley Hills, Sage.

Rubin, K. H. and Clark, M. L. (1983) Preschool teachers' ratings of behavioral problems: observational, sociometric, and social-cognitive correlates, *Journal of Abnormal Child Psychology*, **11**, 273–85.

Rubin, K. H., Hymel, S. and Mills, R. S. L. (1989) Sociability and social withdrawal in childhood: stability and outcomes, *Journal of Personality*, **57**, 237–55.

Rubin, K. H. and Krasnor, L. R. (1986) Social cognitive and social behavioral perspectives on problem-solving, in M. Perlmutter (ed.) *Minnesota Symposia on Child Psychology, Vol. 18*, pp. 1–68. Hillsdale, N.J., Erlbaum.

Rubin, K. H., LeMare, L. J. and Lollis, S. (1990) Social withdrawal in childhood: developmental pathways to peer rejection, in S. R. Asher and J. D. Coie (eds) *Peer Rejection in Childhood*. Cambridge, Cambridge University Press.

Rubin, K. H. and Mills, R. S. L. (1988) The many faces of social isolation in childhood, *Journal of Consulting and Clinical Psychology*, **52**, 955–67.

Schwartzman, A. E., Ledingham, J. and Serbin, L. A. (1985) Identification of children at risk for adult schizophrenia: a longitudinal study, *International Review of Applied Psychology*, **34**, 363–80.

Smith, P. K. (1991) The silent nightmare: bullying and victimisation in school peer groups, *The Psychologist*, **4**.

Smith, P. K., Boulton, M. and Cowie, H. (1989) Ethnic relations in middle school. Final Report to ESRC, Swindon.

Smith, P. K. and Thompson, D. A. (1991) (eds) *Practical Approaches to Bullying*. London, David Fulton.

Stephenson, P. and Smith, D. (1989) Bullying in the junior school, in D. P. Tattum and D. A. Lane (eds) *Bullying in Schools*. Stoke-on-Trent, Trentham Books.

Troy, M. and Sroufe, L. A. (1987) Victimization among preschoolers: role of attachment relationship history, *Journal of the American Academy of Child and Adolescent Psychiatry*, **26**, 166–72.

Yates, C. and Smith, P. K. (1989) Bullying in two English comprehensive schools, in E. Roland and E. Munthe (eds) *Bullying: An International Perspective*. London, David Fulton.

Younger, A. J., Schwartzman, A. E. and Ledingham, J. E. (1985) Age-related changes in children's perceptions of aggression and withdrawal in their peers, *Developmental Psychology*, **21**, 70–5.

CHAPTER 3

A Consideration of Possible Responses to Emotional Abuse of Children by Adults

Sheila Melzak

Introduction

When I first heard the proposed title of this volume, I assumed that I understood clearly that I had been asked to write about certain ways in which children might develop defence and coping mechanisms as a result of emotional abuse. I assumed I had been asked to describe those particular strategies that lead to children avoiding relationships with peers and adults, to avoid social activity, to avoid work etc., and even, in some circumstances, to attempt suicide.

As I began to think more carefully about the title, I realised that when I work with the children, I assume that the variety of responses to emotional abuse which children develop cannot be separated from the context within which they develop. The title of the volume itself begs many questions that are laden with value judgements. My dictionary defines truancy as – 'The action of playing truant' and a truant as 'A lazy, idle person who absents himself from school without leave – hence one who wanders from an appointed place or neglects his duty or business' (Little *et al.*, 1973).

The action of children who absent themselves from school, or indeed from life, can be seen from certain philosophical perspectives to be connected with idleness, lack of discipline, neglectfulness and laziness. I prefer the philosophical and developmental perspectives which assume that children would not absent themselves from school or from life without a good reason.

31

The reason may lie within the child. It may also lie within the school or other social institutions. It is most likely to lie within both.

It is well described in education literature that children leaving school when they are expected to be there are 'talking with their feet'. Schools may be authoritarian, punitive or abusive. They may condone bullying by not providing an active policy against the practice of bullying, thus failing to protect the young victims and perpetrators of this form of abuse. Schools may also fail to provide a curriculum that is meaningful to a large proportion of their pupils or a curriculum and philosophy that is sensitive to the developmental, emotional, intellectual, physical and cultural needs of its pupils (Holt, 1969). Holt wrote a series of books in the late sixties describing the ways in which the institutions of society failed children, and thus, from my perspective emotionally abused children. Other more recent writers take up these ideas, for example, Bryan *et al.*,

> Non-cooperation, disinterest, truancy, strikes and demonstrations, were the ongoing response of many black pupils throughout the seventies to an education which was increasingly seen as irrelevant. While our actions were not always a collective act of conscious resistance, they were nevertheless an expression of our growing disaffection with what the schools and the socieyt had to offer us. (Bryan *et al.*, 1985)

Schools may place constraints and assumptions and myths upon children in terms of class (e.g. having a middle class curriculum), race (e.g. sharing a Eurocentric curriculum) and gender (e.g. expecting girls and boys to conform to different role stereotypes and incorporating these into the school rules), all of which encourage the development of 'apparent' learning (Holt, 1969). In these situations little 'real' learning and development occur at a time when children are best able to grow and develop.

Emotional abuse is thus, from my perspective, institutionalised in various institutions of this society, including families, schools, social services and the law, all institutions which directly affect children. Emotional abuse is also institutionalised internationally in terms of the lack of recognition, acknowledgment and active respecting of the rights and needs of children as laid out in the United Nations' Declaration on the Rights of Children. These 'rights', though agreed by the United Nations (in 1989) are being flouted both in Western and Third World countries. These described rights include the right that their emotional developmental needs are recognised, respected and met. These international laws are openly flouted as adult, economic and military concerns are generally prioritised over the tasks involved in meeting the needs of children who will become the adults of the next generation. It is in this context that I will consider possible responses to emotional abuse.

Children are in contact with many social institutions as they develop. These may include schools, social services, the law and families. Most children grow up within families. Many children grow up within families that superficially appear to function in ways that our conventional morality and standards would consider to be good enough (Winnicott, 1965). However, while good physical care may be provided, some carers fail to meet the child's less observable needs for affection, attention and stimulation (Graham-Hall and Martin, 1987). Some consideration of the quality of the emotional experience of developing children within some families would give any careful observer much evidence of emotional abuse, deprivation and neglect.

In this context, it is perhaps useful to define again 'truancy from life' and 'emotional abuse'. I will assume here that 'truancy from life' involves certain long-term strategies, defences or coping mechanisms that an infant, child or young person develops during the course of childhood (in order to deal with internal or external difficulties, stresses, conflicts or emotional pain) that lead the child to deviate from the broad cultural and developmental achievements and ways of relating to themselves and others, expected for their age group. These age-expectable achievements will be defined in terms of the socially dominant culture. Specifically, I will assume that each child's strategies, defences and coping mechanisms lead the child or young person to avoid or withdraw from large areas of 'normal' experience, and even to wish to die and act on this wish. Again, 'normal' must be defined in terms of the socially dominant culture. As a result of space limitations I am not able to consider in depth here, or in the case material, 'truancy' as an active healthy response and a way of coping with abusive social institutions.

I will borrow a definition of emotional abuse from the pamphlet 'Working Together',

> The severe adverse effect on the behaviour and emotional development of a child caused by persistent or severe emotional ill-treatment or rejection. All abuse involves some emotional ill-treatment. This category should be used where it is the main or sole form of abuse. (DHSS and the Welsh Office, 1988)

Emotional abuse occurs when adults responsible for taking care of children are, over a prolonged period, unable to be aware of and meet their children's emotional and developmental needs. As I wrote previously, I assume emotional abuse to be institutionalised not only within some families but also within other social institutions.

Damage to particular areas of a child's personality at one stage of development can make the child vulnerable to further damage later on. The emotionally abused child, characteristically keeps her experiences secret from both the external world and, more seriously, from herself. It is, in part, the internalisation of this secrecy that leads to distortions in the child's perception and thinking and hence in her capacity to learn, to have relationships and to have a feeling of well-being about herself. In fact those children who early in their development are able to clearly perceive abuse by adults are less likely to be seriously damaged by emotional abuse.

Children show amazing flexibility when they are exposed to trauma. They can withstand enormous external stress with the protection of supportive parents. Emotional abuse involves more than one or two traumatic exchanges between parent and child. Certain chronically negative parent–child interactions can severely limit a child's capacity for healthy development.

Emotional abuse during childhood may lead the abused child to feel emotionally damaged in adulthood or to repeat the style of parenting and adult 'love' relationships that they themselves experienced. As adults they survive, but may unconsciously either repeat primary abusive relationships or compensate for past deprivations and distortions via present relationships, both strategies being unsatisfactory (Miller, 1981; Shengold, 1989; Barocas and Barocas, 1979). Some emotionally abused children develop insight into their experiences and develop strengths as adults and parents. These abused children, as adults are able to think and feel clearly about their abuse and do not idealise or distort the adult world. Other abused children achieve these insights via therapeutic interventions. Garbarino (1989) writes about emotional abuse but calls it psychological maltreatment.

(1) *Rejection* – Children need emotional acceptance, validation, attention and celebration at all stages of their development (see also Covitz, 1986).

(2) *Isolation* – To practise social skills, children need relationships with adults, special parenting adults, peers and children of other ages. Overprotective and possessive parents can seriously impede a child's development.

(3) *Terrorising* – Some parents use fear, humiliation, verbal abuse and threats of violence to manage their children. This can build an internal world of distrust in others. These children are not bound by the normal rules of negotiation with the outside world. They may be withdrawn or bullies. A parent may find ways of terrorising that are effective in forcing the desired behaviour – which makes children particularly vulnerable to this form of abuse. Terrorising may take the form of humiliation or double bind. It may have cultural support in teasing and bullying. It is sometimes used to 'educate' children into the adult's way of thinking and behaving. This form of abuse is often seen in schools.

(4) *Ignoring* – Parents under stress may be more likely to ignore their children. This may occur in situations of separation and divorce (Wallerstein, 1989). Parents in mourning for present or past losses may ignore their children's needs, for example, refugee parents mourning home, family and country (Barocas and Barocas, 1979; Melzak, 1989). Unemployed parents having to adjust to new lifestyles and poverty, isolated parents, mentally ill parents, all may ignore their children's emotional developmental needs. Schools may ignore the learning needs of children from cultures other than the dominant middle class culture, including the needs of working class, immigrant and refugee children.

(5) *Corrupting* – A parent may overwhelm a child with their own unmet needs in the form of sexual corruption, substance abuse and aggression – all resulting in the child's mis-socialisation into the role of the victim or perpetrator of corruption.

The internal and developmental consequences of abuse for a child may be those intended by the parent figure, but more usually the damage caused by emotional abuse is not intended.

Many writers, (e.g. Miller, 1981, 1987) have underlined how the invisible emotional abuse is transmitted from generation to generation as emotionally abused children transform into abusive parents. This transmission can only be stopped if a child or parent allows themselves or is enabled by some facilitating other person to reflect on their experience and gain some insight and capacity to experience and work through forgotten painful relationships, in order to achieve insight or a clear view of reality.

Though statutory provision can provide 'protection' for some children, the child care laws operate on the basis of observable, physical injuries, and it is much more difficult for responsible adults, whether professional or not, to reach consensus on issues involving invisible emotional abuse. Society operates with many conflicting myths about family privacy, the rights of parents and good enough child care (e.g. Parton, 1985; Goldstein et al., 1979). An example of this would be our idealisation of certain kinds of family.

In 1991 there were one million one parent families. Most children from these families grow up to be emotionally well functioning adults. Public opinion is still organised by some myths that two parent families necessarily provide a better and a more healthy emotional environment in which children can develop.

Other myths and fantasies about the strengths of nuclear family life are challenged by the child abuse statistics which reflect the approximate numbers of children neglected and physically abused, and also some of those who are sexually and emotionally abused (NSPCC, 1989). As a result of this, we know that many children dwell in a grey area where their difficult experiences are not recognised or acknowledged by the adult world. They have unhappy childhoods and grow up to be unhappy adults and perhaps abusive parents. This makes the effect of the society on these children emotionally abusive. Emotional abuse can affect every area of the personality of a developing child. It can result in suppression and distortion of feelings, intelligence or morality. Schools can emotionally abuse children. Children abused within their family can underachieve in school, they can have unsatisfying relationships with peers and adults, they can be delinquent. Usually they dislike themselves physically and psychologically. They may feel they have to be adults long before they are emotionally or physically ready for this task. Emotionally abused children can be first noticed as a result of aggressive, overactive, criminal or inconsistent behaviour.

The group of emotionally abused children less likely to be noticed are those who express their confusion and conflicting feelings via quiet withdrawal, avoidance of social activities or work, or extreme passivity. They may be seen as 'weird', rather than 'naughty', as quiet and shy, or ill-at-ease. Some may be seen to be excessively anxious. This group of children are often seen by teachers as lonely, isolated and strange.

There are other children whose truancy from life will take the form of an overt battle with conventional rules and norms. Others will fail to engage with 'life' and stand apart and alone, usually puzzled and bewildered, and often completely uncomprehending of not only social norms but also of both acceptable and of perverse pleasures.

Before illustrating the phenomenon of truancy from life as a result of emotional abuse, it is important to underline that without deep knowledge of a child's internal world such as that obtained by psychoanalytic therapeutic treatment, it is very hard to make a correlation between a certain type of emotional abuse and its consequences. Anna Freud wrote the following about the relationship in child development between environmental conditions and the rate of internal structuralisation of the personality.

> What needs emphasis, though, is the fact there is no one-to-one invariable relationship between the fact of parents being absent, neglecting, indifferent, punitive, cruel, seductive, over-protective, delinquent or psychotic and the resultant distortions in the personality structure of the child. Cruel treatment can produce either an aggressive, violent being or a timid, crushed, passive one. In short, developmental outcome is determined not by the environmental interference *per se*, but by its interaction with the inborn and acquired resources of the child (Freud, 1982).

This frame of reference is useful in considering truancy from life as a response to emotional abuse.

While I briefly mentioned earlier the phenomenon of lack of consensus between adults about emotional abuse and the myths that highest quality care occurs in two-parent families, it is necessary to examine the contradictions and mistaken assumptions within these myths and the myths that imply uncritically that good quality care occurs in all social institutions connected with the care of children.

I start from an assumption that children ideally need continuity of care from one or two committed adults who are aware of their developmental needs and able to meet these needs. It can be argued that child care situations become actively emotionally abusive when adults actively interfere with the emotional development of children or if they become unable to meet children's needs and no adequate substitute parent is provided.

In the latter situation, many questions are raised as to who might hold responsibility for emotional abuse of children. We can speculate that responsibility for emotional abuse may be held at many levels, for example,

(1) With parents.
(2) Within cultural groups and communities.
(3) Within institutions set up by society to educate, protect and care for children.
(4) Within society.

Within many countries children's rights and needs are considered, within national laws, and the United Nations' declarations on the rights of children are accepted and integrated into national laws. It is, however, true that children's emotional and developmental needs are often given low priority and trivialised and marginalised in the face of adult values and activities. This broad statement can be applied to life within various social institutions, such as families, tribes, schools and communities, and more broadly within cultures, nations and internationally.

The concept of emotional abuse and the possible reaction to this abuse of 'truancy from life' can thus be considered with equal validity in terms of one child's experience of emotional abuse within a family. According to DOH figures for 1989 – 2,000 cases of emotional abuse wer recorded on local authorities' Child Protection Registers out of a child population of 11,512,300 (0–17). This is an underestimate. These human rights abuses, measured in terms of the various kinds of interference with a child's development can be caused by repressive and divided societies, wars and their concomitants in terms of terrible and overwhelming exposure to trauma, loss, stress and pain (Carli, 1987; Frazer, 1973; Davidson, 1986). Here I will also consider the reactions of children to this kind of abuse of their rights to have their needs met. This would include situations where social factors prevent parents from carrying out their expectable responsibilities as good enough parents. These social factors may include poverty, physical and emotional illness, etc., at one level, and at another level the particular social divisiveness of some kinds of repressive governments that divide communities, wars, and the creation of refugees. While some families remain in their own country and experience the psychological concomitants of parents' involvement in and reactions to living within a country at war (Davidson, 1986; Carli, 1987; Martin-Barō, 1990), other families are forced to become refugees.

Emotional abuse within families is reacted to in different ways by different individuals, some developing remarkable strengths and coping mechanisms, and others feeling that large parts of their personality have been destroyed, leaving them vulnerable to further stress (Shengold, 1989). In the same way, while most refugee families cope well with considerable loss and trauma and remain emotionally integrated, other refugee families will disintegrate under the stresses of their situation, and emotional abuse of children can occur. The responsibility for the abuse cannot reside with parents but must be set at a social level. The same is true for families affected by social forces, poverty, unemployment, racism, etc.

The effects of emotional abuse on children

In considering possible reactions to emotional abuse, this may have many symptoms, including withdrawal, regression, increased aggression, etc. Suicidal symptoms in a child or adolescent are, for me, the most gross reaction to emotional abuse. As I mentioned above active withdrawal may be the healthiest response to an abusive situation. Suicide is not active but passive withdrawal and may be the only internal solution for some young people. It is in this context that I will briefly describe the internal experiences of two young people, both emotionally abused, one in the context of her family and the other in the context of clear societal abuse and disregard of the needs of children and young people.

As a psychotherapist, I not only consider the societal context of emotional abuse, but also what can be done about this abuse in the form of various kinds of therapeutic work – individual, group or family therapeutic work.

Wendy

Wendy was referred by my clinic at the age of fourteen, after being admitted to hospital with severe stomach cramps for which no physical cause could be found. I was asked to assess her for psychotherapy, and from this time went on seeing Wendy for many years. At the time of her referral, Wendy was living with her father, who was clearly doing his best against many odds to give her both care and opportunities to develop. Wendy's mother had died when she was ten after a long illness. Both parents came from complicated, conflict-ridden families. The story of Wendy's family and her experience of this family unfolded, as it often does, during treatment.

Wendy told me during her assessment that she had taken an overdose and this had caused her painful admission to hospital. She had also tried to throw herself down the stairs. Early on during her treatment, Wendy's conflicts about her family emerged. She hated the fact that her father insisted on paying her paternal aunt for any care she offered to Wendy. She visited her maternal grandmother daily and her grandmother gave her a meal. She ate the meal to please her grandmother, and never had the courage to tell her grandmother that she also cooked and ate a meal with her father.

It is the usual model of work in my centre that when children and young people are involved in psychotherapy once, or, as in Wendy's case, twice a week, the family also attend the centre regularly for family work. Wendy's father refused to come to the centre after attending an initial meeting to sort out the practicalities of the treatment plan.

It was only after the death of Wendy's maternal grandparents, when she was fifteen and sixteen respectively, and her returning home from school one day to find her father collapsed and dying when she was seventeen, that the extent of Wendy's father's problem with alcohol abuse emerged clearly. More significant, of course, were Wendy's various feelings at different stages of her development about the conflicts between her parents and between her grandmother and her separate parents. At the onset of her mother's illness and extensive treatment, which involved a mastectomy, Wendy was moved from her bedroom into her parents' bed and her father was banished to Wendy's room. It also became clear that her father's drinking problems increased when her mother died, and he had violent mood swings and was frequently seriously ill, at home or on the family holidays. In spite of these serious emotional difficulties, he had a regular, well paid job, which he kept until physical illness forced him to stop work a few months before his death.

When Wendy began her treatment, she presented several serious symptoms, including her suicidal wishes. She was just beginning puberty at the time of her referral and hated her developing female body. She refused to participate in sport at school, as this involved undressing, and she refused to wear a brassiere. The onset of her menstruation on a school trip had been hugely traumatic for her, and, significantly, she fainted in a biology lesson during a film about childbirth.

The reasons for Wendy's hatred of large parts of herself are over-determined by her mother's particular debilitating illness and the family conflicts, which both male and female adults seemed helpless to resolve in a productive way to bring about family change. Alongside her psychological symptoms, which indicated the necessity for psychotherapeutic work, Wendy had many good friends, she worked hard and was considered in her school to be very bright. The extent of the emotional abuse to Wendy during the course of her childhood became more and more clear during her treatment. From the time of the onset of her mother's illness when she was seven, neither her relatives nor any adults in the community were able to fully take responsibility for Wendy and be sensitive to her developmental needs, being themselves either preoccupied with their own difficulties or using Wendy to meet their own needs. When her mother died neighbours tried to persuade her father to accept help for his illness and in caring for his daughter, but he refused. When social services were informed and an assessment was made of Wendy's needs, they were not considered to be urgent enough for Wendy to be taken into care, or even for the 'case' to be followed up.

In my opinion, the community failed this child. Wendy had to cope, in addition to the developmental tasks of a young girl becoming a woman, with the loss of her mother at the age of ten and the loss of the three other most important adults in her life before the age of seventeen.

These four significant losses had to be mourned in a family situation where adults did not trust each other and could not talk to each other about their feelings. The family space was crowded with secrets, shame, guilt, recrimination, unhappiness and considerable despair. In this context, Wendy was not only emotionally abused, but she also internalised this atmosphere of secrecy so that she not only, in her state of childish dependency, could not really see and understand the extent to which the adults in her life were abusing her, she also absorbed this atmosphere of conflict and emotional dishonesty and kept secrets from herself. In adult company and in class she was silent and withdrawn. It was easier for her to cope by being silent, as talking might have meant revelation of her family conflicts.

This resulted in Wendy growing up to present only part of herself in the community. She often said to me in sessions that this was the only place where she could be her real self. With her friends and in the community, Wendy was sweet, warm, exceptionally caring, though shy and often sad. In her long periods of time spent alone, Wendy was riddled with anxieties, despair and self-destructive feelings. She felt unvalued and unloved and that she herself could only really love her cat . . . which she doted on.

I am not going to go into any more detail here about Wendy or her treatment. Her tendency towards truancy from life as a result of emotional abuse, was expressed at various levels, most dramatically by her suicidal symptoms. Wendy's difficulties in being open with her friends resulted in her feeling cut off from them sometimes. She avoided, from an early age, any social activities that she felt would make her feel bad. Though she passed very well all her school examinations at sixteen, she did not complete the pre-university exams and she did not find work for years. This was, of course, partly in response to the economic situation in the country and lack of work opportunities for young people. She had an enormously difficult task in making sense of and enjoying the world of adult relationships. She tended to have good female friends, but to choose male friends with emotional difficulties who could not meet her needs or value her.

As her story emerged, it became clear that Wendy had been seriously emotionally abused. Going back to the categories of Garbarino (1989), her complicated emotional developmental needs in various areas had been denied. Wendy, during her development, was rejected, isolated, ignored, terrorised and corrupted, as has become clear from her story. As a result of her parents' preoccupations, Wendy's needs during her early years were not recognised or met, that is, she did not get sufficient attention paid to her emotional needs. She was thus rejected in many ways. Her parents' shame and guilt, and in particular that of her father about his illness, led to Wendy being isolated from social relationships. After her mother's death, he would not allow anyone except one of his brothers to visit their home. Wendy was not allowed to invite friends to the house and learned from her father how to pretend they were not at home.

For me, the most serious aspect of Wendy's emotional abuse, in that it was the most confusing, was Wendy's being alternately terrorised and ignored, especially after her mother died. The various adults in her family only wanted to engage with her in terms of their needs, not hers, thus ignoring her developmental needs. In contrast, her father could be explosive and verbally violent, leaving Wendy terrified, numb and unable to recognise, let alone express, her own needs and feelings.

I have included corruption in the list of Wendy's symptoms in that I think the fact that Wendy slept in her ill mother's bed from the age of seven and that her father moved to her room, had a profound effect on the development of Wendy's relationship with her own body and her sexuality. She was very confused about physical intimacy and sexuality, and was enormously ambivalent about the adult female aspects of her body (Laufer, 1991).

Our work in psychotherapy has been slow but productive. Wendy has worked to value the enormous strengths in her personality, her warmth, her independence and her intelligence, to be increasingly open about her difficulties and to work through these. Our work has involved the difficult unravelling of family secrets that Wendy has both seen and avoided. A huge part of our work has been to resolve her conflict between seeing and avoiding seeing the reality of complicated emotional situations that have resulted in her truancy from life.

In contrast to the family emotional abuse experienced by Wendy, Yusuf's emotional abuse during the course of his development was experienced at a different level. There are many children and young people who do not feel protected by their parents, like Wendy, but for this second group of children, their parents are preoccupied by the concomitants of war, repression and divided societies. Children and young people, who themselves are arrested and tortured, may be angry, not with the 'society' (which is a sophisticated concept for even a young person), but with their parents and family for failing to protect them. This anger is intensified when parents seem to change (as a result of the increased stresses on them resulting from trauma, war, change of lifestyle, etc.) or if parents are absent. This anger may be turned against the self to result in 'truancy from life' as a result of this emotional abuse.

Yusuf

Yusuf was referred to me by one of our psychiatrists, who felt that he could use psychotherapy. Yusuf had made two serious suicide attempts since his arrival in England. He had walked in front of a car and he had tried to gouge out his eyes, both serious symptoms. He was very distressed at these suicidal, destructive feelings inside himself, expecially at what he described as the voices that told him to kill himself and interrupted his studies by interfering with his thinking or by telling him to tear up his essays. He is seventeen.

Yusuf comes from an African country and was in the early stages of pre-university courses towards his wish to study medicine when he was arrested and imprisoned for several months for political activity – activity with which his brothers and sisters had encouraged him to become involved, against the wishes of his parents. He was severely tortured in prison, and eventually escaped and stowed away on a boat bound for Europe. He arrived in England about ten months ago.

When I meet someone for the first time, I have been trained to think carefully about transference and counter-transference. These two useful jargon words, which respectively mean feelings that a person in psychotherapy feels towards his therapist, from all levels of his development, and the latter, feelings that the therapist feels towards her client from all levels of her development. In particular, working with refugees, all of whom have experienced immense loss and trauma and who come from a variety of cultures, countries and political affiliations, I feel there is an onus on the therapist to inform herself about the culture her client comes from. Especially relevant here for the therapist to consider are some observations of the ways in which it is acceptable to express feelings within the culture, class, political group and family of each client. At the same time, I think the emotional developmental processes are generalisable across cultures.

We spent the first few sessions, meeting weekly for one hour each time, with Yusuf recounting his story, all the time with great reservations that talking about the past could do anything to alleviate his great emotional pain. On the contrary, he felt that putting his feelings into words, would actively increase his pain.

There was, of course, little meaning for him that I should say that psychotherapy was the provision of a safe place where we could explore difficult and painful feelings from the past and present and work through these – so that they were more manageable and thus he would feel more in control of himself and free to be himself, but I did say this. As he is very verbal and articulate, I asked Yusuf to take what I was saying about change on trust, even if it seemed weird and crazy and stupid. The onus is on the therapist to make a therapeutic alliance, a working relationship with her client. Yusuf would arrive each week and complain about severe physical pain in his head and limbs (he had been beaten with the dried penis of an ox and on arrival in England had had major abdominal surgery and the removal of a testicle). He wanted to come to see me when he needed to, not weekly as I had suggested. He said he always felt worse in the middle of the week – in between appointments. We gradually put together that he felt bad, guilty and ashamed and worried, like a baby who needs the physical care of his parents. His apparently irrational thoughts and actions made him feel hopeless and helpless. He described how he felt like a drowning man in the middle of a vast sea with no land in any direction.

Yusuf talked about his physical pain, and after he had had several thorough medical examinations which eliminated the possibility that there were continuing physical problems, I talked about the differences between physical and emotional pain. This led on to his clarifying for himself, as a late adolescent, that he felt incomplete as a man in a physical and emotional sense, because his body had been damaged and because he often felt like a mad child. From this discussion we could explore the myths, fantasies, customs, practices and expectations of his culture around young men.

It was clear to me that he longed for the physical and emotional presence of his father, and was struggling with shame and guilt that he had not done what his father wished by avoiding being political and sticking to his studies. It is my job to help Yusuf to become his own man, separate from his father and family, with his own values, ideas and morality, which may or may not coincide with those of his culture and family. To do this, we had to make space to air all the possible choices that he had, the constraints, the regrets and the fears. Our work will take a long time and it is a small part of his life as an exile and a student, looking for accommodation, having little money, making new relationships and struggling to maintain old ones.

To give you a flavour of one meeting, I will describe a session with him.

To this meeting Yusuf arrived on time, having missed the last appointment and not having contacted me. He said it was the snow. He couldn't go out – and studying had been difficult – he was not doing as well as he hoped and he wanted to get high grades for medical school. For the first time he did not say that talking about the past was useless, and said he felt good to be in my room and trying to understand the irrational, crazy feelings inside his head. 'It is like you said last week, like a battle between good and evil inside my head.'

I wondered who was winning this week.

Yusuf smiled, and I assumed that he really felt more in control than before. He had spoken briefly about various practical difficulties and I could direct him to the right people in the community to deal with housing, health, welfare rights, etc. Only then could we focus on our real task, the battle inside him. Why did he have such self-destructive feelings, and where did they come from? Yusuf described the voice in his head that told him to tear up his notes, to kill himself.

My response at this point was to say 'I know you feel crazy inside, but you are a good man living in a crazy world, where there are many battles going on, between Iraq and the Western powers, between the guerrilas and the government, between young men and their brothers and sisters, between young men and their fathers. The battle is outside you and sometimes it feels inside'.

At this point Yusuf said 'But I hate myself – I am helpless here to help my parents – to find my brother (he has been in hiding since leaving prison) – and most of all, I hate myself because I am frightened and lonely and I cry'. I wondered then aloud if good strong men in his country cry – he replied 'Oh no – never. My father would never cry'. We then talked about the myth that strong men never cry.

While my sessions consist of the slow expression of feelings and an exchange of interpretations, containment, confrontation and clarification, they are also spent in the exploration of the area bounded by religion, politics, child development theory, culture and language when two people meet who have separate and unfamiliar language, culture, religion and history, in order that a firm therapeutic alliance might be established between therapist and client. I often spend some part of a session asking for translations of certain words and expressions that I often use and asking about cultural definitions of life cycle processes.

Over the course of some sessions, the central theme emerged that Yusuf felt tormented not so much by his torturers or by British racism, which are of course very important factors, but by his extreme guilt as a young man from his particular culture, that he had disobeyed his father and become involved in politics, the consequence of which was his having to leave his country. This meant for Yusuf that he was also forced to leave his responsibilities towards his parents, that is, in looking after them. If he had voluntarily left his country, as a student for example, and with his father's blessing, he agreed he would feel very differently and not hate himself so much. It is our task together to carefully work through the multiple causes of Yusuf's negative feelings towards himself in order that he might become free to be himself and to survive. We need to understand together the multiple sources of his suicidal feelings.

In this context, as a psychotherapist trained to listen to the internal and unconscious world of children and young adults, I have to be careful not to be too distracted by the horrifying realities of torture, trauma and loss in order to listen carefully and establish the central concern of each individual.

The especially terrible human rights abuse to young children and young people is the interference with the normal healthy process of their development, and this abuse is the consequence of repression and war. Torture is as much a consequence of this repression as are refugees. Characteristic of the treatment of these young people are the secrets in the

44

transference, secrets brought about by the central divisive aim of repression. See the writing of Martin-Barō about El Salvador and the work of other South American writers.

Not only are communities divided and turned against each other, but also, as I mentioned above, races, political groups, classes, sexes and families. For me it is also true that people are turned against their own selves. This process occurs in various ways, using the psychological process of splitting. I need to be aware of the theme of secrets, some being conscious and some unconscious. These young people, at a vulnerable stage in their development, are cut off from themselves – alienated from certain feelings and experiences, and tormented by shame and guilt. The process of torture and repression also makes them consciously untrusting of new adults. They therefore tend to share only a certain part of themselves with the therapist in a mistaken belief that this is what the therapist wants to hear. For effective treatment the therapist must be aware of these processes and must be ready to ask certain questions about the absence of certain feelings and themes that we would expect to find in order to integrate the various split-off parts of the personality.

To clarify this second case study by referring back to Garbarino's categories, Yusuf was over his intense period in prison, terrorised, rejected and ignored. The inadequate social structures for dealing with an unaccompanied young person arriving alone to Britain resulted in further ignoring and rejection by the social system.

Conclusion

Referring back to the quotation from Anna Freud (p. 36), we cannot predict what effect emotional abuse will have on the developing personality. It will have different effects on different individuals in different circumstances, and it may result in life-avoiding strategies and even suicide.

I have tried to illustrate here the fact that the responsibility for emotional abuse of children in our society cannot be located within individuals but is the result of our community and culture not making the needs of developing children a priority.

References

Allsebrook, A. and Swift, A. (1989) Broken promise, in *The World of Endangered Children*. London, Hodder & Stoughton.

Barocas, H. A. and Barocas, C. B. (1979) Wounds of the fathers: the next generation of holocaust victims, *International Review of Psychoanalysis*, 6, 331–40.

Bryan, B., Dadzie, S. and Scafe (1985) *The Heart of the Race*. London, Virago.

Carli, A. (1987) Psychological consequences of political persecution: the effects on children of the imprisonment or disappearance of their parents.

Covitz, J. (1986) *Emotional Child Abuse: The Family Curse*. Boston, Mass., Sigo Press.

Davidson, S. (1986) The clinical effects of massive psychic trauma in families of holocaust survivors, in *Journal of Marital and Family Therapy*, January.

DHSS and the Wesh Office (1988) *Working Together*. London, HMSO.

Frazer, A. (1973) *Children in Conflict*. London, Secker & Warberg.

Freud, A. (1982) *The Psychoanalytic Psychology of Normal Development*. International Psychoanalytic Library, London, Hogarth Press.

Garbarino, J. (1989) Emotional abuse, unpublished talk given at Haifa University, January.

Goldstein, J., Freud, A. and Solnit, A. (1979) *In the Best Interests of the Child*. New York, The Free Press.

Graham-Hall, J. and Martin, P.F. (1987) *Child Abuse Procedure and Evidence in Juvenile Courts*. London, Barry Rose Books.

Holt, J. (1969) *How Children Fail*. London, Penguin.

Korde, N., Diana, R., Edelman, Lucica, I., Lagos, D.M., Nicoletti, E. and Bozzolo, R.C. (1988) *Psychological Effects of political Repression*. South America, Planeta.

Laufer, E. (1991) Body image, sexuality and the psychotic core, *International Journal of Psychoanalysis*, **72**, part 1.

Little, W., Fowler, H.W. and Coulson, J. (1973) *The Shorter Oxford Dictionary*. Oxford, Oxford University Press.

Martin-Barō, I. (1990) War and the psychosocial trauma of Salvadorian children. Posthumous presentation, Annual Meeting of the American Psychological Association, Boston, Massachussetts (presented by A. Aron).

Melzak, S. (1989) 'What do you do when your parents are crying?' Paper given at the Second International Conference of Centres, Institutions and Individuals concerned with the Care of Victims of Organised Violence, 27th November–2nd December, San Jose, Costa Rica.

Miller, A. (1981) *Prisoners of Childhood*. New York.

Miller, A. (1987) For your own good, in *The Roots of Violence in Child Rearing*. London, Virago.

NSPCC (1989) NSPCC statistics, *Child Abuse Trends in England and Wales 1983–7*. London, NSPCC.

Parton, N. (1985) *The Politics of Child Abuse*. London, Macmillan.

Shengold, L. (1989) *Soul Murder: The Effects of Childhood Abuse and Deprivation*. Yale University Press.

Townsend, P. (1980) *The Smallest Pawns in the Game*. London, Granada.

United Nations (1989) United Nations Convention on the Rights of Children.

Wallerstein, J. (1989) *Second Chances*, Men, Women and Children a Decade after the Divorce. London, Bantam.

Winnicott, D.W. (1965) The good enough parent, in *The Maturational Processes and the Facilitating Environment*. London, Hogarth Press.

CHAPTER 4

Bereavement and Withdrawn Children

Ann Drake

Death when it comes brings shock and trauma, even if the death was expected. What follows on can have far reaching effects on all those who are left to cope.

Imagine the ripple effect, when a stone is dropped into water, the disturbance is greatest at the centre most point, it spreads outwards until it disappears.

The main stages of grief are – shock, anger, guilt, denial, loss of status, depression, loneliness and finally acceptance. Of course not every child will experience all these stages, but it is likely that they will pass through most of them, and the time spent on each, will also vary with each individual.

The penalty we all must pay for loving someone is grief, grieving takes its own time, it will not be rushed. Often a child will suddenly realise that a whole year's education has been lost, they have been so busy with their 'worry work' and 'grief work' that the things which were once so important have been left behind. This is a crucial point, when understanding is most needed to avoid a 'panic' situation. Often the child will say things like, 'I have been trying to make sense of it all', or 'I know that my school work is important, but my mind is wandering back to the death'. Unfortunately for some a grief may remain unresolved for many years, for these unfortunate children it may well be the first steps to becoming 'truants from life'.

All adults should be more aware, just how dramatically a death in the family can change a child's life forever, for someone who is offering help it is important to consider all the factors which surround the actual death, the child, and the child's family circumstances.

Learn not to make hasty judgements, especially if the child's behaviour changes. Look for all the outward signs, but learn to read them correctly, misinterpretation can so easily lead you down a false trail.

The child will be filled with insecurities already and to place a label saying 'problem child' will only make matters more difficult. It is up to us, as individuals to learn how to support others, in doing so, we learn to accept death, as a way of life.

Humans in grief could be compared with the chameleon, that very clever lizard who has the ability to change its appearance, it confuses all those who threaten it. Children and adults use similar 'ploys', in order to protect themselves, and those around them, from the painful experience of loss and grief.

How often have you heard the expression, 'she's putting on a very brave face'? Have you ever once considered why this is? It is a form of camouflage, similar to the one used by the chameleon, it conceals and disguises those very real emotions which are often just underneath the surface. There are many reasons why children find it easier to cope in this way, basically they find their own pain too much to cope with, sharing other people's emotions might also be difficult. They misguidedly think that in time, the pain will dissipate, especially if it can be surpressed for long enough.

In some cases tears are still regarded as a show of weakness, and an adult who really believes this, will transfer this view onto their offspring. How many times have you said to a child when he is hurt, 'Don't cry, be a brave boy'? How much healthier the child would be, if a parent could say, 'I know you miss Daddy very much, if you feel like having a good cry, it will help to ease the pain'. Sometimes we have to give children permission to cry and release bottled up emotions. Much of the blame for not showing our true emotions, and expressing them, is due to our early conditioning, during our formative years.

Speech is the most important line of communication, and yet following a death it can be one of the most difficult things to do.

Our entire attitude to death creates another problem, as the topic of death, is still very much a 'taboo' subject. And yet is it not a part of life? It comes as no surprise therefore, to find that the lone parent is unable to share with the remaining members of the family, just how they feel about death of a loved one. The parent is so consumed by their own grief, that there is nothing left to give the siblings. Grief can be very selfish in its nature, and takes a great deal of energy out of those who are left to cope.

Guidelines for supporters

There are several very important factors which must be considered before attempts to support a bereaved child are made. First, the child must be able to relate to the 'supporter', as someone who has an understanding of his or her problems. Second, there must be complete trust, which must work both ways. It is impossible to work with half truths or white lies. Third and perhaps the most important issue, the person taking on the commitment of counselling, must be fully aware of their own attitudes towards death. It is not unknown to hear of a person embarking on helping someone else, only to discover that somewhere in their own past are 'unresolved' grief feelings.

What happens then, is that strong emotions come rushing to the surface. If this happens the person is unable to carry on and this could prove unsettling for both parties. Of course if the person who is acting as facilitator, has life experience as well as counselling skills, this can make the child feel that they have found someone who really does understand.

Some schools already appoint 'tutor counsellors', to help with pupils' problems, but one must still consider that the child may not necessarily relate to this person. A little time spent on trying to find a good 'key' person in the beginning could be regarded as 'preventative medicine', this may in fact lessen the risks of children becoming 'truants from life'.

No-one can have too much support, following a death or major trauma. It has been noticed that a person can need different types of support at various stages of recovery. A parent may benefit from group support or one to one counselling, whilst a child with more intense problems, could well benefit from support from a Child Guidance worker. We have to learn to share the load and be far more flexible in our way of trying to support bereaved people, especially the siblings in the family.

Good relationships with the parent and the child are always of benefit, it is good to encourage the family to trust each other with emotions which are frightening and confusing. It is also important that a parent is aware of any problems arising at school due to a bereavement, and permission of the parent should be sought if counselling is going to be offered to the pupil.

Before we can begin to understand why some children, and adolescents become 'truants from life', we have to understand that every child will deal with a death in an individual way. Some may find it very easy to 'share' their feelings at great depth and in graphic detail, others who are often not as outgoing will internalise things, be unable to share, their grief becomes a heavy load to carry around, and this they will do, for many years unless someone with the right approach can be found.

We must always be aware of what we want to say to a child, and how we go about the way in which we communicate the message.

One child returned home from school a few days after his father's death, and asked his mother, 'Are we a one parent family now?' The mother who was still in a state of shock, thought for a moment and replied, 'Well I suppose we must be'. Can you see how quickly labels start to be attached to a situation. The child had been informed that there would now be free school meals available, unfortunately there is a kind of stigma surrounding a child whose family is now unable to afford the school meal. All families need a great deal of support and encouragement in those early stages of adjustment, even making a christmas card at school which a year before would have been to both parents, must now bear a single name.

Family case study

Consider the following case study in order to see just how many individual feelings, emotions and ways of coping, come into play following a death in a family of five.

The father has died at the age of thirty-eight, the mother has to convey the sad and sudden news to her three children. The eldest son was so distraught that he cried non-stop for many hours, he was inconsolable, falling eventually into a deep sleep from sheer exhaustion. He was fifteen, and had spent many hours enjoying his father's company. The daughter who was fourteen kept her grief and feelings locked away inside of her, she too had had a good relationship with her father, he had been the one to whom she turned with homework problems. It was not until she was studying for her examinations a year later, that her grief suddenly came to the surface. It could have been all the added pressure she was under, that now intensified the loss she felt, by not having him there to help.

To actually witness an unresolved grief suddenly emerge, can be quite a frightening experience, but it brings total relief to the bearer, it is very much like witnessing an exorcism. Once the natural floodgates burst open, communication can be not only improved but built upon, bringing the courage to share feelings which have been kept at bay for so long.

The youngest son when hearing of his father's death, rushed from the confines of his mother's lap and arms, and sought refuge beneath his duvet. He was so angry with his father, it was as if the duvet prevented the outside world and truth from getting to him, if he hid it would all go away. When you are only seven years old, it is a hard lesson to learn that 'dead', really means 'dead', and *no*, he will not be seeing daddy again, and young people die as well as the old and infirmed.

Although this is a painful experience for one so young to learn, it is important to be truthful regarding the manner of death, as it will set a good foundation for the recovery period. We do not help children by telling lies or half truths, just to make death more acceptable.

This little lad needed a father figure to share things with and to show him all the things his elder brother had already learnt from the father. His answer was to adopt people to use as role models, fortunately for him the people he chose were caring and understanding, the relationships grew, and so did he.

We have talked so far about the children in the family, but what of the mother and her grief? She had experienced the loss of a parent through divorce in her teenage years, and strived to keep the family home life as near normal as possible, being there for the children, working hard to keep things just as they were when her husband was alive. She in fact put her family first in all ways, her grief was kept from those around her, and her crying was done when the children were in bed, and she was alone, crying in the shower brought a gentle release.

Like her daughter it was another stressful situation that acted as a cataclysm which enabled her to start her grieving at last.

This case study outlines each member in the family, their immediate reaction to the death, and a mixture of feelings and emotions that each is trying to come to terms with. No family will be the same, as each situation will vary from the next.

Let us now look at some of the more normal changes that we can expect from a child following a death – shock, unable to function normally;

withdrawn; listless; apathy; lack of interest; mood swings; lack of concentration; short term memory impaired; irritability; minor illnesses; agressive behaviour; feelings of guilt; non-acceptance that the parent has died; stealing, telling lies; loss of status (trying to refit into a changed family balance); loss of self esteem; absenteeism in varying degrees.

Younger children may revert back to tantrums, over dependency, not playing with other children, nightmares, not sleeping alone, anxiety, self comfort, natural development impaired, and soiling.

Children in grief will go through the above stages at some time or the other, and you can understand just how easy it would be for someone with little knowledge of grief to believe that a child is behaving *abnormally* rather than *normally*. However one must always be aware that some children can get stuck at a particular stage for too long, and help may be needed to help them to move on. Some may take only a few days to resolve an angry or guilty phase, whilst others could take several months to finally resolve the problem.

It is quite possible that the child who has not actively taken part in the classroom activities, is silent because he finds discussion difficult, he may be confused and frightened by his own feelings. Not all children find it easy to share, and there is this big problem of finding someone who will *really listen*. If help is not sought he could so easily become a 'truant from life', and he will in fact just switch off, because that seems to be the easiest thing to do.

However I do not think that children give up on participating in life necessarily following a bereavement, however traumatic. It is more likely to be determined by the nature of the death, previous losses, and the social and personal circumstances surrounding the child and the entire family. It is not normally just one factor but an accumulation of events which simply brings things to ahead. In fact this child may have been 'switching off' gradually over a period of years, rather than months, this latest event is the final straw. It is as if this child is saying, 'I cannot go on any longer', or 'Is it all worth it?' However hard he has tried to cope in the past, there is now this intense feeling that life has rejected him, and the familiar 'couldn't care less' attitude takes over.

There is a very fine line between normal and abnormal grief and it will become apparent earlier rather than later whether a lay counsellor is able to help a child resolve the bereavement problems. A good indication of a child with more complex issues, is when the child's anxieties and fears about life and death become phobias, making it impossible for them to live a normal life. They become unable to see things as they really are, often these children were anxious and insecure before the death, the death now makes it more difficult for them to function, and they will need help of a professional nature.

Some counsellors feel that they have let the child down if they have to refer on, this is not the case, as it takes a great deal of courage to acknowledge that we all have our limitations, and in some cases we have no more to offer. At the very least the child has been given the insight to his or her own problems and the importance of seeking further help.

Even normal cases can have their own particular issues, and it is the role of the counsellor to help the child to view the problem from all angles, by talking things through, issues become much clearer, often the child finds solutions to their own situation. Many fears and worries are unfounded but the reassurance that a good counsellor can give will often give the child the courage to face up to the painful facts. The main role is to allow a child to grow and learn from the bereavement experience.

Individual case studies

In the following case studies the aim is to illustrate just how each set of circumstances, create different problems for the child. The counsellor has to learn to be flexible. Often it is the counsellor's understanding, patience and expeience which will determine which way to proceed.

Simon aged fourteen

Simon came for counselling a year after his father committed suicide. He was a tall, pale listless child, he stretched and yawned the whole time, as he presented his story. His dialogue was stilted, with long silences. It was always a surprise that he returned each week. Simon placed barriers to protect himself and his dead father. The first barrier protected Simon from feeling pain, and the second was to protect his father's reputation, 'suicide' brings not only a feeling of total rejection, but also the stigma, that the taking of one's own life is a show of weakness and failure.

During one session in particular Simon suddenly asked why I thought there was a strong 'atmosphere' at home? It was so strong that he could almost eat it. I gave his question some thought and explained that humans give off distress signals when they are unhappy, angry, sad and grieving. He had told me about his mother who always seemed to be in a bad mood or depressed, and I realised that after a day at school, he would return to a mother in grief. Later I contemplated the situation again, and wondered if the boy had imagined the 'atmosphere' coming from the dead father's spirit. I planned to discuss this thought with him the following week. As it turned out I had no need to follow these lines, as Simon had changed his attitude towards his mother and decided to discuss his feelings openly, and in doing so the mother also found she could talk about her husband's death with her son.

On another occasion we talked about Simon's other problem which was 'apathy' and general tiredness. He had great difficulty in getting off to sleep, and when he eventually managed to do so, it seemed that the alarm was then going off ready for school.

I showed him some very simple relaxation exercises, just closing the eyes and then concentrating on tightening the muscles from head to toe, and then relaxing them again. These simple exercises can be of great value for children and adults, especially as it is something that can be done either sitting in a chair or lying flat in bed. We also discussed that grief is a heavy load to carry, and sometimes you can get fed up with the weight of it. In fact there comes a time when it is perfectly alright to let go. This simple statement made such an impact on him, that I could almost see the load start to lift. I cannot explain why it is, but in some cases just a right word, at the right time, acts as a 'key' to unlock a particular problem, but you do have to witness this type of reaction to realise that often, it is a very simple technique that can help the child to come to terms with his bereavement.

Thomas aged twenty-two

Thomas was an outpatient at a local psychiatric hospital, during the previous six months he had tried to commit suicide on several occasions. He was withdrawn, shoulders slumped, with little or no eye contact, but at the same time it was possible to feel his intense anger. Although Thomas was in his twenties his bereavement had taken place with he was eighteen, he was in fact suffering from an unresolved grief. As Thomas told his story I found it difficult to imagine how anyone could cope with so many losses in a short life, and not be left with some very deep scars.

He had been placed in a 'foster home' at an early age, due to the break up of his parents' marriage, he had been separated from his brothers and sister, and lost contact with relations and friends. At the age of eleven years he was involved in a bad road accident, which left him in hospital for a year, learning to speak, read and write all over again. During this time his only visitor had been his grandmother, she became an important person in his life, she was the only stable person from his previous family. They supported one another until she died, the shock and trauma was just too much for him to cope with.

It took several years, when he did become a very real 'truant from life', he took to drink, petty crime and attempted suicide before he sought help.

The one thing which stopped his grieving process what that, by a twist of fate, Thomas had been unable to be with his grandmother at the time of her death. He felt cheated and totally rejected. There were so many things unsaid, the most important were 'Goodbye', and 'I love you'.

The basis for my counselling was to get this young man to talk about all his losses in his life. There were many painful memories which we had to discuss, before we could tackle the grieving process for his grandmother. I could feel his anger and this overpowering feeling of rejection, it kept coming to the surface, he felt unloved and unwanted, his self esteem was so low that he considered that he had very little to offer others. He needed a lot of support from myself, his 'key' worker at the hospital, and a social worker who could advise him on financial difficulties and accommodation.

From my standpoint I knew that his grief had to be worked on and then finalised, and the main stumbling block was the 'Goodbye'. I suggested that a special letter containing his feelings could be written down, these feelings are better written on paper, rather than locked away inside. The following week Thomas brought me, not only a letter of farewell, but a beautiful poem, which he read to me. I asked him what he thought we should do with them? Some find a ceremonial burning symbolic, or giving them to someone else to destroy can be helpful. On this occasion he gave me the letter to burn, the poem was to go in his wallet, to keep on his person. Thomas had been a true 'truant from life' in every sense of the word.

This case study not only highlights the importance of all aspects of loss, but the importance of grieving for them, and the way in which voluntary organisations can work alongside the professionals.

Daniel aged nine

Daniel was nine when his father died of a heart attack. He found talking very difficult, but was eager to work with a group of children using paint as a way of 'sharing'.

Daniel's pictures were always tight and painstakingly thought out. He used the smallest brush to cover the largest area of paper, when drawing a line he used a ruler, his own work took the form of a maze. He was convinced that in the centre of the maze was his father, he was not dead, only lost, given time he would find his way back. It was as if Daniel was trying to find a magic formula to return his father to him, the maze gave Daniel breathing space, and a good reason to put off the acceptance of death and the finality it brings with it.

Terminal illness

Saying 'Goodbye' is never easy, especially when a person is going to die. Terminal illness brings with it shock, it is nearly as traumatic as sudden death. We should learn to share, rather than exclude children from the painful issues of terminal illness. Children as young as nine, tell of being 'cheated', because they were not told that a parent was going to die. They feel rejected and unimportant.

A nine-year-old girl told how on the afternoon of her father's death, a neighbour had been asked to take her to the park. She did not really want to go, but did for her mother's sake. When telling her story she said she knew the exact time her father had died, and had mentally said 'goodbye'. On returning to the family home she was met by tearful relations, who informed her what she already knew was a fact. Her anger and resentment simmered for over a year, the anger was directed at her mother for excluding her at the very end. She told how other people's presence had seemed more important than her own, if that were the case then she would withdraw herself, and did in fact spend many hours alone in her own room.

If we are to understand just why some children become withdrawn from life, we too have to consider how and why this starts to happen. If children are excluded by adults on a regular basis, they might well begin to exclude themselves. Bereavement brings with it a kind of 'aloneness', which is quite different from 'loneliness', this coupled with 'withdrawal' would make it very difficult indeed for the child to come to terms with his or her loss.

Some children and teenagers will act out elaborate games of make believe in order to convince themselves that the person who had died, is not dead at all, they are simply not around at that moment, it is this kind of situation which can so easily follow on from a death, where all the facts were not made available.

This child was encouraged to make a special memory book filled with photographs of her father's life from birth until his death. These photographs gave the family a starting point on which to begin 'sharing' again. The child was also left with something which was special to her.

Pressure can often be placed on siblings after a death to change their role within the family. Often when a father or mother dies you can hear well meaning people say, 'Well now you are the man of the house', or 'Now you have to be Mother', how can a child gain a lifetime of experience over night? The answer is that they cannot. They then begin to feel inadequate and often spend hours in their bedroom locked away listening to loud music, which helps to block everything else out. Their room becomes their private place, intrusion from the outside world is met with resentment. Often a notice will be placed on the door, saying 'Private' and 'Keep Out', they dare anyone to go inside and clean up. Often this child shows little or no signs of distress, but underneath the emotions are buried.

Teenagers especially can change the way in which they dress, an adolesent girl may become drab in her clothing, her appearance will border on the unkempt look, it is as if she is rejecting herself as a person. Some teenagers take to wearing the dead person's clothes, although some might find this strange, it is a form of comfort and should not be discouraged.

Other modes of dress may border on the flamboyant, it is all about making a non-verbal statement. What this child is saying to the others in her or his peer group is 'If you cannot accept me as a grieving person. Then accept me for another reason, the way in which I dress creates the attention I need'.

All these very complex issues could be going on in the class room situation without the teacher ever suspecting why. The child may not be able to make contact verbally. In fact it is more often seen as another way of creating tension between the pupil and school authorities, and yet in itself it is another way of crying for help and seeking attention.

Teenage girls can develop eating problems which could possible develop into anorexia, this can be triggered by a death of a parent. It is an attempt to stay at the little girl stage, changes and an increase in responsibilities can be difficult to cope with, but coupled with puberty the problems are increased. Anorexia is often accompanied by phobias which will need professional help and guidance, often teenagers are adamant that they like being the way they are, it is others who wish them to seek help.

Aggressive behaviour is quite common in teenage boys following a death of a parent, the pent up anger and emotions can suddenly be released taking those in the immediate vicinity completely by surprise. In some cases the anger can be directed at themselves with self inflicted injuries or even attempts at taking their own lives, some sadly are successful, causing further pain for the family. Others who are at their angry stage take to destroying or defacing things around them, which are not their property, this can lead to arrest resulting in further complications, which the teenager and his family would find difficulty in coping with.

Unfortunately some young people find alcohol is a way of blocking out emotions and pain, but as we are aware it is only another form of masking the underlying problem. If the drinking goes undetected, then that teenager could eventually end up with two problems, rather than one. Often these children have been brought up in a household where adults use alcohol as a way of unwinding at the end of a busy day, for that particular family it is considered normal. When the lone parent discovers what has been happening, they are usually quite shocked and do not condone their child's actions.

Although drugs can be found fairly easily in most major cities, this is far less common than alcohol abuse. One young teenager who smoked 'pot' as a way of coping, insisted that it never made him aggressive, but more passive. It was explained to him that if he wanted to undertake counselling for his bereavement, he would have to agree to let his true feelings out, rather than suppress them with the use of drugs. He agreed to do this and eventually with support went on to live a normal life, once his grief had been resolved.

Throughout this chapter the aim has been to give the reader an insight into the complexities brought about by a death either in the family itself or of a close friend. It is important to offer good support which all parties involved, feel comfortable with. The overall aim is to enable the child who is in grief to come to terms with his or her loss, to grow through the experience, and then move on with life.

Guidelines for lay counsellors

(1) The task of the counsellor is to give a child the chance to explore and discover ways in which a bereavement can be resolved.
(2) The counsellor must encourage growth, as a loss handled well will become a 'life experience' on which to build.
(3) Counselling is a responsibility which needs commitment from both parties.
(4) Guidelines and a necessary framework should be clear to all those who are involved, e.g. counsellor, client, parent and others.
(5) Written confirmation giving details of 'contact'. Remember those in grief are confused and suffer memory loss.
(6) Confidentiality. If advice or discussion is needed with a third person, then permission should be sought from the clinet.
(7) Supervision for the counsellor. This is important not only for the counsellor but also the client.
(8) Regular reviewal of the case to assess progress made.
(9) Encouraging the client to look back on problems which have successfully been resolved, as well as moving forward. This method of encouragement helps those whose self esteem has been very low.
(10) Make use of all types of communication and sharing, for example,

photographs; making a special memory book; pictures in paint, felt tips, pen, pencil or clay work; all written work, including poetry.

(11) Moving on. 'Saying goodbye'. When a bereaved child has worked through his or her grief, they often feel that they might like to help another who has also suffered a 'loss'. It is at this time that group work can play an important role in the recovery. Some children share their experiences, whilst others seek the reassurances by listening to others. The same rules apply in a small group where consideration, empathy, understanding and confidentiality should be observed.

PART TWO

Assessment

CHAPTER 5

The Psychiatric Examination of Withdrawn Children

Philip Barker

The examination of the child who is emotionally withdrawn presents a challenge to the psychiatrist. Many such children are reluctant or unwilling to be interviewed in the first place. They may have fears they are reluctant to discuss, at least until they have gained confidence in the psychiatrist. Moreover, unlike most adults coming for psychiatric examination, children are usually brought for examination by others, most often their parents. They may have no desire whatever to undergo psychiatric examination.

While the objectives of the psychiatric examination of children vary somewhat according to the clinical situation, similar general principles apply whether the child is withdrawn or outgoing, happy or sad, intellectually gifted or of lesser intelligence, deprived or privileged. The main areas the psychiatrist will wish to explore are:

- The child's emotional state and level of emotional development. Sometimes the question of whether the child presents a suicidal risk is a major issue to be addressed.
- The child's cognitive functioning. Has cognitive development followed a normal path? Are there deficits or areas of precocious development?
- The child's relationships and social skills.
- The characteristics of the child's motor behaviour.
- The child's communication skills, both verbal and non-verbal.
- The child's fantasy life.
- Whether there is evidence of delusions, hallucinations, thought disorder or other abnormal mental processes.
- The subjects that occupy the forefront of the child's mind.

- The child's pattern of psychological defenses – the mechanisms used to deal with emotionally painful or anxiety provoking issues.
- The child's play skills.
- The child's attention span.
- Whether there is evidence of a physical basis for the child's problems.

This list is not exhaustive. In particular circumstances, for example psychiatric examinations conducted for medicolegal purposes, or to assist a child welfare agency in the placement or care of a child, other issues may need to be addressed. It does however include most of the areas a psychiatric examination should cover. We will consider the information to be obtained more fully when the interview with the child is discussed.

While information obtained in the course of the psychiatric examination can be supplemented by the use of standardised psychological and other tests, these are not a satisfactory substitute for a careful clinical psychiatric evaluation. One reason for this is that it can be hard to know what tests to administer to a particular child until a global psychiatric assessment has been completed.

Background considerations

Before we turn to the special considerations that must be taken into account when a withdrawn child is examined, we must consider what the background to withdrawn behaviour may be. Previous chapters have considered certain possible causes, including bullying by other children, bereavement, and abuse of various sorts. In addition we need to consider certain psychiatric disorders which have withdrawn behaviour as part of their clinical picture. These include:

- Infantile autism (referred to in the revised third edition of the Diagnostic and Statistical Manual of the American Psychiatric Association (1987) as a form of 'pervasive developmental disorder').
- Elective mutism.
- Avoidant disorder of childhood or adolescence.
- Separation anxiety disorder.

We will consider these conditions in the final section of this chapter. In addition to children with conditions which can be classified under one of the above headings, we meet others whose withdrawn behaviour seems to be, in large measure, a feature of an inborn temperamental style. The wide variation in temperamental styles found among children has been well documented in the work of Thomas and Chess (1977) and Chess and Thomas (1984).

How can we tell whether a child is displaying withdrawn behaviour primarily because this is his or her inborn, perhaps constitutionally determined, temperamental style rather than for other reasons? An important point is that temperamental styles tend to be established early in life and to persist. Thus Bronson (1970) found that fearful one-year-old boys were still fearful when aged six to eight. In the Fels longitudinal study, the degree of inhibition shown by children in their first three years predicted their behaviour during the next three years, in that they were found to be easily dominated by their peers and were likely to withdraw from peer interactions (Kagan and Moss, 1962).

Studies of twins have also suggested that genetic factors may play significant roles in determining the degree to which children are withdrawn and inhibited in their behaviour. Plomin and Rowe (1979) found that monozygotic twins were more similar, at one year of age, in their degree of behavioural inhibition in the presence of unfamiliar adults than dizygotic twins.

The term 'behavioural inhibition' is used frequently in the research literature to describe behaviour which clinicians would probably consider to be 'withdrawn'. Behavioural inhibition has been studied extensively and intensively in the Harvard Infant Study Laboratory in Cambridge, Massachussetts, by Kagan and his colleagues.

In 1984, Kagan, Reznick, Clarke, Sniderman and Garcia-Coll (1984) studied and compared two groups of children, one of them comprising 28 extremely inhibited children, the other 30 extremely uninhibited children. The children were selected from a larger group at the age of 21 months. In addition to behavioural observations, these authors also made various physiological measurements. Twenty-two of the children who had been classified as inhibited at 21 months, and 21 of those who had been uninhibited, were re-examined at age four. It was found that, in general, they retained the qualities of behavioural inhibition or lack of inhibition. If there was a change it was more likely to be from inhibited to uninhibited behaviour.

(To some extent, therefore, it seems that time is on our side if we choose to delay our examination of these children. However, a further follow-up at age five and a half found that the formerly inhibited children were still more inhibited with peers in both laboratory and school, and with the examiner in the testing situation, and were more cautious in a situation of mild risk (Reznick et al., 1986).)

In a later study Kagan et al., 1989) 100 children were observed in laboratory settings at 14, 20, 32 and 48 months. When the data relating to the entire sample were analysed there was found to be no significant difference between the degree of inhibited behaviour at 14 or 20 months, on the one hand, and that observed at four years. On the other hand, the children who were either extremely inhibited or extremely uninhibited at 14 or 20 months differed significantly at age four. It seems that extremely inhibited children may represent one end of a continuum from 'shyness and restraint to sociability and affective spontaneity' (Kagan et al., 1989).

At seven years of age, a majority of children who had shown 'extreme restraint' at age two were 'quiet and socially avoidant' with both children and adults (Kagan et al., 1988).

In 1990, Biederman and his colleagues reported a study of children with 'behavioural inhibition,' a temperamental category defined by various laboratory measurements, and consisting of constricted behaviour in unfamiliar situations. They found that these children had increased risk of developing multiple anxiety, over-anxious and phobic disorders. Enquiry about children's early temperamental styles seems likely, therefore, to yield information of value in understanding their later psychiatric condition. We need always to consider the question, how far is this a lifelong pattern of behaviour and how far is it a reaction to environmental or other factors such as physical disorders?

Of interest, too, is the evidence reported by Kagan *et al.* (1988) that there is a biological basis for childhood shyness. This may be related to inherited variations in the threshold of arousal in certain sites in the limbic area of the brain. But these authors suggest that 'the actualization of shy, quiet, timid behaviour at two years of age requires some form of chronic environmental stress acting upon the original temperamental disposition present at birth'. They suggest that 'stressors [such as] prolonged hospitalization, death of a parent, marital quarrelling, or mental illness in a family member' may be contributory factors. To this list might be added bullying, other forms of deprivation and abuse in its various forms. Kagan *et al.* (1988) also comment that two thirds of their group of extremely inhibited children were later-born children, whereas two-thirds of their unhibited children were first-borns.

The above findings suggest a number of areas which should be explored during the psychiatric assessment of withdrawn children.

Examination strategies

Many schemes exist for the psychiatric examination of children. In *Basic Child Psychiatry* (Barker, 1988) I have set out one which I have found to work well. *Clinical Interviews with Children and Adolescents* (Barker, 1990) discusses ways of conducting interviews with young people. I have found that the principles and techniques set out there facilitate the obtaining of needed information in an efficient manner, while retaining respect for the young person. There is however more to the psychiatric assessment of a child than the interview, or interviews, with the child.

Because children are so dependent on their environments, a psychiatric assessment that focuses only on the child must inevitably miss information of relevance to the child's psychiatric condition. Moreover, young children have limited verbal communication skills. The younger they are the more this is the case; and withdrawn children are often reluctant to use the verbal communication skills they do possess. For all these reasons the psychiatric examination of a child or adolescent should, as a minimum, include the following:

- A meeting with the whole family group.
- An interview with the child on his or her own.
- A meeting with the parents or other caregivers, in the absence of the child.

Without going through at least the above three processes it is not usually possible to obtain the information needed to make a sound psychiatric assessment.

In many cases it is helpful to supplement the information obtained as above with reports from the child's school, or – better – interviews with teachers; with reports from other caregivers who may have been involved – foster parents, daycare staff, those responsible for recreational or sports groups the child attends and so on; or with information from any child welfare or other social agencies that are or have been involved with the child or the child's family. Although the possibility of obtaining information from these other possible alternative sources must always be borne in mind, the process for doing so will not be discussed further here.

The interview with the family

There are two main classes of information which should be obtained from the interview with the family. There is factual information about the family and its history, and information about the functioning of the family *as a system*.

The family and its history

Understanding of a child's psychiatric condition is greatly facilitated when the examiner has a good understanding of the nature of the family in which the child is a part. Under the above heading we should consider the following:

- The composition of the family.
- How long the parents have been married.
- Whether either parent has been married previously.
- Whether there have been any marital separations.
- Whether the family is a nuclear family, a blended one or a single parent one.
- The family's economic status and living conditions.
- The life, medical and psychiatric histories of the parents and other family members. It is important to enquire for any history of alcoholism or drug abuse in the family, since such problems are often associated with emotional disorders in children. In view of the findings summarised above concerning the possible biological basis of shyness, it is a good idea to enquire for a history of similar personality characteristics in first degree relatives.
- Any history of physical, sexual or emotional abuse in the family.

I find it helpful, during the process of obtaining this information, to have the family help me construct a genogram or family tree. The family members provide the information while I record it. This process is described further in *Basic Family Therapy* (Barker, 1986) and in *Genograms in Family Assessment* (McGoldrick and Gerson, 1985).

The information listed above may not always be readily available. While many families are open and frank when telling us their stories, others are not. This may especially be the case when issues such as abusive behaviours within family groups, and drug and alcohol use are discussed. These are often minimised and sometimes denied entirely, even though they may be major problems.

The family system

An assessment which does not take account of a young person's social system is unlikely to yield an adequate understanding of that person's psychiatric condition. This is true whatever the age of the patient being assessed, but the younger the patient, the truer it is likely to be. Preschool children, and to an even greater extent infants, are so much dependent on those caring for them that their conditions and emotional problems cannot be properly understood without an understanding of the emotional climate in which they are living.

For most children the social system we need to pay the greatest attention to is the family. Some children, however, are encountered who are not living with their families. They may be in hospitals, group or 'children's' homes, residential schools, or institutions for delinquent or behaviourally disturbed young people. In these cases we must pay as much attention to the social system of the institution as we normally do to that of the family.

Among the most extreme examples of emotional withdrawal by children is that reported by Spitz (1946). He described what he called 'anaclitic depression', an extreme state of withdrawal with failure to thrive and a high mortality rate in children who were institutionalised and lacked stimulation. Many of us thought this was a thing of the past, but recent reports from Romanian orphanages have shown, alas, with their horrifying pictures and TV images, that this is not the case. These reports should remind us of how vital are the roles of children's social environments and the social stimulation they receive.

It is relevant to point out here that the behaviour of most children is quite situation specific. Epidemiological studies, for example that were conducted in the Isle of Wight (Rutter *et al.*, 1970) and also the Ontario Child Health Study (Offord *et al.*, 1987), have shown that disturbed behaviour is often manifest differentially either in the home or in school. The phrase 'withdrawn child' should therefore be supplemented by a description of the situations in which the child is more, or less, withdrawn.

The assessment of family systems is a major subject in its own right and it is not possible to go into it in death here. I have described approaches to family assessment in *Basic Family Therapy* (Barker, 1986) and there are many other textbooks on the subject. The examiner is a participant observer and must discover the patterns of interaction of the family members; who relates to whom and in what way; what subsystems exist in the family; how rigid or flexible the boundaries between subsystems are; what are the roles of the different family members; and, if a child is the 'identified patient', what is the role of that child in the family.

If our withdrawn child displays the withdrawal within the family circle, it may well be that this is the role assigned to him or her in this system. The assignment of family roles is a complex process. It must suffice here to say that the temperamental and other characteristics of each family member predispose the member to adopt a particular role. To this is added a complex of dynamic factors. It is possible to understand many emotional and behavioural problems as related to the attempts of individuals to fit into roles 'required' of them by the nature of the family system of which they are part.

Examples of the so-called 'idiosyncratic' roles (Epstein *et al.*, 1978) which family members may play include scapegoat, 'parental' child, martyr, 'family angel' (Gross, 1979), sick member, handicapped person, 'crazy' member and, of course, withdrawn child.

It is important to bear in mind that the behaviour of children tends to be quite context specific. The meeting with the family provides an opportunity to see the extent of any withdrawal that is evident in that situation. The child may also be more or less withdrawn when relating to different family members. The behaviour observed may be compared to that observed when the child is interviewed individually, and with that reported to be displayed in other situations – for example school, other groups and with peers in the community.

The interview with the child

The meeting with the child is the central act in the psychiatric assessment. The impressions and opinions of others are important but they can be misleading. There is no substitute for a one-to-one interview with the child who is the subject of the assessment. Some children present, in this situation, in ways substantially different from that the examiner had been led to expect.

In this section I will first outline an approach to the interviewing of children generally, with emphasis on the special points which need to be considered when a withdrawn child is encountered. In the following sections I will consider how our approach may be modified when we are dealing with children with certain specific disorders.

Every interview has at least three stages (Barker, 1990, Ch. 4); or perhaps it is more accurate to say that it is necessary to go through three processes. The stages/processes are:

- An introductory stage, a major feature of which is the establishing of rapport.
- A period during which information is exchanged. It is well to bear in mind that every interview is a two-way process. While we obviously wish to obtain information from the child we are interviewing, we inevitably give information, both verbal and non-verbal. Even if we are parsimonious about the information we impart verbally, we communicate much in non-verbal ways.
- The termination process.

The above processes are not mutually exclusive. Indeed they normally overlap to a great extent. Thus the building of rapport should be something that is occurring at all times; and the termination process really starts as soon as a time frame for the interview is mentioned. Also, information is inevitably exchanged between the participants throughout the interview. Indeed it sometimes happens that important information, which until then has been witheld, emerges during the termination process. For example, the discovery that the child does not wish to end the interview and return to the parents may be of great significance; and the child who has been wanting to reveal a piece of information but has hesitated to do so for fear of possible adverse consequences, may blurt it out at the last minute. This may be because it seems to the child that this may be the last opportunity to say what is on his or her mind, or because it is 'safe' since there is now little time left to discuss what may be a painful and anxiety laden subject.

We will now consider these three processes in greater depth, with particular reference to interviews with withdrawn children.

The introductory stage and the building of rapport

The first thing to be considered is the matter of confidentiality. This is an important issue in all clinical interviews. Any person carrying out such an interview must be clear about the limits of confidentiality that apply. This must also be made clear to the person being interviewed. One reason why children (and others) are sometimes reluctant to divulge information is because they do not know what will happen to it.

In many clinical situations it is not necessary to reveal to parents or others details of what the child has said. It is usually sufficient to give the parent(s) only a very general account of how the interview went, together with an opinion on the child's mental state and recommendations for any further investigations or treatment that are considered to be indicated.

There are three principal exceptions to this general rule. First, when the child reveals information that the parents or other responsible adult *must* know about. This covers such things as a child's intention to commit suicide or engage in other behaviour which would put the child or others in serious danger. Second, when the interviewer is compelled to report information because of a legal requirement to do so. Most jurisdictions have legislation that makes it mandatory for all people – whether professionals in the helping fields or not – to report, usually to the statutory child welfare agency, anything that gives them grounds to believe that a child has been physically or sexually abused. Some jurisdictions have laws that cover also emotional abuse. Third, when the assessment is being done for medicolegal purposes, as for example when it is done at the request of a court to which the psychiatrist must submit a report.

The action that might be necessary when the above three situations arise should be explained to and discussed with the young person early in the interview and any questions answered. This clears the air and ensures that the child knows where he or she stands. It is important, too, that the points are explained in language the child can understand. These matters may be of special importance when we are dealing with withdrawn children. Part at least of their inhibited behaviour is sometimes due to a reluctance to divulge information which they feel might lead to their getting into some sort of trouble if it falls into the wrong hands.

Once the confidentiality ground rules have been explained and clarified the process of actively developing a trusting relationship can proceed further. Trust is a major part of that hard-to-define quality we call rapport. Careful attention to the process of establishing rapport is of especial importance when one is examining an emotionally withdrawn subject. Withdrawn children are inclined to limit severely the amount of information they are prepared to communicate to others, especially those they do not know. They are often reluctant to trust unfamiliar figures – and sometimes even familiar ones. They may also be fearful or anxious about being separated from their parents or whoever it is that has brought them to the interview.

A central point which cannot be over emphasised is that rapport is built by starting where the subject is. By this I mean that the child's point of view and wishes should initially be accepted. And not only that. It is also helpful to adopt, as far as is practical, the child's posture, manner of speaking, tone of voice, and speed of movement.

In deciding which activity to start with it is usually best to accept the child's wishes. Most withdrawn children are not great conversationalists. Therefore starting the interview by attempting to engage them in a conversation, especially about matters of emotional significance, will probably be counter productive. They may prefer to play, or perhaps to engage in something quite 'safe' such as looking at a picture book.

While the approach to interviewing a child will always be determined in large measure by the age of the child, a wide range of options exists. There is talk and there is play. There is free play and there is structured play. There are board games, cooperative games and competitive ones. There is sand tray play and there is water play. Other options are drawing, painting, modelling and puppetry. And this list is not exhaustive. Not all these options may be available in the place in which the interview takes place, nor need they be. But a range of materials, games and activities should be available and initially the child should be allowed to choose from among them. The interviewer accepts the child's choice and, in due course, gets involved in the activity in which the child is engaged.

Some children like to play and much can be learned from the form and content of their play, even if they do not talk at all. Others like to talk, or at least are willing to talk, though we find fewer in this category among withdrawn children. In any case one should always try to get a conversation going during the interview. It is best to start with non-threatening subjects. After greeting the child, the interviewer might go on to ask about how the child got to the clinic or office, the child's age, date of birth, place of residence, school, school grade or class, and leisure time activities and interests. The latter may serve as a main topic of conversation during the early stages of establishing rapport and gaining the child's confidence.

Whether in play or conversation the interviewer should be appropriately responsive to what the child is doing or saying. This involves accepting the child's feelings and views. Thus it is not usually helpful to question a child's emotional responses to things discussed – at least during an assessment interview and when a good degree of rapport has yet to be developed. Many children express anger towards others – parents, siblings, peers, teachers or other people. Such children's angry attitudes may not appear (and in reality they may not be) constructive or useful. One may feel tempted to point out the destructiveness of such attitudes but to do so at an early stage in one's relationship with the child is likely to work against the establishment of rapport.

The processes of setting the stage for interviews with children, and establishing rapport with them, are discussed more fully in *Clinical Interviews with Children and Adolescents* (Barker, 1990).

Once rapport has been established, the process of exploring the child's state of mind can proceed. This should be done gently, sensitively and in a flexible manner. Information may be obtained either by means of question-and-answer interchanges, in the course of more informal conversation, or less directly through play, drawing, painting and modelling. In many cases a combination of play activities and conversation yields the best results. Comments on the child's play may be offered and this may lead to the child's explaining his or her views on the issues being played out, or on other topics.

The content of the interview will depend in part on the purpose of the interview but there are certain areas which a psychiatric assessment should always cover. These, reproduced from *Basic Child Psychiatry* (Barker, 1988), are:

(1) *General appearance* Are there any abnormalities of facial appearance, head, body build or limbs? Are there any bruises, cuts or grazes? Mode of dress and appropriateness for the climate and time of year? Does the child look happy or unhappy, tearful or worried? Attitude to the examiner and the consultation?

(2) *Motor function* Is the child overactive, normal or underactive? What motor activities are carried out? Are they performed normally, or clumsily, quickly or slowly? Abnormal movements such as tics? Right- or left-handed? Can the child distinguish right from left? Is the gait normal, and if not, in what way is it abnormal? Can the child write, draw and paint, and if so, how well?

(3) *Speech* Articulation, vocabulary and use of language should be noted. Does the child speak freely, little or not at all? Any stuttering? Receptive and expressive language? Ability to read and write?

(4) *Content of talk and thought* What does the child talk about? How easy is it to steer the conversation towards particular topics? Are any subjects avoided? Does the stream of thought flow logically from one thing to another? Is there any abnormal use of words or expressions? Is there evidence of hallucinations or delusions?

(5) *Intellectual function* A rough estimate of the child's level of intelli-

gence should be made, based on general knowledge, conversation, level of play, and knowledge of time, day, date, year, place and people's identity, taking into account what is normal for the child's age.

(6) *Mood and emotional state* Happy, elated, unhappy, frankly depressed, anxious, hostile, resentful, suspicious, upset by separation from parents and so on? Level of rapport which has been established. Has the child ever wanted to run away, or to hide, wished to be dead or contemplated suicide? Does the child cry, and if so, in what circumstances? Specific fears and if present how are they dealt with? Appropriateness of emotional state to subject being discussed?

(7) *Attitudes to family* Indications during conversation about family members or during play.

(8) *Attitudes to school* Does the child like school? Attitudes towards school work, play, staff, other pupils? Child's estimate of own abilities and progress in school?

(9) *Fantasy life* The child's three magic wishes. The three most desired companions on a desert island. What kind of dreams are reported or made up? What is the worst thing – and the best thing – that could happen to the child? What are the child's ambitions in life? Material expressed in play, drawing, painting, modelling and so on.

(10) *Sleep* Does the child report any difficulty in sleeping? Fear of going to bed or to sleep? Nightmares, night terrors (not usually reported by children unless they have been told they have them by others), pleasant dreams?

(11) *Behaviour problems* Does the child reveal anything about behaviour problems, delinquent activities, illicit drug use, running away, sexual problems or appearance in court?

(12) *Placement away from home* Has the child been placed, or lived, away from home? If so where, when, for how long, and what is the child's understanding of this? Child's reaction to this experience?

(13) *Attitude to referral* How does the child see the referral, and the reasons for it? Is he or she aware of a problem, and if so, what is it?

(14) *Indications of social adjustment* Number of reported friends, hobbies, interests, games played, youth organisations belonged to, how leisure time is spent. Does the child feel a follower or a leader, or bullied, teased or picked on? If so, by whom?

(15) *Other problems* Do any other problems come to light during the interview, for example worries, pains, headaches, other somatic problems or relationship difficulties?

(16) *Play* A general description of the child's play is required. What is played with and how? To what extent is play symbolic? Content of play? Concentration, distractibility and constructiveness?

(17) *The child's self-image* This cannot usually be assessed directly, but must be inferred from the sum total of what the child does and says, the ambitions and fantasy ideas expressed, and the child's estimate of what others think of him or her. There is evidence that disturbed children may overrate their self-esteem, as compared to ratings by adults,

whether these are parents, therapists or teachers (Zimet and Farley, 1986).

Children's behaviour should always be described as objectively as possible. A good account of how to do this is provided by Savicki and Brown (1981, Ch. 15).

The interview with the parents

In addition to the interviews with the whole family group and with the child, it is helpful to see the parents (or other caregivers in the case of children who are not living with their parents) on their own. This interview is concerned mainly with the parents' own issues. Their own family backgrounds, which tend to be major factors powerfully influencing how they rear their own children, should be explored. How were they brought up? What were the models of parenthood provided for them during their childhoods? What are their philosophies of child rearing? Were they abused as children? Their own personal and psychiatric histories, if these were not fully covered in the meeting with the whole family, should be explored further. Many disturbed children come from extended families with strong histories of alcoholism and drug abuse.

Any of the above issues may be of relevance in gaining an understanding of the emotional state and behaviour of a child undergoing psychiatric examination.

Other sources of information

The information obtained as set out above often requires to be supplemented by contacts with others concerned with the child. Especially if problems are reported in school, a report from the child's teacher(s) should be obtained or, better, a visit to the school carried out. There may be others who can add useful information about the child's behaviour, emotional state and reactions, or home or other environment. These may include social workers, daycare staff and youth group leaders. The consent of the parents and, if possible, the child is normally necessary if one is to contact such people – the exception being when child abuse is suspected, in which case communication with statutory child protection agencies does not require consent.

Some special categories of withdrawn children

Autistic children

Children suffering from autistic disorders (American psychiatric Association, 1987) display, among other features, extreme withdrawal. This disorder (more probably it is a group of disorders with varying causes) almost certainly has a neurological basis, though this is not fully understood. Many accounts of autistic disorders exist (see, for example, Barker, 1988, Ch. 7; Rutter, 1985a, b; Frith, 1989).

These are socially withdrawn children who seem to lack empathy for others and are content to remain in their own worlds, often engaging in repetitive, stereotyped activities. Their speech development is delayed and abnormal. Their psychiatric examination often has to be carried out by close observation of their behaviour in different situations, and by detailed history taken from those familiar with their behaviour and reactions to others. How much they are able to communicate verbally varies, but attempts to engage them in conversation should always be made. I have described elsewhere (Barker, 1990, Ch. 11) some strategies which can be helpful in entering the world of the autistic child.

The electively mute child

Elective mutism is a relatively rare condition, with a prevalence rate of perhaps 0.8 per 1000 seven-year-olds (Kolvin and Fundudis, 1981). The main feature is a failure to talk in most situations, despite the ability to do so. Characteristically these children decline to respond verbally when in school, public places, clinics, doctors' offices and indeed anywhere except at home or alone with their families elsewhere. They are often reluctant or quite unwilling to communicate nonverbally, such as by play, drawing or painting. As with autistic children, it is important to be aware of the existence of the condition. In carrying out a psychiatric assessment we usually have to be content with observing the reactions of the child to the various phases of the interview process. Obtaining a good history from others is particularly important in these cases.

Avoidant disorder of childhood

The third edition (revised) of the Diagnostic and Statistical Manual of the American Psychiatric Association (1987) (DSM-III) describes and defines a category which is given the above name. It is characterised by 'excessive shrinking from contact with other people' and 'desire for social involvement with familiar people' such as family members and peers the child knows well. A diagnostic category of 'avoidant personality disorder' is also described, being characterised by similar but more extreme behaviour.

Many of the children meeting the criteria for 'avoidant disorder' probably have 'avoidant' temperamental styles, and may also have been born into families where such behaviour has been accepted or even reinforced. In examining these children it is necessary to pay particular attention to the building of rapport, to proceed slowly and in a non-threatening manner, and to accept that they may take a while, perhaps a number of interviews, to gain trust and confidence in the examiner.

Separation anxiety disorder

Children exhibiting the features of this DSM-III-R disorder (American Psychiatric Association, 1987) become excessively anxious when separated from those to whom they are attached, most often their parents. They may refuse to go to school or sleep away from home. When seen for psychiatric examination, they are usually reluctant to separate from their parent(s) and may appear withdrawn. They may cry or become angry if the examiner insists upon separation. Initially it may be wise to interview such a child in the presence of a familiar figure (often the mother). Similar considerations apply to the examination of these children as to those with avoidant disorder.

The diagnostic formulation

Once the various procedures outlined above have been carried out the psychiatrist's task is to develop a diagnostic formulation. This should take into account all the information that has been obtained and should explain how the various relevant factors are seen as having worked together to produce the clinical situation that exists. It usually leads logically to a treatment plan.

The formulation should consider *predisposing, precipitating, perpetuating* and *protective* factors in each of the following categories:

- The child's temperamental style.
- The child's constitutional endowment. This will include any genetic factors that may be thought to be operative.
- The effects of any physical diseases or disorders.
- Psychological factors (anxiety, fears, depression, cognitive limitations, speech difficulties and difficulties or strengths in other areas of functioning).
- Environmental factors, especially the family, but including also the school and neighbourhood environments.

The formulation is more than a listing of factors. It should describe their relative importance and how they are believed to have interacted, and currently to be interacting, to produce the clinical picture the child presents.

Summary

The psychiatric examination of withdrawn children follows the same general lines as that of children generally. Special attention needs to be paid however to the establishment and maintenance of rapport. Also, in view of the reluctance of many of these children to talk, there is a particular need to obtain independent accounts of the child's behaviour and reactions from others.

Knowledge of the factors which predispose to emotional withdrawal enables the psychiatrist to focus special attention to relevant aspects of the child's and the family's history. A knowledge of those psychiatric syndromes of childhood which have emotional withdrawal as part of their clinical picture is also necessary.

References

American Psychiatric Association (1987) *Diagnostic and Statistical Manual of Mental Disorders* (3rd edn, revised). Washington, DC, American Psychiatric Association.

Barker, P. (1986) *Basic Family Therapy* (2nd edn). Oxford, Blackwell; New York, Oxford.

Barker, P. (1988) *Basic Child Psychiatry* (5th edn). Oxford, Blackwell.

Barker, P. (1990) *Clinical Interviews with Children and Adolescents.* New York, Norton.

Biederman, J., Rosenbaum, J. F., Hirshfeld, D. R., Faraone, S. V., Bolduc, E. A., Gerston M., Meminger, S. R., Kagan, J., Sniderman, N. and Reznick, J. S. (1990) Psychiatric correlates of behavioral inhibition in young children of parents with and without psychiatric disorders, *Archives of General Psychiatry* **47**, 21–6.

Bronson, G. W. (1970) Fear of visual novelty, *Developmental Psychology* **2**, 33–40.

Chess, S. and Thomas, A. (1984) *Origins of Behavior Disorders from Infancy to Early Adult life.* New York, Brunner/Mazel.

Epstein, N. B., Bishop, D. S. and Levin, S. (1978) The McMaster model of family functioning, *Journal of Marriage and Family Counselling* **4**, 19–31.

Frith, U. (1989) *Autism: Explaining the Enigma.* Oxford, Blackwell.

Gross, C. (1979) The family angel – the scapegoat's counterpart, *Family Therapy* **6**, 133–6.

Kagan, J. and Moss, H. A. (1962) *Birth to Maturity.* New York, Wiley.

Kagan, J., Reznick, J. S., Clarke, C., Sniderman, N. and Garcia-Coll, C. (1984) Behavioral inhibition to the unfamiliar, *Child Development* **55**, 2212–25.

Kagan, J., Reznick, J. S. and Gibbons, J. (1989) Inhibited and uninhibited types of children, *Child Development* **60**, 838–45.

Kagan, J., Reznick, J. S. and Sniderman, N. (1988) Biological bases of childhood shyness, *Science* **240**, 167–71.

Kolvin, I. and Fundudis, T. (1981) Electively mute children: psychological development and background factors, *Journal of Child Psychology and Psychiatry* **22**, 219–32.

McGoldrick, M. and Gerson, R. (1985) *Genograms in Family Assessment.* New York, Guilford.

Offord, D. R., Boyle, M. H., Szatmari, P., Rae-Grant, N. I., Links, P. S., Cadman, D. T., Byles, J. A., Crawford, J. W., Blum, H. M., Byrne, C., Thomas, H. and Woodward, C. A. (1987) Ontario child health study: prevalence of disorder and rates of service utilization, *Archives of General Psychiatry* **44**, 9–19.

Plomin, R. and Rowe, D. C. (1979) Genetic and environmental etiology of social behavior in infancy, *Developmental Psychology* **15**, 62–72.

Reznick, J. S., Kagan, J., Sniderman, N., Gersten, M., Baak, K. and Rosenberg, A. (1986) Inhibited and uninhibited behavior: a follow-up study, *Child Development* **57**, 660–80.

74

Rutter, M. (1985a) Infantile autism and other pervasive developmental disorders, in M. Rutter and L. Hersov, (eds) *Child and Adolescent Psychiatry: Modern Approaches* (2nd edn). Oxford, Blackwell.

Rutter, M. (1985b) The treatment of autistic children, *Journal of Child Psychology and Psychiatry* **26**, 193–214.

Rutter, M., Tizard, J. and Whitmore, K. (1970) *Education, Health and Behaviour*. London, Longman.

Savicki, V. and Brown, R. (1981) *Working with Troubled Children*. New York, Human Sciences Press.

Spitz, R. A. (1946) Anaclitic depression, *Psychoanalytic Study of the Child* **2**, 113–17.

Thomas, A. and Chess, S. (1977) *Temperament and Development*. New York, Brunner/Mazel.

Zimet, S. G. and Farley, G. K. (1986) Four perspectives on the competence and self-esteem of emotionally disturbed children beginning day treatment, *Journal of the American Academy of Child Psychiatry* **25**, 76–83.

CHAPTER 6

The Psychological Assessment of Withdrawn Children

David Jones

Withdrawn children do not belong to a single diagnostic category. The term withdrawn is a descriptive label applied to children who fail to meet the expectations of others in terms of social interactions and the forming of relationships. The features of these children most frequently referred to are sadness, being excessively shy, quiet and difficult to communicate with, easily frightened, having few or no friends. They may also develop an unusual number of physical ailments and express fears about social situations. The assessment of withdrawn children is one of the most challenging tasks of all for clinical and educational psychologists. Many of the principles of test administration following a standard form as prescribed in the manuals and not deviating from set rules may have to be abandoned. Often the withdrawn child does not want to be in the assessment situation and the parents find it hard to say why they are seeking help. More so than in most referrals the parents may seem to be unsure about when they started worrying about the child.

Unfortunately psychological assessment is always a time-consuming process even with willing and cooperative children. Drawing valid inferences from test results depends upon the psychologist being able to establish rapport with the child. In the case of withdrawn children initial cooperation on testing is often not forthcoming. The goals of the assessment may need to be adjusted according to the time available and the first session may produce little more than a cautious opinion on the case. Nevertheless the goals for assessment do need to be defined carefully. Often the child's difficulties are impairing functioning at school and it may be necessary to reach a conclusion on whether the child has special educational needs. The Education for All Handicapped Children Act, PL94–142, which was passed in 1975 in the US, refers to serious emotional handicap (SEH) as a condition for which special educational services may need to be provided. Examples of characteristics referred to in the Act as conditions which might adversely affect educational performance are 'An inability to build or maintain satisfactory relationships with peers or teachers', 'A general pervasive mood of unhappiness or depression' and 'A tendency to develop physical symptoms or fears associated with personal or school problems'. These could well be descriptions of withdrawn children in the sense that the term is used in this chapter. The situation for withdrawn children with educational problems is less clearly spelled out in the UK, but the 1981 Education Act indicates that a child has a 'learning difficulty' if 'he has a significantly greater difficulty in learning than the majority of children of his age'. The learning difficulty may be a consequence of cognitive, emotional or social problems. The psychological assessment of the withdrawn child will need to address two separate questions. First, whether the child's intellectual functioning is in the learning difficulty range on standardised tests; and second, whether emotional difficulties are seriously handicapping the child's educational performance. Further goals for the assessment are to provide evidence of any specific cognitive or emotional difficulties and optimistically to come up with possible explanations for aspects of the withdrawn behaviour.

It is worth reflecting briefly on what it is typically possible to achieve in a fairly full psychological assessment so that the problems involved in the assessment of withdrawn children can be seen in this wider context. Usually it is possible to obtain objective measures of the child's present level of functioning on a range of cognitive and linguistic tasks together with an estimate of the child's academic attainments, particularly in terms of literacy and number skills. In addition an evaluation is made of the child's emotional development and level of self-esteem and whether appropriate social skills have been acquired. The overall evaluation of development involves a consideration of the child's strengths and weaknesses as revealed in the test scores and judged in the context of an awareness of family background and parental expectations of the child. It is also important to obtain information on the child's educational history from the parents or others and to know whether or not there have been adequate opportunities at school. Almost always the measurement and observation of present functioning obtained in the assessment will be used to estimate potential or to allow predictions to be made about future performance.

Beginning the assessment

The first priority in assessing the withdrawn and uncommunicative child is to attempt to measure comprehension of spoken language to estimate how much the child is able to understand. A multiple choice picture vocabulary test such as the British Picture Vocabulary Test (BPVT) (Dunn *et al.*, 1982) is quite a good instrument to begin with. The test has a standard Long Form which provides a measure of Receptive Vocabulary for children in the age range two and a half years to fifteen years. The child is required to indicate by pointing which of a set of four line drawings on a page represents the single word spoken by the tester. For the younger age ranges the stimulus words begin with concrete nouns for the child to identify but the scale quickly brings in action verbs, adjectives and abstract nouns. There are clear instructions about when to stop testing and the raw scores can be converted into percentile ranks for each age group or into an Age Equivalent which is the expected mean level of performance of children of that age. The Long Form of the BPVT correlates quite well with tests of Verbal Intelligence. Whilst some withdrawn children will cooperate on the Long Form of the test an early decision needs to be taken as to whether it would be more appropriate to begin with the Short Form which samples the whole age range with a set of 32 words and often allows an estimate of the child's Receptive Vocabulary to be made from fewer than 20 responses. Whilst the Short Form is less accurate than the Long Form it does provide an estimate of the child's level of understanding and there is also considerable reinforcement for the child, who has perhaps grudgingly and reluctantly pointed at the pictures, to find that one test has been completed with so little effort. In extreme cases it is possible to complete the Short Form of the BPVT with the child sitting on the parent's knee and firmly hanging on with one hand. With pre-school children who are unwilling to attend to the pictures or to choose between them, it is sometimes possible to demonstrate that they are capable of responding to commands by encouraging them to point to parts of the body. The somewhat out-dated large picture of a doll taken from the Stanford-Binet Intelligence Scale sometimes proves an effective stimulus to release pointing responses (Terman and Merrill, 1961). The norms for this test require four correct responses to seven named parts of the body for a pass at the two year level and six correct responses for a pass at the two and a half years level. Even young children who are so unresponsive that they will not respond to the doll picture will sometimes respond to direct requests to show parts of their own body or clothing.

Failure to obtain responses from the child on any or all of the above attempts to demonstrate comprehension should not be taken as evidence of language deficit or learning difficulty. In these very withdrawn children it will be necessary to return to attempts at measurement at some later stage. The unlikely possibility of undiagnosed deafness should always be kept in mind and careful observation of the child should reveal whether there is an appropriate startle response to some external incidental noise. It would be ill-advised to distress the child even more by creating an unexpected noise just for the purposes of eliciting a startle. Similar caution must be taken in interpreting the scores of withdrawn children who have responded in varying degrees on the pointing and picture vocabularly tasks. Their scores should be seen on most occasions as a minimal estimate of their capacity to understand spoken language. On this basis a child who obtains a score within the average range for his or her age level could at least be excluded from the category of general learning difficulty and the assessment would proceed to seek further evidence of the child's cognitive abilities.

Estimating cognitive abilities

Those psychologists who still feel that an assessment should include as many of the sub-tests of the Wechsler Intelligence Scale for Children – Revised (WISC-R) as possible will at this stage attempt to administer the Information or Similarities sub-tests (Wechsler, 1974). However, both of these sub-tests require the child to give verbal responses and it is essential that the withdrawn child is not allowed to feel powerful in the withholding of verbal cooperation. It is well worth moving on quickly to the Performance Scale of the WISC-R and presenting the Picture Completion sub-test. Although in normal use this test requires the subject to name the missing parts of simple line drawing pictures, it is possible to obtain a minimal estimate of the child's capacity to respond to the material by allowing a pointing response. A child who begins in this way and finds that the test is not unduly threatening will then often make the occasional verbal response almost without being aware of the change. If the child is now beginning to participate adequately it may well be possible to move on to the rest of the Performance Scale of the WISC-R since none of the remaining sub-tests require verbal responses. Again any results should be taken as minimal estimates of potential since Picture Arrangement, Block Design, Object Assembly and Coding all involve timing of responses and withdrawn children may not give their best effort. Many withdrawn children will shrink away from these tests because they involve such a degree of movement and effort and it may be necessary to move on to less confrontational tasks.

A wide choice of alternative tests can be selected from the British Abilities Scales (Elliott, *et al.*, 1983). For example the Matrices Scale could be given to sample Reasoning and both Block Design Scales could be taken from Spatial Imagery. It is also worth observing the child on Speed of Information Processing whilst accepting that a less than optimum performance may be the outcome. For children younger than six years of age sub-tests requiring minimal verbal responses could be selected from the McCarthy Scales of Children's Abilities (McCarthy, 1972).

Assessing children's drawings

The assessment of drawing ability and the interpretation of drawings are both techniques which can be especially useful in the case of some withdrawn children who are reluctant to respond verbally. Each of these topics could well take a chapter on its own. They are discussed together here partly for convenience and partly to emphasise that an assessment can sometimes be adapted to use the same material to estimate cognitive functioning and aspects of the child's emotional experiences. There are several versions of the instructions for administration of the Draw-A-Person type of test and there are variations in scoring criteria. One of the simplest forms of this test to use and score is the Draw-A-Child sub-test from the McCarthy Scales of Children's Abilities. If the child is a boy he is invited to draw a boy and if the child is a girl she is invited to draw a girl. In each case the child is told to 'Do it as nicely as you can. Be sure to make all of him or her'. Scoring concentrates on the child's use of anatomical detail and not on artistic skill. The Goodenough-Harris Draw-A-Man Test has a far more detailed scoring system involving over 70 items and normative data has been collected allowing an estimate of IQ to be obtained for children from three to fifteen years of age (Goodenough, 1926; Harris, 1963). For younger children the Stanford-Binet has simple measures of the capacity to draw a circle, square and diamond and also at the five year level, a simple test of the ability to finish an incomplete drawing of a man. Both the McCarthy Scales of Children's Abilities and the Wechsler Preschool and Primary Scale of Intelligence (WPPSI) have simple measures of the ability to copy geometric designs (McCarthy, 1972; Wechsler, 1963). A much used copying test in the past was the Bender Visual Motor Gestalt Test (Bender, 1946) which requires the child to copy nine separate geometric shapes and can usually be completed in less than ten minutes. A detailed procedure for analysing possible errors in responses to the Bender drawings was devised by Koppitz and age norms for normal children are available (Koppitz, 1963, 1975). The use of the Bender Gestalt to diagnose brain damage is more controversial. Withdrawn behaviour can occasionally be a reaction to experiences of failure or criticism by 'clumsy children'. If there is concern about the child's eye-hand control or other aspects of perceptual development a separate session for the child to complete the Frostig Developmental Test of Visual Perception should be considered (Frostig, 1966).

The use of children's drawings to make judgements about the child's emotional difficulties moves the assessment into the more uncertain area of projective testing (Cummings, 1986). Children draw people they are most concerned about and one system of interpretation focuses on three groups of features: Quality Signs such as the overall size of the figures and the integration of body parts, Special Features such as the position and size of arms, legs or other body parts and Omissions of specific body parts (Koppitz, 1968). Another approach to interpretation assumes that the child's internal view or body image may be reflected in drawings (Machover, 1949). The head is taken to represent both the expression of emotion and social communication and the method of representation or absence of eyes or mouth could be important signs. The position and size of the hands may represent interaction with the environment, etc. More recently interest has moved to the potential value of children's drawings in the diagnosis of child sexual abuse. It is necessary to be aware that children who have not been abused will occasionally show unusual expressions of interest in genital areas in their drawings. Clearly when withdrawn and non-communicative children indicate an unusual interest in genital or anal features and activities the findings should be treated with due caution and concern in the context of what is already known about the history of the case. If there are serious suspicions that a child has been sexually abused and there is a possibility that the abuse is still continuing then the Social Services Child Protection Team will need to be informed. Any attempt at a disclosure interview with the child should be fully videotaped and independently observed. Sometimes with withdrawn children the history of past abuse is already documented and the use of projective drawing techniques in the assessment is a prelude to therapy.

The withdrawn child's willingness to draw can be exploited further to provide an estimate of visual memory. The Revised Visual Retention Test (Benton, 1974) measures the child's ability to reproduce geometric designs by drawing from memory immediately after a ten seconds exposure. Again the normative data allows conversion of the results into an estimate of IQ. Another version of a Memory For Designs Test by Graham and Kendall (1960) provides normative data to aid diagnosing children with brain damage.

Further projective testing

In addition to the problems of unestablished validity projective tests such as the Rorschach (Francis-Williams, 1968) have the problem of relying too much on the child's willingness to respond verbally to the stimulus cards to be of use with uncommunicative children. A similar difficulty applies to the use of the Children's Apperception Test (Bellak and Bellak, 1957) which invites children to create stories in response to potentially ambiguous picture material. Such material may be of value in providing hypotheses for therapeutic intervention if the child becomes willing to respond. A projective technique which will sometimes produce responses from withdrawn children is The Family Relations Test (Bene and Anthony, 1957). The test has versions for younger and older children and is suitable for the age range three to fifteen years. The projective element of the test comes at the start when the child has to select a set of line drawing figures to represent family members. Behind each figure is an attached box. A series of statements on cards is read out to the child who has the task of posting the card into the box associated with the figure the statement best applies to. Older children are given the opportunity to read the cards for themselves. A 'Mr Nobody' figure provides the child with the option to avoid involving a family member. The statements refer to a range of positive and negative feelings some of which are outgoing and some incoming. Scoring the responses provides a matrix of the intensity of the child's interaction with the other members of the family and a guide to the extent of denial of feelings. The popularity of this test is somewhat limited because it can be quite time consuming to administer and emptying the boxes to score the responses is also a fairly tedious process. Nevertheless it is a useful procedure in situations where it is felt important to explore the child's feelings and involvement with other members of the family in a non-threatening way.

There is an extensive literature on the use of dolls and toys as materials in structured or semi-structured interviews or play sessions. Different approaches vary in the amount of freedom given the child to select toys and activities. An example of guidelines for a diagnostic play interview which encourages the use of toys to give a dramatic enactment of important events is given by Greenspan (1981). The highly specialised techniques for using anatomically complete dolls to explore the possibility of sexual abuse in young or non-communicative children are discussed by Vizard and Tranter (1988).

Self report measures of personality

Discussion of the problems of assessment so far has tended to concentrate on work with the more extremely withdrawn children who show an unwillingness to respond to verbal questioning. There are many withdrawn children who will cooperate enough to give 'yes' or 'no' responses to questionnaires or to fill in the forms themselves. For these children the assessment session can be used to collect information about their personality characteristics and social skills. The choice of scales is large and many of the measures have sound psychometric properties, but there remain serious concerns about the clinical validity of questionnaire measures for individual children. This section will give some indication of the range of measures available. In any individual assessment it is likely that only one or two of these scales will be used to supplement clinical impressions of the child.

Much attention has been focused on ways of measuring anxiety in children (Finch and Rogers, 1984; Jones, 1984). The majority of questionnaires for use with children have been developed from instruments used first with adults. Mostly the child is required to respond by expressing agreement or disagreement with each of a series of items. It is critical that the tester is aware whether or not the child's reading level is sufficient to allow independent completion of the questionnaire or whether the items should be read aloud to the child. Most of the anxiety scales are trait measures of anxiety, that is, they refer to how the child usually feels, or to the tendency to feel anxious. The Children's Manifest Anxiety Scale (CMAS) consists of 42 items covering a range of possible worries and difficulties (Castaneda et al., 1956). Items are in the form of statements which the child can respond to by agreeing or disagreeing, for example, 'I worry when I go to bed at night'. The General Anxiety Scale for Children (GASC) measures general anxieties by asking the child a range of questions, for example, 'If you were to climb a ladder, would you worry about falling off it?' (Sarason et al., 1960). The Defensiveness Scale for Children (DSC) is a further scale developed partly from items in the GASC to detect the child's tendency to deny negative feelings, such as, 'Are there some people that you don't like?'. Many of the anxiety scales have associated Lie Scales or similar attempts to measure denial.

No account of the measurement of anxiety in children would be complete without reference to the extensive work of Cattell and his colleagues on the multidimensional IPAT Scales. One example is the Children's Personality Questionnaire (CPQ) designed for children aged eight to twelve years which provides scores on fourteen primary source traits (Porter and Cattell, 1963). The six primary traits which are used to calculate an anxiety score are: phlegmatic vs excitable; self-assured vs apprehensive; relaxed vs tense; casual vs controlled; affected by feelings vs emotionally stable and shy vs venturesome. A big problem with the use of the CPQ is the lengthy testing time. There are two equivalent forms available, each of which can take up to fifty minutes to complete. For clinical use the administration of both forms is recommended. Younger children aged six to eight years can be given the Early School Personality Questionnaire (ESPQ) which samples thirteen primary source traits (Coan and Cattell, 1966). Partly to overcome the need to use such a large questionnaire the Child Anxiety Scale has been developed as a scale of only twenty items based on the criterion of the ESPQ anxiety factor (Gillis, 1980).

The Junior Eysenck Personality Inventory (JEPI) provides British norms for both boys and girls aged seven to sixteen years (Eysenck, 1965). Anxiety is measured on the neuroticism (N) dimension which is also referred to as emotionality. The second dimension of the JEPI is extraversion–introversion (E) which is in part a measure of sociability. Taken together the scores on the N and E scales can provide insight into the functioning of the withdrawn child which is more valuable than a single anxiety measure. A further alternative to the JEPI is the Junior Version of the Eysenck Personality Questionnaire (EPQ) which in addition to measuring N and E provides a score on psychoticism (P) (Eysenck and Eysenck, 1975). The P score is considered to be a measure of 'toughmindedness' rather than psychoticism and just occasionally shows up at a high level in withdrawn children with aggressive tendencies.

In addition to measuring trait anxiety it can be valuable to obtain a measure of state anxiety, that is, how the child is actually feeling at the time of assessment. The State-Trait Anxiety Inventory for Children (STAIC) provides a quick method for measuring both state and trait anxiety (Spielberger *et al.*, 1970). The A-State scale consists of twenty statements about their present feelings with three possible choices for each, for example, I feel . . . 'very frightened', 'frightened' and 'not frightened'. State measures are an invaluable part of assessment and it can be very useful to adopt an informal single case design to monitor the feelings of the withdrawn child both within a single session and across sessions. For example the child can be invited to estimate how tense he or she is feeling at the present time on a ten point scale with ten representing very tense and one representing very relaxed. The ratings can then be extended to other situations if appropriate, such as, how the child might feel before getting up in the morning or just before a games lesson.

Several scales have been designed to be specific measures of anxiety in school situations. The Test Anxiety Scale for Children (TASC) is similar to the GASC referred to above, but all of the thirty questions refer to some aspect of test or classroom situations (Sarason *et al.*, 1960). A more detailed measure is available in the 74 item School Anxiety Scale (SAS) which includes a factor identified as Fear of Assertiveness and Self-Expression which is a measure of social anxiety (Phillips, 1978). Other identified factors on the SAS are Test Anxiety, Lack of Confidence in Meeting Expectations of Others and Physiological Reactivity Associated with Low Tolerance of Stress.

Several other rather specific scales are of interest in the assessment of withdrawn children. The Loneliness Scale attempts to measure social anxiety in terms of the child's perceived loneliness (Asher *et al.*, 1984). The Children's Self-Efficacy for Peer Interaction Scale (CSPIS) measures the child's beliefs about his or her ability to persuade or influence others to participate in social activities (Wheeler and Ladd, 1982). Again the wording of items on this scale needs adapting for British use.

Assessment of childhood depression

It is beyond the scope of this section to discuss the basis for clinical diagnosis of depression in children. The view is accepted that depression is not a single symptom or condition but rather a cluster of symptoms. The features of this syndrome are typically an inability to obtain pleasure from normally pleasurable activities, cognitive distortions in the form of lowered self esteem, self blame and feelings of worthlessness, social withdrawal, low energy level sometimes combined with feelings of agitation, possible disturbances of appetite or sleeping pattern and in some cases recurrent thoughts related to suicide or death. Many withdrawn children will show some of the features of a depressive condition but often the similarity is only superficial. From the outset the assessment needs to be sensitive to the quality of the behaviour shown by the child in the assessment situation. The quick defensive avoidance behaviour shown when some anxious and withdrawn children turn away or cling to their parents is very different from the reluctance to participate shown by some depressed children. Speed of response on cognitive tests will not on its own be diagnostic but it is important to note the occasional bursts of speed shown when the anxious withdrawn child finds that he or she is actually quite good at some activity.

Several scales have been devised to measure depression in children. The Children's Depression Inventory (CDI) has been developed as a children's version of the widely used Beck Depression Inventory (BDI) (Kovacs, 1980-1). The CDI consists of 27 items which require children to choose one from several alternatives to best describe themselves for the past two weeks. A fairly wide range of symptoms is covered including feelings of sadness, ideas related to suicide and self-injury, and patterns of eating and sleeping. The general impression of the validity of the CDI from a large number of research articles is that it is effective in being able to distinguish between emotionally disturbed and non-disturbed children, it is less effective at dis-criminating between different categories of emotional disturbance. The Children's Depression Scale (CDS) consists of 66 statements to be rated by the child (Lang and Tisher, 1978). In addition to an overall depression score it provides separate measures of different ways in which children might show their depression together with a Pleasure and Enjoyment Scale. There is also a separate CDS-Parents Questionnaire. Yet another feature of depressive behaviour is measured in the Hopelessness Scale for Children (Kazdin *et al.*, 1986). The children are required to make true or false responses to seventeen statements mostly about how things will be in the future.

Assessing the autistic child

Some of the features of the withdrawn child which have been described in this chapter are also features of the behaviour of autistic children. The diagnosis of autism depends on the overall clinical evaluation of the child. Kanner (1943) referred to autistic aloneness to describe the impairment in social interaction and the acquisition of social skills, but it is important to recognise that autistic 'aloofness' is different from social withdrawal in children with emotional disturbances. Another important criterion for making a diagnosis of autism is the qualitative impairment of speech and communication skills. Psychological assessment of autistic children can be difficult, especially when speech is almost absent or distinctly unnatural in quality. Current opinion is that the majority of autistic children function in the learning difficulty range on tests of intellectual abilities although they may have higher scores on some abilities, particularly on some performance measures. Occasionally some cognitive abilities in autistic children may be highly developed. It has been suggested earlier that the assessment of emotionally withdrawn children, who show reluctance to communicate a satisfactory estimate of their language abilities, may be made from their comprehension and performance scores. In contrast the language abilities of autistic children should not be estimated from scores on tests of other abilities. Other work on autistic children indicates that they are poor at imaginative play and have difficulty in recognising that there are alternative views of the world from their own (Frith, 1989).

Developmental dysphasia

Just occasionally qualitative aspects of the withdrawn child's language or lack of language will indicate the possibility of linguistic difficulties at the level of central processing. Children with developmental dysphasia or specific language impairment show evidence of difficulties in their use of spoken language. They tend to use short simple sentences and to avoid using adjectives. However, they also have difficulty in understanding the structure of quite simple sentences spoken by others (Cromer, 1978; Bishop, 1982). Fortunately such conditions are relatively rare, but when they are suspected in the withdrawn child a much more detailed investigation of language skills is indicated.

Information from parents and teachers

Whilst the majority of clinicians prefer to gather information about the child from the parents by conducting semi-structured interviews, it is sometimes of value to gather this information more systematically in the form of responses to standard questionnaires or inventories. It can be particularly instructive to observe the degree of concordance between the parents in their perceptions of the child and of the withdrawn behaviour. In a sense the wide range of instruments available is a sign that this sort of information gathering is very much a supplement to the assessment procedure. The Conners Parent

Symptom Questionnaire is one of the most frequently used methods in the US for obtaining parents' ratings on their children (Goyette *et al.*, 1978). Adaptation for British use requires minor changes to the wording of some of the items. Analysis of the responses to the 48 item scale gives scores on six scales of which psychosomatic problems and anxiety are the most relevant to an evaluation of withdrawn children. Just occasionally it is revealing to find that the withdrawn child is perceived by a parent to be impulsive or to show conduct problems in some situations. The Personality Inventory for Children (PIC) is a much more detailed instrument constructed on the principles of the Minnesota Multiphasic Personality Inventory (MMPI) and requires parents, usually the mother, to complete 600 true/false items about the child's behaviour (Wirt *et al.*, 1977; Lachar *et al.*, 1986). Selected sub-scales can be used to focus on withdrawal, anxiety, depression, and social skills. A final choice of instruments to use with parents is the Child Behaviour Check List (CBCL) which has been the subject of a number of factor analytic studies (Achenbach, 1985). Responses to the 118 behaviour items can be analysed to give scores on dimensions such as uncommunicative behaviour, depression, somatic complaints and social withdrawal.

In addition to obtaining information from parents it is valuable to obtain information on the child's behaviour in the school situation from teachers. The Rutter Children's Behaviour Questionnaire is a brief screening instrument which most teachers are prepared to complete although not many of the items cover withdrawn behaviour (Rutter, 1967). If the teachers have the time to complete a more detailed checklist of the child's behaviours it is possible to use the Bristol Social Adjustment Guides (Stott, 1974). Separate scores are obtainable on the five core syndromes of Unforthcomingness, Withdrawal, Depression, Inconsequence and Hostility.

Testing literacy skills

It is often difficult to decide where to insert the assessment of reading and spelling abilities in the overall sequence of tests. With most children a brief screening of the ability to read aloud can be given early in the proceedings to determine whether more detailed investigations of reading will be necessary. As in so many other areas the extremely withdrawn child may be so quiet or hesitant that an adequate estimate of oral reading accuracy is not possible. In these cases an attempt should be made to estimate spelling ability using the Schonell Graded Word Spelling Test (Schonell, 1955). Reading comprehension can be estimated using an appropriate silent reading test for the child's age or a word gap filling test. Often the withdrawn child can be drawn into conversation for the first time by asking them about the last book they read or had read to them.

Overview

A range of procedures has been indicated for estimating the abilities of the more severely withdrawn child. The assessment should always aim to avoid confrontation if the child is unwilling to respond. In early questioning an attempt should be made to allow the child to choose between simple alternatives whilst taking every care not to ask leading questions. Observation of the child can sometimes provide as much information as the actual test responses. In some cases it may be helpful to practise simple relaxation exercises with the child early in the session. Often it will be appropriate to attempt to integrate therapeutic intervention into the assessment.

References

Achenbach, T. M. (1985) *Assessment and Taxonomy of Child and Adolescent Psychopathology*. Beverly Hills, Sage.

Asher, S. R., Hymel, S. and Renshaw, P. P. (1984) Loneliness in children *Child Development, 55*, 1456–64.

Bellak, L. and Bellak, S. (1957) *The Thematic Apperception Test and the Children's Apperception Test in Clinical Use*. New York, Grune & Stratton.

Bender, L. (1946) *Bender Gestalt Test*. New York, American Orthopsychiatric Association.

Bene, E. and Anthony, A. J. (1957) *The Family Relations Test*. London, National Foundation for Educational Research.

Benton, A. L. (1974) *Revised Visual Retention Test*. New York, Psychological Corporation.

Bishop, D. (1982) Comprehension of spoken, written and signed sentences in childhood language disorders, *Journal of Child Psychology and Psychiatry, 23*, 1–20.

Castaneda, A., McCandless, B. and Palermo, D. (1956) The children's form of the Manifest Anxiety Scale, *Child Development, 27*, 317–26.

Coan, R. W. and Cattell, R. B. (1966) *Early School Personality Questionnaire*. Champaign, Illinois, Institute for Personality and Ability Testing.

Cromer, R. F. (1978) The basis of childhood dysphasia: a linguistic approach, in M. Wyke (ed.) *Developmental Dysphasia*. London, Academic Press.

Cummings, J. A. (1986) Projective drawings, in H. M. Knoff (ed.) *The Assessment of Child and Adolescent Personality*. New York, Guilford Press.

Dunn, L. M., Dunn, L. M., Whetton, C. and Pontille, D. (1982) *British Picture Vocabulary Scale*. Windsor, NFER-Nelson.

Elliott, C., Murray, D. J. and Pearson, L. S. (1983) *British Ability Scales – Revised*. Windsor, NFER-Nelson.

Eysenck, H. J. and Eysenck, S. B. G. (1975) *Manual of the Eysenck Personality Questionnaire*. London, Hodder & Stoughton.

Eysenck, S. B. G. (1965) *Manual of the Junior Eysenck Personality Inventory*. London, University of London Press.

Finch, A. J. and Rogers, T. R. (1984) Self-report instruments, in T. H. Ollendick and M. Hersen (eds) *Child Behavioral Assessment: Principles and Procedures*. New York, Pergamon Press.

Francis-Williams, J. (1968) *Rorschach with Children*. Oxford, Pergamon Press.

Frith, U. (1989) *Autism: Explaining the Enigma*. Oxford, Blackwell.

Frostig, M. (1966) *Developmental Test of Visual Perception*. Palo Alto, Consulting Psychologists Press.

Gillis, J. S. (1980) *Child Anxiety Scale Manual*. Champaign, Illinois, Institute for Personality and Ability Testing.

Goodenough, F. L. (1926) *Measurement of Intelligence by Drawings*. New York, World Book, Inc.

Goyette, C. H., Conners, C. K. and Ulrich, R. R. (1978) Normative data on revised Conners parent and teachers rating scales, *Journal of Abnormal Child Psychology*, **6**, 221–36.

Graham, F. K. and Kendall, B. S. (1960) Memory-For-Designs Test: revised general manual, *Perceptual and Motor Skills*, **11**, 147–88.

Greenspan, S. (1981) *The Clinical Interview of the Child*. New York, McGraw-Hill.

Harris, D. B. (1963) *Children's Drawings as Measures of Intellectual Maturity: A Revision and Extension of the Goodenough Draw-a-Man Test*. New York, Harcourt, Brace & World.

Jones, D. (1984) Recognition of anxiety by psychometric tests, in V. P. Varma (ed.) *Anxiety in Children*. London, Croom Helm, pp. 15–34.

Kanner, L. (1943) Autistic disturbances of affective contact, *Nervous Child*, **2**, 217–50.

Kazdin, A. E., Rodgers, A. and Colbus, D. (1986) The Hopelessness Scale for Children: psychometric characteristics and concurrent validity, *Journal of Consulting and Clinical Psychology*, **54**, 241–5.

Koppitz, E. M. (1963) *The Bender Gestalt Test for Young Children*. New York, Grune & Stratton.

Koppitz, E. M. (1968) *Psychological Evaluation of Children's Human Figure Drawings*. New York, Grune & Stratton.

Koppitz, E. M. (1975) *The Bender Gestalt Test for Young Children: Research and Application, 1963–1973*. New York, Grune & Stratton.

Kovacs, M. (1980–1) Rating scales to assess depression in school-aged children, *Acta Paedopsychiatrica*, **46**, 305–15.

Lachar, D., Kline, R. B. and Boersma, D. C. (1986) The Personality Inventory for Children: approaches to actuarial interpretation in clinic and school settings, in H. M. Knoff (ed.) *The Assessment of Child and Adolescent Personality*. New York, Guilford.

Lang, M. and Tisher, M. (1978) *Children's Depression Scale*. Victoria, Australia, Australian Council for Educational Research.

Machover, R. (1949) *Personality Projection in the Human Figure*. Springfield, Illinois, Thomas.

McCarthy, D. A. (1972) *Manual for the McCarthy Scales of Children's Abilities*. San Antonio, Psychological Corporation.

Phillips, B. N. (1978) *School Stress and Anxiety: Theory Research and Intervention*. New York, Human Sciences Press.

Porter, R. B. and Cattell, R. B. (1963) *The Children's Personality Questionnaire*. Champaign, Illinois, Institute for Personality and Ability Testing.

Rutter, M. (1967) A children's behaviour questionnaire, *Journal of Child Psychiatry and Psychology,* **8**, 1–11.

Sarason, S. B., Davidson, K. S., Lighthall, F. F., Waite, R. R. and Ruebush, B. K. (1960) *Anxiety in Elementary School Children*. New York, Wiley.

Schonell, F. J. (1955) *Reading and Spelling Tests*. Edinburgh, Oliver & Boyd.

Spielberger, C. D., Edwards, D. C., Montouri, J. and Lushene, R. E. (1970) *The State-Trait Anxiety Inventory for Children*. Palo Alto, Consulting Psychologists Press.

Stott, D. H. (1974) *The Social Adjustment of Children: Manual of the Bristol Social-Adjustment Guides*. London, Hodder & Stoughton.

Terman, L. and Merrill, M. A. (1961) *Stanford-Binet Intelligence Scale: Manual for the Third Revision Form L-M*. Boston, Houghton Mifflin Co.

Vizard, E. and Tranter, M. (1988) Helping young children to describe experiences of child abuse – general issues, in A. Bentovim, A. Elton, J. Hildebrand, M. Tranter and E. Vizard (eds) *Child Sexual Abuse Within the Family*. London, Wright, pp. 84–104.

Wechsler, D. (1963) *Manual for the Wechsler Preschool and Primary Scale of Intelligence*. San Antonio, Psychological Corporation.

Wechsler, D. (1974) *Wechsler Intelligence Scale for Children – Revised*. New York, The Psychological Corporation.

Wheeler, V. A. and Ladd, G. W. (1982) Assessment of children's self-efficacy for social interaction with peers, *Developmental Psychology,* **18**, 795–805.

Wirt, R. D., Lacher, D., Klinedinst, J. K. and Seat, P. D. (1977) *Multidimensional Description of Child Personality: A Manual for the Personality Inventory for Children*. Los Angeles, Western Psychological Services.

CHAPTER 7

Attachment and Withdrawal in Children's Friendships

John Simmonds

The development of policy and practice in child care social work over the last fifteen years has moved uneasily between a focus on the needs of children and the rights of parents. Numerous internal and public enquiries have shown that child care professionals have been overconcerned to meet the needs of the child's parents or to maintain a relationship with them at the expense of protecting the child (Blom Cooper, 1985; Lynch and Roberts, 1982). This has in turn led to a social work practice that has become dominated by the initial investigation and protection of children and the meeting of various procedural requirements such as case conferences and child protection registers. At the same time, the development of permanency planning has led child care professionals to focus more clearly on the urgent and time limited developmental needs of children (Goldstein *et al.*, 1973; Adcock, 1980) particularly in relation to the development of attachment and bonding between the child and its adult caretakers. As such, time limited and focused interventions have been called for (DHSS, 1986) to replace the lengthy and unfocused interventions of professionals in trying to improve the parenting capacity of birth parents to the long term detriment of the child. The results of such work was often seen to be a lengthy period where children 'drifted' in and out of care and for some to find themselves in the end 'drifting in care' (Rowe and Lambert, 1973) without clear plans or a secure base (Bowlby, 1988).

While such child centred policies have clearly had laudable aims in attempting to both protect child and ensure their proper development, there has also been considerable controversy surrounding these policies. This has largely stemmed from the arguments of those (Family Rights Group, 1982) who saw such policies as disadvantaging families who as a result of multiple deprivations such as poverty, racism and poor medical and educational facilities were subject to the rash and unreasoned actions of large state bureaucracies. The controversial nature of child protection work in particular was highlighted most dramatically in the Cleveland Report (Butler Sloss, 1988) and recently in Rochdale where the hasty and ill-conceived actions of child care professionals in diagnosing and removing children where there was a suspicion of sexual abuse caused much public consternation and outcry. The immediate effects of this were outlined in many recommendations of the Report itself but come more fully into view in the philosophy underpinning the Children Act 1989. Here the government's principle of minimum state intervention unless positively beneficial, of parental responsibility undiminished by subsequent events such as divorce, of partnership between welfare agencies and parents emphasises unequivocally the central place of the family and particularly its duties and obligations in the socialisation of children.

The preoccupation with parents as critical to a child's development and socialisation cannot be challenged and must remain at the heart of any interventive efforts that helping agencies make with families. Yet there has also been active concern in the assessment of families not only with the capacity and competence of its immediate membership – the 'nuclear family' – to raise children, but also with the strength of the wider network – the extended family, friends, community, work and agencies such as schools and health services to support and sustain families through their normal developmental and life crisis. Indeed one area that has emerged from much of the research in child abuse and neglect has been the relative isolation and lack of social support networks (Garbarino, 1977) of families identified as abusing. Understanding a family's ecology through the use of graphic aids such as ecomaps and family trees can add an important if not vital dimension to any assessment work that is undertaken. Withdrawn and isolated families are 'high risk' families and their children likely to be 'high risk' children who have experienced marked amounts of individual and social rejection.

However, in using an ecomap in making an assessment of a family, it is a common experience to find much of the concern focused on the isolation of the parents and little on the position of the children in relation to their own support and friendship network. If the concern is focused on the children themselves, then it is likely to be focused on the nature of their relationships with adults – parents and grandparents first but the teachers, and then maybe social workers or doctors. If rejection is a cause for concern, then it is likely to be rejection by the parents of the child although the child may be withdrawn in consequence at school or from friends. But as important as these relationships are, the adult–child dimension will, from the child's point of view especially as he or she grows older, take its place alongside the relationships the child has with other children – siblings and peers. Indeed the capacity to make age appropriate friendships is a mark of developmental progress and maturity (Ellis *et al.*, 1981; Hartup, 1983; Asher and Parker,

1989). However, for some children, these relationships will come to be marked by escalating difficulty with rejection by peers and the prospect of isolation and withdrawal another disadvantage to be added to many others. added to many others.

This chapter reviews some of the research in the field of children's friendships. The paradigms that have evolved over the last twenty years for understanding the subject have approached it from different directions and have not always been compatible. However sufficient evidence is now accumulating from studies in child abuse, peer rejection and attachment theory to give some pointers to future directions in both practice and research. In particular, this chapter stresses the need to look at children's withdrawal from peer relationships as a complex phenomenon with different pathways and different consequences.

It is important to have some measure of what is important in children's relationships. Mueller and Silverman (1989) describe them as marked by the progressive development of equality, a value which comes to have an increasingly important subjective meaning to the child, and the measure of his or her satisfaction with these friendships. This view is consistent with Piaget's (1926, 1932) view of cognitive development moving from the egocentric stages of early childhood towards the ability to 'take the other's point of view' on the basis of equality and reciprocity. Asher and Williams (1987) approach the issue more directly and suggest that children come to look for six qualities in a friendship –

(1)   Is the other child fun to be with?
(2)   Is the other child trustworthy?
(3)   Is the other child similar to me?
(4)   Does the other child help and join in with my games and activities and not disrupt them?
(5)   Does the other child make me feel good about myself?
(6)   Do we influence each other in ways that I like?

However, in describing children's friendships, it is important to recognise the wide range of experiences that these encompass. Some friends will be 'special' and the relationship will be long lasting with a considerable degree of closeness and companionship. Others will be more task centred around a particular activity such as a sport or hobby. Other friendships will be transitory and superficial. At another level some relationships will be based on shared and reciprocal feelings and activity, others on a shared antagonism to another child or group of children. Sometimes friendships will be on a one-to-one basis and other times in small groups. The notion of friendship is simple enough to say but much more difficult to describe given these different dimensions. They must of course also be related to both appropriately drawn developmental norms placed within the child's cultural and social setting.

The complexity of the skills that children need to learn from an early age in order to develop successful relationships is impressive – indeed, it would make an hefty curriculum for a course for any trade union negotiator or foreign relations diplomat. What to say, how to negotiate, to share, how to handle fun, conflict, aggression, jealousy, competition, intimacy, defeat etc. It is through the opportunity that children have to test out their competence in these encounters that stimulates a considerable part of social, cognitive and emotional development.

In discussing children's peer relationships and especially those children that become rejected by their peers, we are not dealing with the Victorian image of innocent children who move painlessly through childhood untroubled by conflict, rejection or unhappiness in their friendships with individuals and their place within groups of peers. Although any developmental framework must contain both a set of norms and a broad pathway, they are not intended to create ideals. It is safe to assume that most children will at some time find themselves falling out with their best friend, feeling lonely or rejected or be subject to teasing or bullying or indeed teasing or bullying others. However, for some children these problems will become so severe, that they will withdraw from social contact with peers. Hymel and Asher (1977) estimate this to be about 10 per cent, Bukowski and Hoza (1989) estimate an even higher figure. Coie and Dodge (1983) in a longitudinal study demonstrate that between 30 per cent and 50 per cent of these children continue to remain rejected over five years. Rubin (1990) found 66 per cent of children identified as showing extremely isolated behaviour at five continue to do so at seven.

One of the most significant factors in the development of the capacity to make relationships is the child's attachment to his or her principal caretakers (George and Main, 1979; Bowlby, 1973; Bronfenbrenner, 1979; Bronfenbrenner and Crouter, 1983). A securely attached child is likely to be in the best position to explore the social environment and make friendships. While this is a self evident notion in many respects, much of the early research on peer relations has studied the subject independently of parental influence.

The centrality of attachment in the development of sociability can be readily connected to the three patterns of response identified by Ainsworth and others in the Strange Situation Test (Ainsworth *et al.*, 1978; Stayton and Ainsworth, 1973; Tracy and Ainsworth, 1981; Bretherton and Waters, 1985). Infants and mothers are brought into a comfortable room. When they have settled down, the mother leaves the room and observations are made on the child's responses. Mother then returns and observations are made of their reunion. Ainsworth reports in the first group B (66 per cent, N = 106), that infants separated from their mothers showed signs of distress and sought physical contact and interaction with her when she returned to the room. These infants were classified as securely attached. In the second group, group A (20 per cent), the infant showed little or no distress on separation and on their mother's return avoided making any contact with her. In the third group, group C (12 per cent), the infant was anxious prior to the separation, very upset during it but resisted making contact when mum came back into the room. A further group of responses has subsequently been identified as disorganised/disorientated (Main and Solomon, 1990; Main and Hess, 1990; Greenburg *et al.*, 1990). Evidence varies as to the stability of these patterns, some showing quite clearly the persistence of all three patterns from 12 to 18 months (Main and Weston, 1981), from age one to age six (Main *et al.*, 1985) while others show the extent to which life events can lead to both positive and negative changes in attachment classification. In one study of abused children (Egeland and Sroufe, 1981a,b) the psychological unavailability of the mother was found to be strongly correlated with insecure attachment with 43 per cent of infants being classified as group A at 12 months but 86 per cent at 18 months. Further, Egeland and Farber (1984) report that maternal unavailability was associated with and predictive of avoidant (Group A) attachment patterns.

The development of these non-optimal attachments is of crucial significance. Although there may be some uncertainty about cause, most of the evidence for the direction of effect suggests that it is the primary attachment figure's capacity to be appropriately sensitive and responsive to the needs and feelings of the infant (positive and negative, good and bad) that is crucial. Whether the paradigm is empirical/behavioural or psychoanalytic, the intensity of the relationship and the capacity to sustain it by the parent lays the foundation for the child's future development. One feature that is vividly described in the psychoanalytic literature is the capacity particularly during feeding to sustain joint attention on a common experience that involves intensive and primitive emotions (Miller *et al.*, 1989).

The development within attachment theory of the concept of internal working models of the attachment relationship has been very important (Bowlby, 1982). In particular, the notion that the child internalises both sides of the relationship which comes to affect both the way the child feels about himself and the expectations he has about the responsiveness and safety of those around him. However, it is clear that this model is not based on any unified picture as the experiences of all infants will involve some frustration and difficulty. The development of these models in children who have been abused will be particularly complex as it involves incorporating quite contradictory experiences in that proximity seeking behaviour and emotion will have incurred violence and abuse.

How far attachment theory provides a base for understanding children's relationships with each other is difficult to determine. Its primary goal is the maintenance of proximity and 'felt security' in the early years but while as a system it continues to be active under conditions of stress throughout the life cycle, its appearance as a system in other relationships must be in a modified form with other factors becoming significant. However, there do seem to be basic issues which are common to the operation of the attachment system which have also been found to be signficant in rejection by and withdrawal from peers. However, before exploring this in more detail, some preliminary statements need to be made about child abuse.

Child abuse covers a multiplicity of inter-related acts in a multiplicity of inter-related circumstances, and as a result makes any accurate description of developmental consequences difficult to describe with any accuracy (Lynch and Roberts, 1982; Lynch, 1988; Farrell, 1989). Even when patterns of behavioural consequences are identified, it is not possible to attribute that consequence to the abusive acts themselves (even when they are discrete entities) as opposed to other more pervasive issues such as the quality of attachment or indeed general environmental and social deprivation such as poverty, racism and poor health and education services (Hufton and Oates, 1977; Elmer, 1977). However, certain characteristics do stand out in a number of studies. Gray and Kempe (1976) identify two patterns in children at the time of diagnosis. They found that 75 per cent of children exhibit signs of 'frozen watchfulness', the compliant, eager to please behaviour that seems to be an attempt to avoid further abuse. The other pattern shown by 25 per cent of children is aggressive and provocative behaviour. Longer term they say, the problems are likely to be anti-social behaviour. Lynch and Roberts (1982) describe the behaviour of children during developmental testing in their follow up study showing distractability, extreme manipulation of the tester, resistance and rebelliousness, elective withholding of speech and passive denial. Martin and Beezley's (1977) study of 50 children four and a half years after diagnosis found 66 per cent with an impaired ability for enjoyment, 62 per cent with symptoms such as sleeping problems, enurisis, temper tantrums and 52 per cent with poor self esteem.

Although not all abused children show long term effects (Morse *et al.*, 1970; Martin and Rodeheffer, 1976), Lynch and Roberts conclude 'the implications are clear: children from abusing families can very quickly grow into difficult and disturbed individuals, disliked by their peers and frustrating and antagonizing adults who try to care for them' (1982: 112). Erickson *et al.* conclude similarly,

> These children have histories that lead them to expect that they will not be cared for and/or that they will be hurt or taken advantage of, and they have learned to expect that they are not worthy of being treated otherwise. Thus they behave in ways that perpetuate those expectations. (Erickson *et al.*, 1989: 679)

The use of family centres and day nurseries as a means of working with abused and neglected children has become well established and is likely to increase under the Children Act 1989. The objectives of working in these group settings can be numerous. At a simple level it can be seen as one way of protecting a child during the day from possible harm and giving the parent(s) a break from the stresses of childcare. At another it may provide direct help to the parents in their parenting practices as well as giving them some opportunity for social contact and social support. However, for the children themselves, they are likely to provide opportunities to play with other children not just as a time filling activity but with either the explicit or implicit intention of developing their social, emotional and behavioural skills. Indeed the amount of time spent in interaction with other children is likely to far exceed the actual amount of time the child spends with the parents in the centre. Similarly, when the child enters school, while the explicit aim will be educational and much of the focus on the activity of the teacher, social activity in the classroom and playground will be the context in which this happens. If this context is positive with the child enjoying on the whole a rich pattern of friendships, then it is likely to facilitate the educational objectives, if it is negative, it may well seriously interfere with them. Indeed the failure to become reasonably proficient in this area for whatever reason, is likely to become a source of considerable stress for the individual child and may indeed have serious consequences for his or her future social and cognitive development and directly or indirectly contribute towards patterns of school withdrawal, delinquency and mental health problems (Kupersmidt *et al.*, 1990).

The extent to which parents and other significant adults such as teachers and family centre staff involve themselves directly in children's friendships is difficult to estimate. Undoubtedly most become involved at some stage in local difficulties such as arguments and fights. Others may well become involved in more protracted problems such as bullying or isolation, especially when a child is at risk or unhappy. For many children, their own developmental maturation in favourable circumstances such as school and organised children's activities will provide them with the opportunity to develop the social skills of friendship. Undoubtedly a small number of children will be referred for specialist help through psychologists or psychotherapists. However, although the consequences of problems in this area can be severe and escalate with age, how far efforts by adults to help children with their social difficulties involve sustained and programmed attempts to intervene directly with individuals or groups of children is doubtful.

The image of the scapegoated figure in the playground or the boarding school dormitory is well established in children's literature. Billy Bunter's greed, size, laziness and manipulative habits have been the object of generations of amusement and ridicule. What it felt like to be Billy Bunter is another matter – unhappy, rejected, frightened – but a sympathetic and understanding approach to him as a person was never called for so we will never know. However, his experiences demonstrate the consequences for a child of being the odd one out, unhappy on the inside and a social outcast in the group.

The kinds of problems that Billy Bunter exemplifies can be understood as an interaction between two areas. First, his problems can be seen as problems particular to him as an individual that have both a developmental history to them and developmental consequences in terms of his social, cognitive and emotional competence. Billy's view of himself, his self esteem and identity will be expressed through his behavioural repertoire of social skills. Second, Billy will have an identity in the eyes of the other boys he has contact with – his reputation. The interaction between these – how Billy sees himself and how he is seen by others is complex – he may see himself as one thing and be known or have a reputation as something else. This distinction is an important one for while there may not be much of a divergence for many children, indeed social adjustment would require that a child is comfortable in himself and his social setting, the problems of peer relationships needs to be understood as both an individual child's problem and the interaction between the child and the group. Which is primary will be returned to later. What makes this distinction more complex is the possibility that how the child sees himself and is seen in one social situation is different to how he sees or is seen in other situations. Children may be happy in the friendship group at home but miserable in their friendship group in class. It would be wrong to assume without further evidence that children develop a unitary and unified picture of themselves that is constant across all situations and for all time.

While the research cited above points to the kinds of problems likely to be experienced by children in their friendships who have been abused and mal-treated, research into peer relations among children approaches the problem from a wider angle. As such, it provides important insights and puts the difficulties of abused children into a wider context. In particular, it provides important evidence about the nature of becoming a 'rejected' child in the eyes of peers.

Much of the research on peer relationships has started by identifying children who have problems with their friendships through measuring their social status in the classroom. Identifying these children has been based on four methods

(1)   Sociometric tests.
(2)   Peer assessment.
(3)   Teacher assessment.
(4)   Behavioural assessment.

Sociometric tests assess the status of individual children and their friend-ship patterns in a group setting such as a classroom (Hymel and Rubin, 1985; Coie *et al.*, 1982; Putallaz, 1987). Children are asked to identify those other children with whom they like to play and those they do not. A number of classifications arise out of such a procedure, the most typical one being those identifying popular children, those frequently identified as friends; neglected children, those who are infrequently identified as friends and rejected children, those who are not identified as friends.

Other evaluations such as the Revised Class Play (Masten *et al.*, 1985) and the Pupil Evaluation Inventory (Pekarik *et al.*, 1976) are based on reports from children themselves using a more detailed set of questions about behaviour and roles. Other evaluations use teacher ratings (Behar and Stringfield, 1974; Edelbrock and Achenback, 1984). However, while all of these measures are important assessment tools, some caution needs to be exer-cised in using their results as they all need to be validated by correlating them against an analysis of the observed activities of withdrawn children appropri-ately set against both age norms and their generalisability across different social situations – classroom, playground, home etc.

However, although caution is important, the three categories 'popular', 'neglected' and 'rejected' have proved to be significant in identifying the respective characteristics, consequences and stability over time of children in these groups. The majority of such studies demonstrate quite clearly that on many measures of behavioural and cognitive performance, it is children in the 'rejected' group who have the severest problems with the severest con-sequences.

On the basis of one study of 848 children in three age groups eight, ten and thirteen, Coie *et al.* (1982) identified five groups:

- Popular children
- Average children
- Socially neglected children
- Controversial children

'Popular' children were rated highly in terms of cooperative behaviour, an ability to follow rules, display leadership and low for disruptive behaviour, starting fights and asking for help. 'Rejected' children were rated at the opposite end of the scale for all these items. 'Average' children scored an overall mean and 'neglected' children below the mean. 'Controversial' children were rated highly in terms of leadership but were on a par with 'rejected' children as far as disruption and aggression were concerned. Gender differences showed themselves as independence and lack of overt aggression in boys and cooperativeness in girls.

The striking finding from this and other research is the distinction between children with 'rejected' status marked by aggressive and disruptive behaviour and those with 'neglected' status whose behaviour is shy and withdrawn.

The extent of the problem of aggressive and disruptive behaviour is vividly demonstrated in a series of observations reported by Calum and Franchi (1987) from their study of a family centre for abusing families. In this study they present a detailed analysis of the behavioural activity of four of the children who were attending the centre. The children were between three and four years old. All four children had been subject to abuse and were considered to be severely at risk. All four lived in families where both historically and in the present there were severe difficulties. Over a period of two hours of observation, the children were seen to engage in play activities for between 58 per cent and 66 per cent of the time. Of this time, the children spent between 18 per cent and 24 per cent of the time in direct play with other children, of which the greater proportion – 77 per cent – was spent in interaction with one other child. During this time, the observers noted the large numbers of acts of hostility the children directed towards each other. In the period under observation, one child directed 31 hostile acts towards other children, was on the receiving end of 13 acts from other children and directed a further 6 acts at adults. At the other end of the scale, another child directed 9 acts towards other children, was on the receiving end of 6 acts and none at all towards adults. Similar findings in day care settings have been found by George and Main (1979), Main and George (1985) and Herrenkohl and Herrenkohl (1981).

Lynch and Roberts (1982) describe similar behaviour in a slightly older child. Simon, a seven year-old had been seriously abused by his father. Therapy with the family had improved the situation dramatically but Simon still continued to feel himself the odd one out. Lynch and Roberts say

> Simon tended to withdraw into his own shell, fearing rejection . . . [he] was expressing all his anger, hostility and disappointment at school . . . unless [he] received individual help and therapy to improve his social relationships, then he would proceed to destroy any friend-

ships made and expect not to be liked, getting into deeper and deeper trouble. (Lynch and Roberts, 1982: 197)

Although aggressive and disruptive behaviour seem to be one of the clearest marks of those children who attain 'rejected' status, a number of qualifying statements need to be made about such behaviour. First, it is not global – these children are not aggressive all the time. In fact observations of preschool children in therapeutic day care suggests that it is related to the lack of familiarity of other children in the group, the extent to which activities are structured and is a particular reaction to distress in other children (Howes, 1984, 1985a,b). With nine-year-old boys Coie and Kupersmidt (1983) observed that those with 'rejected' status made as many hostile comments and fought as much as those in the 'average' group. However, when the boys themselves were asked who it was that started the fights, it was the boys in the 'rejected' group who were most frequently identified. Reports by adult observers revealed that what distinguished the two groups was the justifiability of the aggression – 'average' status boys might engage in as much fighting but did so when they needed to defend themselves or there was reason for them to do so.

Another dimension to this issue is added by exploring 'entry behaviour'. On the basis of children's sociometric status, researchers have studied what it is about 'popular' children that makes them more able to enter into and be accepted by a group of children already at play. Fairly consistent patterns have been found. The most important feature is the ability of the child to be able to perceive and understand what activity the group is already engaged in – determining its frame of reference (Phillips *et al.*, 1951). In order to do this, the child spends some time 'hovering' outside the group passively observing it. After this, his behaviour is directly group orientated – he does not do or say anything to draw attention to himself as an individual. In other words the child is sensitive to the activity outside of himself and is orientated towards joining it rather than overturning it. Successful entry behaviour is dependent on the child's capacity to put the group and the other children before himself in order to meet his own needs in the longer run rather than to have the group attend to his own needs immediately. The strategy in itself is fairly low risk as the child has not exposed himself to any serious degree so that if rejection by the group is the result, it does not lead to overwhelming loss of face or status. This strategy is quite different to that observed in children with 'rejected' status. Here they tend to make an immediate bid for leadership of the group by making claims about their own status, attempting to change the activity of the group or by taking a leadership role (Putallaz and Gottman, 1981). They put themselves and their own needs first and in doing so adopted a strategy that because of the disruptive effect on the other children's activity, put them at high risk of being rejected. Children with 'neglected' status tended to engage in a lengthy period of 'hovering' which is low risk in terms of the individual child feeling rejected, but unpredictable in terms of being eventually accepted by the group.

However, although the mark of successful entry behaviour is sensitivity to the group's activity, the importance of assertive behaviour is demonstrated by observing the difference between the way that some six-year-olds can explain and find positive solutions to theoretical social problems, such as acquiring a toy from another child, in a test situation but be unsuccessful in translating this knowledge into actual skills in play situations (Rubin and Krasnor, 1986). In observed play, they defer to the wishes of others and if they do attempt to take the lead, are less successful in doing so. Rubin *et al.* (1990) argue that in such children, it is their social anxiety that inhibits them from using what they know and leads over time to them developing a poor picture of their social competence, hence their withdrawal.

In terms of the criteria of reciprocity and equality, it is clear why aggressive and disruptive behaviour generally and in entry behaviour in particular is unsuccessful. However, there is an important distinction to be made here between children who behave aggressively and disruptively in their interactions with friends, and those children who are withdrawn in terms of social activity. Part of the explanation for this comes from seeing the development of 'rejected' status as moving through different stages. Coie (1990) talks of peer rejection as having three stages:

(1)   the precursor stage
(2)   the emergent stage
(3)   the maintenance stage

In the first two stages, the child's behaviour is primary and as an individual he or she may act in aggressive and disruptive ways some of the time. However, whatever problems this causes other children, they can be forgiven and the child will not be marked out by the peer group as unpopular. However, over time the aversive consequences of such behaviour for other children becomes more and more significant and the child builds up a reputation which becomes a significant part of the framework that guides the interaction. In the maintenance phase, the child's status is of a different order to that in the preceding two phases and the operation of the group's dynamics become an important part in maintaining the child's status and behaviour. The child then not only has a poor repertoire of social skills but has also to deal with the experience of a negative social identity and the rejection that results from this. What might start out as a problem to the individual child and relatively opaque to other children, will as expectations about appropriate and acceptable social behaviour increase, become issues which are problematic for other children and a reason 'not to be friends'. They are a victim of their own individual difficulties and a victim of the dynamics of the group. Withdrawal in these circumstances is a response to rejection.

The stability of this behaviour is clearly demonstrated by Coie and Kupersmidt (1983) who observed the effects of aggressive and disruptive behaviour in a school based group of nine-year-old boys. In an arranged out of school playgroup, boys from different status categories – popular, rejected, neglected and average – were placed in one group in which they were known by their reputation at school and one group where they were not known. Although the rejected boys showed themselves to be well behaved in the first session, in the second week in the familiar group and in the third week in the unfamiliar group they had reverted to their previous status category. Boys from the neglected group however, showed a divergence in the unfamiliar setting towards being more assertive and showing higher levels of leadership behaviour. In the familiar group however, they also reverted to their previous status. The distinction between these two groups suggests that while behaviour associated with neglected status is responsive to the social setting in which it occurs, behaviour associated with rejected status is independent of it.

However, as often as aggressive and disruptive behaviour appear in reject- ed children, they account for only 50 per cent of children so identified (Coie, 1990; French, 1988). The other behavioural cluster is that of isolation and withdrawal but its appearance in the literature on peer relations is less than clear on its developmental significance. In an early study by Wickman (1928) and later by Hollins (1955), groups of teachers were asked to rank symptoms of maladjustment in order of severity. In comparison with acts of aggression and hostility, the quiet, withdrawn child was seen to be of far less concern and much less at risk. Similarly, it was children who exhibited aggressive and acting-out behaviours who were considered to be most at risk by teachers in Lynch and Roberts' (1982) follow up study of abused children at Park Hospital. The reason that probably explains this is that aggression and dis- ruption are more noticeable and more problematic to parents and other children and in the classroom challenges teachers in their authority and control. Yet severely isolated children spend significantly more time alone and uninvolved in constructive play. Rubin *et al.* (1990) observing children from age four to age nine identified 15 per cent of their school based sample as isolates, with children in the younger age range spending only 12 per cent of their time playing with friends. Overall their social activity was significantly inhibited and their cognitive competence less mature, imagin- ative and flexible.

The reason this does not appear so clearly as a factor in the peer rejection literature is that it is not of great significance to other children until they become nine, ten or eleven years old. Developmentally it is common for younger children to spend time playing alone and in itself it is not behaviour that is aversive. These children may be regarded as 'strange', or 'odd' but it is more likely that they will just not be noticed.

This gives us two reasons why children withdraw from relationships with peers. In the first, children withdraw because they have been rejected by peers because of their aversive behaviour. However, their withdrawal may be circumscribed by their involvement with other children who are rejected despite some of the negative consequences that may accrue from developing friendships with other rejected children (Dishion, 1990). In the second, child- ren avoid social contact because of behavioural inhibition and social anxiety, lacking both opportunity for developing a network of friends and the social skills to sustain them. However, it is only when sociability has a higher profile – pre and early adolescence – that they become marginalised.

What this implies is that phases to the development of 'rejected' status with different pathways (see Rubin *et al.* (1990) for a detailed exposition) are dependent on whether the original behaviour is aggressive and disruptive or anxious and inhibited.

The impact of the development of an interactive pattern of insecure attachment on the child is clear – the insecurity, expressed through an unwillingness to seek out mother reinforces her negative experiences of herself and her role which in turn reinforces her psychological unavailability and in turn her child's experience of her. It is from this base, that the child develops complex and contradictory internal working models of himself and the world outside. If the capacity to give joint attention is the basis for cognitive, emotional and social development and is rooted in a consistent internalised working model built on a secure pattern of attachment, then any disruption in this will be likely to cause difficulty. The frequently reported observation of abused children who attack other distressed children is a clear example and the behavioural disorganisation manifested in hostility and aggression that results when abused children are approached by other children is another. The link between this and successful 'entry' behaviour also seems particularly strong. If children need to adopt the frame of reference of the group in order to join it, then this must be on the basis of a capacity to be sensitive to the needs of others internalised from the working model of a secure attachment.

The impact of the child's early attachment history and the development of internal working models for relationships are a clear basis for the development of friendships. In particular, the internal development of a picture of a responsive and available parent generalisable to an expectation of a responsive and available network of other relationships. The development of both a social identity and associated self esteem along with their associated skills are the basis for the way the child feels about himself as well as providing the general expectation that he will be positively received by others. Of course there is likely to be some variation in the extent to which the child has positive and negative feelings about himself and the confidence that he feels in entering new social situations. It is entirely conceivable that any child however socially orientated will find some social situations difficult and be unable to find a way into them. Similarly some children who are less confident and have fewer social skills will be positively accepted in some groups and not so in others. These are the normal if difficult swings and roundabouts of childhood development. Most children find a way through these set-backs through a combination of developmental maturity built on an internal working model of a secure attachment. However, for other children, through their attachment history they learn that people are not responsive or sensitive to their needs and they learn to avoid or resist having positive expectations of them. Their lack of self esteem and poor social skills will make friendships more and more difficult as the expectations of other children become more demanding and exacting as they grow older. Whether they go on to fight the world or avoid it, they withdraw.

References

Adcock, M. (1980) The right to a permanent placement, *Adoption and Fostering*, 4–1.

Ainsworth, M. D. S., Blehar, M. C., Waters, E. and Wall, S. (1978) *Patterns of Attachment: A Psychological Study of the Strange Situation.* Hillsdale, New Jersey, Elrbaum.

Asher, S. R. and Parker, J. G. (1989) The significance of peer relationship problems in childhood, in B. H. Schneider *et al.* (eds) *Social Competence in Developmental Perspective.* London, Kluwer Academic Publishing.

Asher, S. R. and Williams, G. A. (1987) *Helping Children Without Friends in Home and School.* Urbana, Ill., ERIC.

Behar, L. and Stringfield, S. (1974) A Behavioural Rating Scale for the pre-school child, *Developmental Psychology*, **10**, 601–10.

Berndt, T. J. and Ladd, G. W. (1989) (eds) *Peer Relationships in Child Development.* New York, Wiley.

Blom Cooper, L. (1985) A child in trust. London Borough of Brent.

Bowlby, J. (1973) *Attachment and Loss: Vol. 2. Separation.* London, Penguin.

Bowlby, J. (1982) *Attachment and Loss: Vol. 1.* London, Penguin.

Bowlby, J. (1988) *A Secure Base.* London, Routledge.

Bretherton, I. and Waters, E. (1985) (eds) *Growing Points of Attachment Theory and Research.* Monographs of the Society for Research in Child Development, **50**, 1–2.

Bronfenbrenner, U. (1979) *The Ecology of Human Development: Experiments by Nature and Design.* Cambridge, Ma., Harvard University Press.

Bronfenbrenner, U. and Crouter, A. C. (1983) The evolution of environmental models in developmental research, in Kessen, W. (ed) *Handbook of Child Psychology: Vol. 1. History, theory and methods* (pp. 357–414). New York, Wiley.

Browne, K., Davies, C. and Stratton, P. (1988) *Early Prediction and Prevention of Child Abuse.* New York, Wiley.

Bukowski, W. M. and Hoza, B. (1989) Popularity and friendship: issues in theory, measurement and outcome, in T. J. Berndt and G. W. Ladd *Peer Relationships in Child Development.* New York, Wiley.

Butler Sloss, I. J. (1988) *Report of the Inquiry into Child Abuse in Cleveland 1987.* London, HMSO.

Calum, R. and Franchi, C. (1987) *Child Abuse and Its Consequences.* Cambridge, Cambridge University Press.

Children's Social Development: Information for Teachers and Parents. Urbana, Ill., ERIC, Clearing House on Elementary and Early Childhood Education.

Cicchetti, D. and Carlson, V. (1989) *Child Maltreatment.* Cambridge, Cambridge University Press.

Coie, J. D. and Dodge, K. A. (1983) Continuities and change in children's social status: a 5 year longitudinal study, *Merrill-Palmer Quarterly*, **29**, 261–81.

Coie, J. D. and Kupersmidt, J. B. (1983) A behavioural analysis of emerging social status in boys' groups, *Child Development*, **54**, 1400–16.

Coie, J. D. (1990) Toward a theory of peer rejection, in S. R. Asher and J. D. Coie, *Peer Rejection in Childhood*, Cambridge, Cambridge University Press.

Coie, J. D., Dodge, K. A. and Coppoteli, H. (1982) Dimensions and types of social status: a cross age perspective, *Developmental Psychology*, **18**, 557–70.

Coie, J. D. and Koeppl, G. (1990) Intervention and aggressive – rejected children, in S. R. Asher and J. D. Coie (op. cit).

Department of Health and Social Security (1986) *Social Work Decisions in Child Care*. London, HMSO.

Dishion, T. (1990) The peer context of troublesome child and adolescent behaviour, in P. E. Leone *Understanding Troubled and Troubling Youth*. Sage Publications.

Edelbrock, C. and Achenbach, T. M. (1984) The teacher version of the child behaviour profile: 1 boys aged 6–11, *Journal of Consulting and Clinical Psychology*, **52**, 207–17.

Egeland, B. and Sroufe, L. A. (1981a) Attachment and early maltreatment, *Child Development*, **52**, 44–52.

Egeland, B. and Sroufe, L. A. (1981b) Developmental sequelae of maltreatment in infancy, in P. Rizley and D. Cicchetti *Developmental Perspectives in Child Maltreatment*. Jossey-Bass.

Egeland, B. and Farber, E. A. (1984) Infant–toddler attachment: factors related to its development and changes over time, *Child Development*, **55**, 753–71.

Ellis, S., Rogoff, B. and Cromer, C. C. (1981) Age segregation in children's social interactions, *Developmental Psychology*, **17**, 399–407.

Elmer, E. (1977) A follow-up study of traumatized children, *Pediatrics*, **59**(2), 273–314.

Erickson, M. F., Egeland, B. and Pianta, R. (1989) The effects of maltreatment on the development of young children, in D. Cicchetti and V. Carlson *Child Maltreatment*. Cambridge, Cambridge University Press.

Family Rights Group (1982) *Fostering Parental Contact*.

French, D. C. (1988) Heterogeneity of peer rejected boys: aggressive and non-aggressive subtypes, *Child Development*, **59**, 976–85.

Garbarino, J. (1977) The human ecology of child mistreatment, *Journal of Marriage and the Family*, **39–4**, 721–35.

George, C. and Main, M. (1979) Social interactions of young abused children: approach, avoidance and aggression, *Child Development*, **50**, 306–18.

Goldstein, J., Solnit, A. and Freud, A. (1973) *Beyond the Best Interests of the Child*. New York, Free Press.

Gray, J. and Kempe, R. (1976) The abused child at time of injury, in H. P. Martin (ed.) *The Abused Child*, Ballinger.

Greenburg, M., Cicchetti, D. and Cummings, M. (1990) (eds) *Attachment in the Preschool Years*. Chicago, University of Chicago Press.

Hartup, W. W. (1983) Peer relations, in E. M. Hetherington *Handbook of Child Psychology, Vol. 4*. New York, Wiley.

Herrenkohl, R. C. and Herrenkohl, E. C. (1981) Some antecedents and developmental consequences of child maltreatment, in R. Rizley and D. Cicchetti *Developmental Perspectives in Child Maltreatment*. Jossey-Bass.

Hetherington, E. M. (1983) *Handbook of Child Psychology, Vol. 4, Socialization, Personality and Social Development*. New York, Wiley.

Howes, C. and Eldredge, R. (1985) Responses of abused, neglected and non-maltreated children to the behaviours of their peers, *Journal of Applied Developmental Psychology*, **6**, 261–70.

Howes, C. and Espinosa, M. P. (1985) The consequences of child abuse for the formation of relationships with peers, *Child Abuse and Neglect*, **9**, 397–404.

Howes, C. and Farver, J. (1984) Toddler responses to the distress of their peers. Paper presented to the International Conference on Infant Studies, New York.

Hufton, I. W. and Oates, R. K. (1977) Non-organic failure to thrive: a long term follow-up, *Pediatrics*, **59**, 73–7.

Hymel, S. and Asher, S. R. (1977) Assessment and training of isolated children's social skills. Paper presented at the biennial meeting of the Society for Research in Child Development, New Orleans (ERIC Document Reproduction Service No ED 136 930).

Hymel, S. and Rubin, K. H. (1985) Children with peer relationships and social skills problems: conceptual, methodological, and developmental issues, in G. J. Whitehurst (ed) *Annals of Child Development*. JAI Press.

Kupersmidt, J., Coie, J. and Dodge, K. (1990) The role of poor peer relationships in the development of disorder, in S. R. Asher and J. D Coie, (op. cit).

Lynch, M. and Roberts, J. (1982) *Consequences of Child Abuse*. London, Academic Press, p. 194.

Lynch, M. (1988) The consequences of child abuse, in K. Browne *et al. Early Prediction and Prevention of Child Abuse*. New York, Wiley.

Main, M. and George, C. (1985) Responses of abused and disadvantaged toddlers to distress in agemates: a study in the day care setting, *Developmental Psychology*, **21**(3), 407–12.

Main, M. and Hess, E. (1990) Lack of resolution of mourning in adulthood and its relation to disorganization in infancy: speculations regarding causal mechanisms, in M. Greenburg *et al. Attachment in the Preschool Years*. Chicago, Chicago University Press.

Main, M., Kaplan, N. and Cassidy, J. (1985) Security in infancy, childhood and adulthood: a move to the level of representation, in I. Bretherton and E. Waters *Growing Points of Attachment Theory and Research*. Monographs of the SRCD.

Main, M. and Soloman, J. (1990) Procedures for identifying infants as disorganized–disorientated during the Ainsworth strange situation, in M. Greenburg *et al. Attachment in the Preschool Years*. Chicago, Chicago University Press.

Main, M. and Weston, D. R. (1981) The quality of the toddler's relationship to mother and to father: related to conflict behaviour and the readiness to establish new relationships, *Child Development*, **52**, 932–40.

Martin, H. P. (1976) *The Abused Child*. Ballinger.

Martin, H. and Beezley, P. (1977) Behavioural observations of abused children, *Developmental Medicine and Child Neurology*, **19**, 373–87.

Martin, H. and Rodeheffer, M. (1976) Learning and intelligence, in H. Martin *The Abused Child*. Ballinger.

Masten, A. S., Morison, P. and Pellegrini, D. S. (1985) A Revised Class Play method of assessment, *Developmental Psychology*, **5**, 523–33.

Miller, L., Rustin, M. and Shuttleworth, J. (1989) *Closely Observed Infants*. London, Duckworth.

Morse, C. W., Sahler O. J. Z. and Friedman, S. B. (1970) A three year follow-up study of abused and neglected children, *American Journal of Diseases of Children*, **120**, 439–46.

Mueller, E. and Silverman, N. (1989) Peer relations in maltreated children, in D. Cicchetti and V. Carlson (eds) *Child Maltreatment*. Cambridge, Cambridge University Press.

Pekarik, E. G., Prinz, R. J., Liebert, D. E., Weintraub, S. and Neale J. M. (1976) The Pupil Evaluation Inventory: a sociometric technique for assessing children's social behaviour, *Journal of Abnormal Child Psychology*, **4**, 83–97.

Perlmutter, M. (1986) (ed.) *Minnesota Symposia on Child Psychology* (Vol. 18, pp. 1–68). Hillsdale, New Jersey, Erlbaum.

Phillips, E. L., Shenker, S. and Revitz, P. (1951) The assimilation of the new child into the group, *Psychiatry*, **14**, 319–25.

Piaget, J. (1926) *The Language and Thought of the Child*. London, Routledge & Kegan Paul.

Piaget, J. (1932) *The Moral Judgment of the Child*. New York, Free Press.

Putallaz, M. (1987) Maternal behaviour and children's sociometric status, *Child Development*, **58**, 324–40.

Putallaz, M. and Gottman, J. M. (1981) An interactional model of children's entry into peer groups, *Child Development*, **52**, 986–94.

Rizley, R. and Cicchetti, D. (1981) (eds) *Developmental Perspectives in Child Maltreatment*. Jossey-Bass.

Rowe, J. and Lambert, L. (1973) *Children Who Wait*. ABAFA.

Rubin, K. and Krasnor, L. R. (1986) Social cognitive and social behavioural perspectives on problem solving, in M. Perlmutter *Minnesota Symposia on Child Psychology*. Hillsdale, New Jersey, Erlbaum.

Rubin, K., LeMare, L. and Lollis, S. (1990) Social withdrawal in childhood, in S. R. Asher and J. D. Coie (op. cit).

Schneider, B. H., Attili, G., Nadel, J. and Weissberg, R. P. (1989) (eds) *Social Competence in Developmental Perspective*. London, Kluwer Academic Publishing.

Stayton, D. J. and Ainsworth, M. D. S. (1973) Individual differences in infant responses to brief everyday separations as related to other infant and maternal behaviours, *Developmental Psychology*, **9**, 226–35.

Tracy, R. L. and Ainsworth, M. D. S. (1981) Maternal affectionate behaviour and infant mother attachment patterns, *Child Development*, **52**, 1341–3.

Whitehurst, G. J. (1985) (ed.) *Annals of Child Development* Vol. 2, 251–97. JAI Press.

Wickman, E. K. (1928) Children's Behaviour and Teachers' Attitudes. Teachers' College Contributions to Education.

CHAPTER 8

Language and Communication in Withdrawn Children

David Jones

Withdrawn children are characterised by fundamental difficulties in their ability to communicate with others or a reluctance to use communication skills in social interaction. The distinction between these two types of condition is often much harder to make when assessing a non-communicating child than would be expected at first sight. Typically withdrawn children use very little speech in the presence of strangers. Close observation often reveals that the problems extend to other modes of communication as well as a lack of conversational skills. They tend not to use the changes in facial expression which are such an important part of many verbal exchanges. Frequently they have a sad or detached expression and they fail to signal interest in others. They rarely smile appropriately during social interactions. The problem sometimes extends to a deliberate avoidance of eye contact or a failure to maintain eye contact if it is established. A mood of depression or sadness may be signalled by general body posture or the absence of limb gestures. In other cases tension and irritability may be shown in agitated or jerky movements, or the child may avoid communication by indulging in repetitive or stereotyped behaviours. When speech is used qualitative aspects of the production such as the rate of production or the lack of intonation may suggest disordered language functioning. Non-verbal sounds may also reveal some of the child's feelings and distress. Laughter like smiling is likely to be absent. Sighing, grunting, gentle sobbing or even crying may punctuate periods of silence.

All of these problems indicate the complexity of human language. They provide a clear illustration that the development of communication skills involves a great deal more for the child than learning to talk and building up a vocabulary. Yet one of the most impressive aspects of human development is how quickly an integrated pattern of communication skills complete with cultural variations is acquired and becomes functional. There is now evidence from a range of sources that infants have an inbuilt ability to respond to social and linguistic stimulation. But it is important to emphasise that the attainment of the capacity to communicate is much more than a sequence of stages determined by maturation. Development depends upon interaction and the nature and quality of the stimulation provided by the child's caretakers. For most children the early stages of learning to communicate are an integral part of being cared for and forming first relationships. There is no formal period of instruction but a suprising amount is learned well before the child starts school.

A brief consideration of some of the very earliest features of adult–child interaction will serve to draw attention to the urge to communicate which is almost bursting out of the normal child. These same processes may be functioning atypically from an early age in withdrawn children or may be disrupted as a consequence of adverse environmental experiences. The onset of smiling is a good example to begin with as it is almost certainly innately determined. By around six to eight weeks of age most babies seem willing to smile at many things, it has been suggested that the most effective stimulus for eliciting a smiling response at this time becomes the nodding, talking, head (Wolff, 1963). This is a stimulus that is complex and social in origin. The baby in smiling may be signalling back a readiness to participate in social interactions and in turn we as adults seem to be predisposed to take pleasure from being smiled at. Further evidence that the onset of smiling is innate comes from observations that blind babies show fleeting smiles at around the same age as sighted infants when they are talked to and that babies who are both blind and deaf smile when they are handled and jostled affectionately (Freedman, 1964). It would seem that the primitive innate response can be released by a number of forms of social interaction, but that visual contact facilitates the continued development of social smiling. Again there is evidence that babies cared for in institutions where they receive less consistent interaction with adults reach a peak in social smiling a little later than home reared babies. It is tempting to speculate that if the baby does not experience satisfaction or is inappropriately reinforced or is often ignored then withdrawn behaviour may be a more likely reaction to later childhood stresses.

The extensive literature on the study of visual perception in very young babies indicates that other important processes may be functioning well before the onset of smiling. Controlled observations suggest that some babies during the first few days of life may be more likely to track a moving target with their eyes when it is a schematic face than when it is a jumbled stimulus of the same complexity level. Debate continues over the precise age at which it is possible to demonstrate such preferences, but there is little doubt that the infant's propensity to look at faces and to listen to voices is reinforced by nurturant interactions with the mother. These early social interactions are providing the baby with experience of turn-taking and the foundations of what to expect from others in communication. Also from an early age babies show a willingness to imitate facial expressions and gestures. Communication seems to be giving them pleasure even before it has acquired meaning. Sadly some autistic children show a deficit at the level of failing to attend to others in social interactions even when they are very young.

Attachment and dependency

Further evidence from studies of the development of smiling suggests that at around 16 to 20 months of age many babies start becoming much more selective in their smiling. They respond less readily to strangers than to those they are already familiar with. In terms of attachment theory this change in behaviour may be taken as an indication that the child is becoming able to recognise others, an essential requirement for the establishment of social relationships. The development of a healthy wariness to strangers at this point in development is seen as age appropriate behaviour and in evolutionary terms may represent the vestiges of a behavioural system which increased the prospects of survival for the young of the species (Bowlby, 1969). There are at least two major sources of anxiety for the child in these early social contacts. One is concern related to separation from the mother figure and the other is the more specific fear of strangers. These anxieties may increase during the second half of the first year after primary attachment bonds become more firmly established. A healthy and secure attachment provides the child with the confidence to explore the environment and tolerate brief separations, whereas a high level of dependency inhibits exploratory behaviour and as a consequence reduces opportunities for learning. The overly dependent infant is perhaps showing early signs of withdrawn behaviour and an avoidance of social interactions. An insensitive approach to dependency weaning at whatever age is often a causal factor in precipitating withdrawn and uncommunicative behaviour.

Operational measures of the security of attachment at around 12 months of age based on observations of the reunion behaviour with the mother following brief separations have shown that children signal insecurity in different ways (Ainsworth and Bell, 1970). Some show avoidant behaviour, not seeking contact on reunion and others appear to be ambivalent mixing clinging and demanding behaviour with anger and rejection. This diversity of responses reveals the difficulties which pre-verbal children experience in coping with feelings of insecurity. At least for some of these children the longer term consequences will be a tendency to withdraw from social contact during periods of emotional distress. Certainly not all children who experience early attachment difficulties will become withdrawn, it is more appropriate to think of them as a vulnerable group and if the problem is detected early enough the mother can sometimes be helped to focus on the development of the baby's communication skills. The problem at this stage is not seen as in the child or the mother, but in the transaction between them. A striking example of the consequences of separation from the mother during the second half of the first year is given by Spitz and Wolf (1946). They refer to a period of anaclitic depression during which the child is unresponsive and fails to thrive. Further anecdotal evidence of the disastrous effect which adverse environmental experiences can have on the development of communication skills and social behaviour is to be found in the reports of the so-called attic and cellar children (Skuse, 1984).

The origins of language and thought

What does the non-communicating withdrawn child think about? Whilst there is no simple or single answer to this question it is helpful to consider the capacities of withdrawn children in terms of what other children at similar ages and stages of development are able to do. Piaget has put forward an elaborate stage theory of cognitive development which, although it has been challenged on many aspects of detail and may underestimate the cognitive capacities of younger children, provides a useful framework for evaluating ways in which language and thought may be related at different ages. According to Piaget early representations of the external world are in the form of sensorimotor schemes which are action based. This Sensorimotor Period of development covers the first 18 months to two years of life. A major attainment during this period is the acquisition of the 'object concept', an awareness that objects and other people have a degree of permanence in their existance and that they continue to exist independently even when they are not being directly perceived. In attaining object permanence the young child also becomes aware of the position of objects in space and time and begins to have some knowledge of causality. It is interesting that this model of early cognitive development lends an element of credence to some of the processes hypothesised for the formation of attachment bonds.

According to Piaget's theory the child has a knowledge of objects and other people before words or symbols are acquired. The child must learn that the word can represent an object or action but is still separate from the object. In these terms symbolic thinking becomes possible when the child reaches the Preoperational Period usually by around two years of age (Piaget, 1952). Language is seen as dependent upon cognitive development and will develop in part to meet the need to convey thoughts and ideas to others and to receive information from them. Language may facilitate thinking but in the absence of a shared language system more idiosyncratic symbol systems may develop. A theoretical position of this sort which does not see cognitive development as dependent upon linguistic skills allows us to consider that many withdrawn children will have age appropriate abilities at least during the pre-school period. As the child gets older language becomes more important in indirect ways, particularly as a means to gaining information from others by asking questions, a skill which is so often lacking in withdrawn children.

Piaget also considered that the Preoperational child is egocentric. By this he meant that at this stage children are unaware that others have viewpoints or perspectives which are different from their own. Egocentrism in the use of language means that the child fails to take adequate account of the needs of the listener (Piaget, 1926). The evidence to support this claim is that young children are generally poor at explaining things to each other and frequently indulge in the use of monologues during play. Critics of Piaget have demonstrated that even quite young children are capable of showing an awareness of the viewpoints and needs of others under some conditions and consequently that they may have greater underlying competence than he predicted. Nevertheless what Piaget has described is a fairly accurate account of the ways in which children under eight years of age usually behave. The significance of this discussion for our understanding of withdrawn children is that they show an even greater tendency than other children to be egocentric. They are often unwilling to listen to the views of others when these differ from their own. They cannot be talked out of irrational fears and anxieties. Withdrawn children showing extreme phobic or avoidance behaviour are extremely resistant to explanations that other children are safely able to do the things which they themselves are afraid of. The withdrawn child with needle phobia is unimpressed by the apparant bravery of others and may also lack the cognitive capacity to appreciate the purposes of treatment which induces pain and lack of control. There is a further emotional element to the egocentric behaviour of some children to the extent that they actively resist attending and refuse to attempt to consider alternative states. Cognitive behaviour therapy with withdrawn children is often employed to help the child attain a low anxiety level by relaxation or other means and then gradually introducing imagery of successful behaviour.

A somewhat different account of relations between language and thought during development is provided by Vygotsky (1962). He expressed the view that language and thought have separate origins and like Piaget took the position that the primary purpose of language was for communication. As the young child develops, language is used increasingly for social communication but also acquires a directive function in thought processes. The monologues of the young child during play are seen as part of the transition to use language to facilitate thought in inner speech. Some withdrawn children seem to become dominated by this inner speech to the exclusion of normal social interactions. Also during normal development the child perceives that the use of language in social situations allows a degree of influence and control over the behaviours of others. Communication is seen to have valuable functions. Withdrawn children with poor self-esteem rightly or wrongly may feel that they are unable to influence others and they back away from attempting to communicate. The Vygotsky interpretation of the development of thinking does not label inner speech as egocentrism, nor does it regard inner speech as abnormal. Healthy functioning involves the use of communication and directed thinking. It can be helpful to draw on the ideas of both Piaget and Vygotsky to interpret disturbed behaviour rather than expect all cases to fit neatly into a single explanation.

Another insight into cognitive development which we get from Piaget is that there are likely to be several modes of representation of knowledge about the external world. This point is taken up by Bruner et al. (1966) who suggested that actions and motor skills could be represented in the enactive mode which has a degree of similarity to Piaget's sensorimotor schemes. Bruner also proposed an iconic mode giving an image-like representation of aspects of visual experience and a symbolic mode allowing representation by language or symbol systems. There may be individual differences in the reliance placed on each of these modes during thought processes. Most of us know some people who seem to be very good at visual imagery. For most children the symbolic mode would be based on the predominant language of the child's culture. However, limited experience of language may result in highly efficient individual versions of symbolic representation being developed. For example, it has been observed that some profoundly deaf adolescents who have had limited conventional linguistic input have been able to develop to the Period of Formal Operations, the highest of the stages of cognitive development identified by Piaget (Furth, 1969).

The clinical implications of these observations on cognitive development are several. It is possible that the thought processes and cognitive capacities of withdrawn children may often be at an age appropriate level. We should not assume the absence of ability because the child fails to communicate. However, we should remain cautious about inferring language abilities in withdrawn children until at least we have been able to demonstrate the presence of an age appropriate level of comprehension. In extreme cases the child who has withdrawn from communication may be shutting out the anxieties of the world by directing thought processes through excessive use of inner speech. Even more distanced from social contact will be the child who is directing thought processes mainly through the use of non-verbal modes of representation or through highly idiosyncratic symbolic modes. If children function in this detached and isolated way it is possible to understand how some of them can attain outstanding skills and expertise in very specialised areas. It is possible that withdrawn children who frequently indulge in repetitive behaviours with toys or other objects are in some way locked into complex hierarchies of enactive representation. There has been a lot of recent speculation over the possibility that non-verbal modes of representation may be subserved by right hemisphere functioning, and that in some way the so-called silent hemisphere may play a greater role when the left hemisphere which normally controls language functions, at least in right-handers, is less active.

Language in autistic children

Whilst autistic children show many features which would almost universally be labelled as withdrawn behaviour, they also show a number of distinctive features which place them quite clearly in a separate category from other types of childhood disturbance. Early childhood autism has attracted an enormous amount of attention ever since the first description of the condition by Kanner (1943). The clinical diagnosis is usually based on the identification of three distinctive patterns of behavioural abnormality in the child. The first is a severe developmental disorder of language. The second is delayed and deviant social development. The third is the presence of rituals which are exceedingly difficult to change. These conditions may occur singly or in modified forms in other withdrawn children but the combination of symptoms is striking. The diagnosis of autism is usually restricted to cases of early onset, usually in the first two years of life, although there has been recent interest in the condition of disintegrative disorder or 'late onset autism' involving regression after a period of apparent normality in development (Volkmar and Cohen, 1989). In contrast to most other conditions involving withdrawn behaviour the research evidence tends to rule out a psychogenic explanation for autism. The parents of autistic children do not appear to lack parenting skills and the children themselves behave very differently from children who have suffered prolonged neglect or emotional abuse. The evidence indicates that the most likely explanation for the condition is to be found at a biological level.

In severe cases of autism language may be absent. More frequently there is both an element of language delay and a variety of unusual features. Often there is an absence of the first person pronouns 'I' and 'me' and the child may refer to himself or herself as 'you' or by the first name. Another common feature of autistic language is echolalia, the repetition of the last word or words of a speaker's utterance. Echolalia is also occasionally shown by children with moderate learning difficulty or high anxiety levels, but is not used to the same extent as autistic children. It usually signals that the child has not properly comprehended what has been said and has focused instead on the sound pattern of the words perhaps in an attempt to maintain contact with the speaker. The spontaneous speech of autistic children tends to have a poor quality of intonation and the syntax may be inaccurate. Also striking is the poor and inappropriate use of language in social interactions. Autistic children make relatively few spontaneous remarks and they use fewer gestures and other forms of non-verbal communication than children with developmental language delays. From an early age these children fail to show the urge to communicate, which was noted above as such an important feature of normal infant development. They are noted for failing to maintain eye contacts with others and for not readily cooperating in turn-taking or giving joint attention in pointing and labelling activities.

From among the many attempts to identify cognitive and attentional deficits on autistic children came the observation that they find it difficult to distinguish between their own belief and someone else's belief. The proposal which followed was that autistic children lack a theory of mind since they are unable to take account of beliefs. A vivid test of the theory of mind hypothesis was carried out in the 'Sally-Anne experiment' (Baron-Cohen *et al.*, 1985). The child was shown two dolls, the one labelled as Sally had a basket and the one called Anne had a box. Sally has a marble which she puts into her basket and then goes out for a walk leaving the basket behind. Anne takes the marble and puts it in her box. The question for the child is 'Where will Sally look for her marble?' Most of the autistic children in the study pointed to the box indicating that they failed to understand Sally's belief. Other simple but ingenious tests of the theory of mind give the same result even though the autistic children were able to solve problems of greater cognitive complexity correctly. It is clear that if autistic children have such an inadequate understanding of others and what happens to them, they will also have difficulty using language and communication to convey information or in attempts to influence the behaviour of others.

Elective mutism

In many ways elective mutism can be viewed as an archetypal form of withdrawn behaviour. The condition is elective in the sense that the child appears to be exerting volitional control in refusing to use speech to communicate with others. This is especially true when speech is used in interactions with the mother or one or two favoured contacts but not more generally. This is one of the few types of behavioural disturbance in which the incidence is slightly higher for girls than for boys. The condition is usually characterised by extreme shyness in the presence of strangers and most frequently it begins when the child is around three to five years of age. The problem may attract attention when the child starts nursery school or infant school. It is qualitatively different from a transitory state of stubbornness in that the symptoms may persist over a period of years, although fortunately severe forms of the condition are rare.

Case example

Helen was a little girl aged six years from a bilingual Greek Cypriot family. When she was referred she would not speak to anyone outside the home or to anyone other than her immediate family when she was within the home. She had a brother aged eight years and a sister of twelve years both of whom were able to speak both English and Greek and were very protective towards Helen. The mutism had apparently started when Helen was three and was being taken on a holiday by her grandmother in an aeroplane. This was her first separation from her mother and she became extremely frightened by the noise. The holiday had to be cut short but the problem was contained within the family until Helen started school. She would not speak to the teachers or to the other children in her class and although she followed instructions from the teachers, she never asked any questions or gave any answers. She was accepted as different by her class mates some of whom helped her in the playground and collected her coat. She had almost become a sort of class mascot or toy and was protected by the two toughest boys in the group. A persisting symptom at the time of referral was a fear of loud or high-pitched noises and the brother occasionally teased her by chasing her with a vacuum clearner. She would nod or shake her head in response to questions from other children and would sometimes point or touch them. She would not even communicate at that level with her teachers and ducked her head whenever they addressed her. Initially the parents of this girl were not as concerned about her as the teachers. They had felt that she would probably grow out of it and the father commented that his wife had been a very quiet lady when he first met her. So it seems there was not a strong emphasis on verbal communication within the family. However the two elder children had not been impaired by this environment. On the initial interview it was clear that a formal assessment of abilities would not be possible but an informal administration of the British Picture Vocabulary Test was carried out with Helen sitting on her mother's knee (Dunn *et al.*, 1982). She was found to have a Receptive Vocabulary in the Low Average Range which confirmed the impression that she could at least follow simple instructions and given her reluctance to cooperate with a stranger even by pointing at pictures was probably an underestimate of her comprehension ability. Her silence was absolute and she would not even speak to her parents in the clinic setting. Treatment involved a combination of play therapy and behaviour therapy together with several family interviews and active collaboration with the school. No pressure was put on Helen to communicate but she was talked to normally and given the opportunity to look at pictures and handle toys. The breakthrough came after six weeks when Helen used words quietly to enact contact between two toy zoo animals. She first spoke to the play therapist through the medium of a glove puppet and became quite animated in her movements. A week later the therapist conducted a session at the school with the door of the room open. Two weeks later Helen began asking her class teachers questions very quietly. She remained a shy and rather timid girl but the change at the level of a readiness to communicate was impressive.

Not all outcomes with elective mutes or other withdrawn children are so favourable or achieved so quickly. If the underlying stresses and anxieties are still present in the child's life then the intervention will need to address these first.

Specific language impairments

In a small number of withdrawn children it becomes clear that language acquisition is delayed and that there are no likely emotional or environmental explanations for the problems. Also the clinical picture indicates that the child is not autistic. Cases of this sort are sometimes referred to as developmental dysphasia or specific language impairment. It must be emphasised that not all children with these language problems will show withdrawn behaviour although their communication problems may give rise to difficulties in social relationships. Careful examination of children with language problems usually shows that the difficulties can be detected at a variety of levels. They tend to make errors at a syntactic level, that is, in the structure of their sentences and even have difficulty in repeating the correct structural form of sentences read out to them. For example they make mistakes on the use of negatives and in forming the plurals of irregular nouns, etc. They also may show difficulty at the semantic level, that is, in adequately conveying the meaning of the message they wish to communicate. They may have trouble with comprehension of speech spoken by others. They may have difficulties in learning to read and write. Recent evidence also suggests that they may have subtle problems with the pragmatics of communication, that is, properly understanding the function of communication, the purposes of communication. Distinguishing between children with mild forms of these disturbances and others who have experienced minimal environmental disadvantages which have delayed language acquisition is not easy and requires careful assessment.

Literacy problems

A final word should be said about the complex task of assessing the role of emotional problems as determinants of reading difficulty. Some withdrawn children are unhappy because they are having problems coping at school. As a consequence their self-esteem suffers and they avoid challenges by retreating into themselves in the classroom situation. This is particularly true of children who experience early difficulty in the acquisition of reading skills. Children with developmental dyslexia frequently go through a period of considerable unhappiness until the condition is properly diagnosed and remedial support is provided. In marked contrast there are some withdrawn children who are exceptionally good at reading and spend much of their time at it. These precocious readers as they are sometimes called avoid the stresses of social interaction with others by retreating into the fantasy world of books and make-believe. A last group of children to challenge the teachers are those whose emotional problems interfere with the acquisition of learning skills. This condition should not be confused with dyslexia and will require therapeutic intervention followed by remedial support.

References

Ainsworth, M. D. S. and Bell, S. M. (1970) Attachment, exploration and separation: illustrated by the behavior of one-year-olds in a strange situation', *Child Development*, **41**, 49–67.

Baron-Cohen, S., Leslie, A. M. and Frith, U. (1985) Does the autistic child have a 'theory of mind'? *Cognition*, **21**, 37–46.

Bowlby, J. (1969) *Attachment and Loss: Volume 1 Attachment*. New York, Basic Books.

Bruner, J. S., Olver, R. R. and Greenfield, P. M. (1966) *Studies in Cognitive Growth*. New York, Wiley.

Dunn, L. M., Dunn, L. M., Whetton, C. and Pontillie, D. (1982) *British Picture Vocabulary Scale*. Windsor, NFER-Nelson.

Freedman, D. G. (1964) Smiling in blind infants and the issue of innate versus acquired, *Journal of Child Psychology and Psychiatry*, **5**, 171–84.

Frith, U. (1989) *Autism: Explaining the Enigma*. Oxford, Blackwell.

Furth, H. G. (1969) *Piaget and Knowledge: Theoretical Foundations*. Englewood Cliffs, N. J., Prentice-Hall.

Kanner, L. (1943) Autistic disturbances of affective contact, *Nervous Child*, **2**, 217–50.

Piaget, J. (1926) *The Language and Thought of the Child*. New York, Harcourt Brace.

Piaget, J. (1952) *The Origins of Intelligence in Children*. New York, International Universities Press.

Skuse, D. (1984) Extreme deprivation in early childhood: II. theoretical issues and a comparative review, *Journal of Child Psychology and Psychiatry*, **25**, 543–72.

Spitz, R. A. and Wolf, K. M. (1946) The smiling response: a contribution to the ontogenesis of social relations, *Genetic Psychology Monographs*, **34**, 57–125.

Volkmar, F. R. and Cohen, D. J. (1989) Disintegrative disorder or 'late onset' autism, *Journal of Child Psychology and Psychiatry*, **30**, 717–24.

Vygotsky, L. S. (1962) *Thought and Language*. Cambridge, M.I.T. Press.

Wolff, P. (1963) Observations on the early development of smiling, in B. M. Foss (ed.) *Determinants of Infant Behaviour*, Volume II. London, Methuen.

PART THREE

Treatment

CHAPTER 9

A Withdrawn Child in the Classroom Referred to an Educational Therapist

Muriel Barrett and Merkel Sender

When a child is withdrawn from his class because his behaviour is withdrawn how might he respond to an educational therapist?

The label 'withdrawn' is probably rarely used to describe classroom behaviour, yet it is an immediately recognisable description. A medical viewpoint provides a summary of this state of mind. 'A child's withdrawal can be a manifestation of a variety of underlying processes – constitutional, biological, developmental, social, emotional and familial – that occur either alone or in combination' (Lewis and Blotchky, 1987).

To withdraw, an individual, consciously or unconsciously, makes a decision to behave in a particular manner. Paradoxically, withdrawal from interaction is in itself a form of communication; what Robert Weiss refers to, albeit in a very different context, as communicating by not communicating (Weiss, 1975).

If we take an imagined spectrum of this behaviour within the limits of various educational settings, the most extreme is probably autism (Tustin, 1981). Failure to make eye contact, communicating by farting, or curling into a foetal position under a table, may result in misunderstanding, and alarm or anger us. These actions on the part of a child seem to be reflecting a state of mind that is defending against having to relate to others: it provides a barrier that can seem impenetrable to those seeking interaction.

We often find withdrawn behaviour irritating, therefore can we assume that it is an unconscious reflection of true feelings of anger, despair, depression or a wish to maintain a degree of helplessness/dependency? It seems probable also that there has been a failure to experience or attach meaning to symbols.

Children who have formed anxious attachments to their parental – or attachment figures – are more likely to continue to behave in an anxious manner in school. Secure children make the transition into school with an expectation that teachers will provide a continuity of care and understanding which is similar to that experienced at home. (The concept of attachment behaviour is taken from the work of John Bowlby, *Attachment and Loss* (1969, 1973, 1980).)

Children's withdrawn behaviour in the classroom may arise from earlier experiences of being rejected, ignored or 'smothered' by their attachment figures. The memory of early rejection may result in withdrawal into silent anger which becomes entangled with an unconscious fear of revealing a wish to retaliate. Interaction with teachers could be thought too risky, or a threat that will undermine attempts to maintain an angry equilibrium.

Those who sink into despair, and sometimes depression, may feel that any attempts to elicit the response they most want will not be forthcoming. A mother described her experience of feeding her infant 'I can't be bothered. What is the point when he loses interest?' How can this child enter a classroom with the expectation that his teacher can 'be bothered'? He no longer believes that he is worth 'bothering about', and retreats within himself.

Many withdraw into a state of dependency. A symbiotic relationship with an attachment figure disallows for goal-seeking or exploratory behaviour. If these children could not depend (on mother), they are less likely to reach a state of independence. (This can lead to a withdrawal from childhood and adopting a parenting role (Bowlby, 1977).) A teacher may inadvertently respond by attempting to 'mother' the dependent child in a similar manner, by not expecting him to carry out age-appropriate scholastic tasks.

A child who makes no eye contact may be ignored or rejected, leaving a teacher in turn feeling ignored or rejected. Whatever feelings are projected into teachers they can be left questioning why their professional skills are not good enough to engage or teach these children. Some may believe that they will elicit a response from a child who withdraws. If a child spends his school day curled up under a table he could be said to have adopted active passivity. He has chosen to act-out his state of mind by refusing to hear or react. Naturally, this behaviour can make teachers feel inadequate, and at times as helpless as the child himself.

These children are not easy to hold in mind in the Winnicottian sense and are frequently overlooked in the classroom and any of these behaviours can evoke feelings of guilt in teachers. They can feel that they should be able to give them more or different attention. A few may feel angry with them because they never asked for help. A study (Sroufe, 1983) of the patterns of attachment behaviour in pre-school children demonstrates how teachers react to those who have no strategies for eliciting a positive response from them; the ones most in need of help are the least likely to gain it. A switched-off manner or impassive face can make teachers feel frustrated and infuriated when their efforts to communicate fail. They may, unconsciously, be reflecting back to the child the very behaviour that he has experienced while interacting with his attachment figures at home.

Numerous educationally-based studies of withdrawn behaviour compare the children in this group with those exhibiting withdrawn/aggressive or aggressive behaviour. Others include teachers', or a peer groups', assessments of withdrawn behaviour and its effect on the class. A more dynamic approach to the problem is shown by studies that include an evaluation of self-esteem, emotional development or implementing changes in interactive behaviour.

Two such studies that correlate with our clinical experience as educational therapists, emphasise the importance of a child's pre-school patterns of behaviour. The first considers patterns of anxiety and withdrawal either since infancy, or since the transition into school (Byrnes, 1984). She regards these children as being 'forgotten', once they are in the classroom. A second longitudinal study, examines aggressive and passive–withdrawn behaviour by looking at the history of insecure attachment; inadequate or hostile parent care; and chaotic or stressful life circumstances (Renken *et al.*, 1989).

When the withdrawn behaviour of a child in class is taken seriously a referral to a psychologist or psychiatrist usually reveals an emotional 'problem', in addition to a cognitive one. Before giving an account of an educational therapist working with a nine-year-old which illustrates these two facets of withdrawn behaviour we give a brief introduction to the practice of this intervention.

Educational therapy

This intervention is practised by either qualified teachers or child psychologists who have undertaken a clinical training. They work with children with severe learning disabilities, individually, in peer groups, and with their families. (We will not consider group and family work here.)

The focus is on the dyadic interaction both at a conscious and unconscious level. Each child is encouraged to recover his capacity for learning by understanding how his feelings can facilitate or inhibit the use of his ability. Feelings are expressed by use of the metaphor in stories, models and drawings. One author (Caspari, 1974) suggested that appropriate educational 'food' is offered in a way that is similar to a mother offering her infant appropriate food, at each stage of his development. Barrett and Trevitt (in press) extended this thinking by comparing the dynamics of 'second-chance' learning of a school child/educational therapist dyad to the first dyadic learning of an infant with his mother. These authors also propose that an educational therapist adopts the role of an 'educational attachment figure' to enable children, (and sometimes their parents) to re-discover feelings related to learning.

Alex: his family and school experience

Alex was the only son of a two-parent family. He was cared for by a succession of inexperienced girls. Mother spent a short period at the end of each day with him, but reported that he showed no interest in her, and 'never played with any toys'. He would not breast feed and later refused solids.

His withdrawn behaviour caused concern in his nursery class: he was unwilling to communicate verbally, made no eye contact and very rarely interacted with either peer group or adults. His teacher noted that he rarely interacted with mother who she described as 'trying to be invisible'. Alex was monitored by an educational psychologist; his hearing was tested and found to be normal; he responded well to speech therapy.

In mainstream school he reverted to his non-communicative behaviour by withholding speech. No language delay or low overall ability were diagnosed but 'psychological' problems were thought to be preventing him from co-operating in situations where demands were placed on him. It was noted that he continued to have difficulty in separating from his father, who, 'denigrated his son almost as if he was denying his very existence and yet at the same time identified himself with him in a way that suggested a symbiotic relationship'. After three years Alex had made no progress socially or in basic skills and was transferred to a Special Needs unit. Shortly afterwards he was referred to an educational therapist by a consultant child psychiatrist.

The following account focuses on the work that took place for one hour a week, over a period of almost two years, after which time the family were offered further help.

The first session with Alex: anxious attachment

My introduction to Alex took place in the clinic waiting room when he came for his first session. In view of the anticipated difficulty of separation from father, I invited both upstairs to the room where Alex and I would be working. With encouragement from his father, and me, Alex sat down on a chair next to a small table on which I had placed his box containing a variety of materials for his use. I sat beside him and invited father to sit on the other side of the room, which he did. Alex perched on the edge of his chair, ill at ease with an axious expression on his face. He didn't look at me at all. He ignored my neutral questions about school, except to whisper the name of his teacher. Alex's father often answered for his son. I sensed that he, and I, were finding Alex's withdrawn behaviour discomfiting.

I drew Alex's attention to his box, and wondered aloud whether he might like to find out what was inside it. He nodded, almost imperceptibly. This glimmer of interest made me feel that this was an opportune moment to ask father to wait downstairs. As he left the room Alex's facial expression displayed even more dejection; he uttered an almost inaudible 'No', and his eyes filled with tears. However he did not cry and was able to remain in the room. While looking at the contents of his box he made no attempt to get anything out himself, but when I did so, he indicated his interest by gestures only.

What came across so powerfully in my first session with this boy was his lack of spontaneity and a feeling I had that for him, people and things were frightening. I was aware of the effect his anxiety had on his thought and language processes. He could not count four objects correctly and when we looked at the animals in his box he was unable to name them, but said repeatedly, 'I know, I know'. His behaviour made me feel anxious and inadequate.

The second session

I expected Alex to resist separation from father in the waiting room and was therefore surprised when he came upstairs with me. (On all subsequent occasions separating from father did not cause this boy any anxiety. That Alex had been able to separate from father during the initial session proved to be important for Alex's parents also. They described the separation as a 'major breakthrough'.)

During the session I observed some tentative exploratory behaviour, when Alex showed an interest in a game called Connect Four. He proceeded slowly and carefully to drop counters into a frame, one colour following another until the supply was exhausted, and then began again. Although he concentrated and appeared to be absorbed in the activity the repetitive almost obsessional way in which he emptied and filled the frame had a mindless quality about it. I felt shut out – Alex was filling up the space for himself. He could not play *with* me; there were no connections.

Subsequent sessions

Alex's anxiety about keeping me, the therapist, and the sessions under his control, seemed to impel him into verbal communication, demonstrated when a simple number activity was introduced. This involved matching counters to numbers. He enjoyed this until I gently questioned a mismatch. He immediately said he didn't want to do it any more and would 'leave it until next week'. This did not suggest to me that he had any feeling of continuity about the sessions, but rather his need to be omnipotent. He could not bear to be helped; my offers seemed to arouse a feeling of helplessness in him. He was too anxious to learn; his potential capacity for learning was channelled into defensive control.

I think many of the educational tasks I had attempted to teach him were irrelevant. My own anxiety prevented me from being sufficiently aware of Alex's state of mind.

The reference to an infant's 'subjective experience' is seen as essential to the discovery of 'a central role for a sense of self' (Stern, 1985). This experience seems almost to have eluded Alex. It is difficult to imagine how much loving care could have been reflected back to him as an infant by his attachment figure, a mother who was so fleetingly glimpsed each day.

Finding a secure base

Alex's play with animals displayed qualities of omnipotence. During one session he intimated that he would like to play with them and I suggested he might like to join the plastic fences together, but he quickly abandoned a half-hearted attempt. When I recognised that this suggestion was reflecting my wish to make links, it made me think that Alex's inability to join anything together was an indication of his fragile ego-relatedness (Winnicott, 1965). He was willing to accept my help on this occasion, and formed a square which he filled with as many animals as possible. He then removed them and placed them in a straight line, outside the square. A few moments later some were returned to the square, then he got up and peered out of the window stating that he no longer wished to play with the animals.

This activity was repeatedly begun and then abandoned. I continued to be excluded, until he vacillated between making use of me in the Winnicottian sense (1971), and ignoring me. He acknowledged some dependent feeling when he indicated, non-verbally, that he wanted to know which were farm and which were wild animals and allowed me to help him to distinguish them, reminiscent of a child playing at a much earlier stage of development. I used this interest in classification to move on to a basic skill task, matching groups of objects to numbers, all under five. We did the first page together but when he was unable to manage the next page he changed the task rather than ask for, or accept, help. He continued to show his reluctance to read, draw or write. He had great difficulty in listening to stories.

I found this boy's withdrawn behaviour very difficult to cope with and became aware that I had resorted to a didactic approach even with play materials. I did not feel Alex was being compliant, it was just that he seemed to be going through the motions of playing, leaving me with an impression that he had to do what I suggested in order to learn *how* to play. It seemed to lack any symbolic quality. It was as if he was using the animals to fill a void, reflecting his own feeling of emptiness. I experienced this play as passive, purposeless. I too felt a sense of helplessness, sometimes taking refuge in being a teacher.

Despite my misgivings I attempted to become attuned to Alex's feelings. I felt he conveyed to me his early experience of worthlessness and emptiness. After a panic reaction to being asked to draw, 'I can't, I can't draw', he nevertheless communicated a feeling of his early experience.

Alex drew three strange immature shapes – figures encased in circles – and labelled them baby, mum, and daddy. The three separated figures of this 'family' made me feel there was no means of communication available to them. When invited to tell a story about them in the next session he nodded enthusiastically but then seemed at a loss. With my help he dictated: 'The baby and the mum and the daddy are sleeping. I like the dad and babies and mums. They are sleeping in a circle.'

In the following session the theme of unrelatedness continued. (If a child is reluctant to use material an educational therapist may take the initiative.)

Alex watched as I began rolling some modelling clay. He decided I was making a pram. He began to help me and at his instigation we made a baby – the first time he took any initiative. This figure was quite out of proportion and so it wouldn't fit into the pram. He became very perturbed; my response was to make the pram bigger and ask if we should make someone to push it. 'No', he said, 'it's all alone . . . no-one's pushing it . . . it's sleeping'. He then turned his attention to the animals. Later I asked if the baby would like to see the animals. He said only the daddy would push the baby. He moved the pram towards the animals and I commented that perhaps he could tell the baby the names of the animals. 'You don't talk to babies', was Alex's immediate and emphatic response.

The establishment of a secure base, represented by the therapist and the sessions enabled this boy to show some tentative exploratory behaviour.

Alex began for the first time to play as though attaching some meaning to it. The animals were dropped into the square plastic fence and he laughed when everything fell over. Then he covered the square with his head and arms. I asked what he was doing. 'Magic' he replied. This was repeated a number of times until he told me he wanted to go. When we replaced the animals in his box Alex said he wanted to keep the pram. In a subsequent session the pram and baby were placed close to the animals, but ignored. At the end of this session he squashed both baby and pram and told me the pram had 'slipped'.

I felt that dropping the animals was related to his unconscious feelings aroused by the plasticine baby. It made me think of Winnicott's idea of an infant 'infinitely falling' and not having an experience of being 'held'. I felt the destruction of the baby and pram was because the feelings these models aroused were so intense that he had to destroy them. I was very moved by Alex's communications about the baby. The drawing and story of the foetus shaped family, the model of the baby and pram, suggested to me a baby who had not had his needs adequately met; his efforts had brought no response so he had given up hope. I felt the parental figures represented a mother and father who were asleep and therefore unable to think about their baby; a baby who was isolated and to whom no attention was paid. Alex's two comments 'He's all alone' and 'You don' talk to babies', seemed to confirm that all the baby could do was to sleep and show no interest in his surroundings. I was reminded of Bion's theory of the container and the contained, his reference to the role of a mother and her baby (Bion, 1962) His contention was that the baby's capacity to be curious and to think, depends upon the baby's experience of being thought about by a mother who makes him feel understood.

Alex felt secure enough to reveal both painful and ambivalent feelings, that may have paralleled the reality of his early experience, but his anxiety about separation is shown by his continuing denial of the meaning of breaks, while at the same time making indirect references to them. The concept of the Emergent Self (Stern, 1985) encapsulates the next phase of the process of Alex's development within the context of the sessions, when he resumed his rather inhibited play with the animals until he said he wanted to 'feed' them.

I noted his good fine motor control when he cut out irregular pieces of sticky paper, far larger than the animals, which he coloured black on the reverse side then announced that he had finished with both. In the following session he placed the dog in one enclosure and separate ones for the wild and farm animals. 'We must feed the animals' he said, giving me some paper and a second pair of scissors. I had no feeling of being involved just controlled. This feeling was confirmed when I commented on the amount of food Alex was giving the animals. 'They must be very hungry', I said. 'Make food', was the reply. When all the food had been distributed, I said, 'I wonder what they are going to do now?' He looked at me in a perplexed way and muttered, 'I'm finished', which was then changed to, 'I'm going to do magic'. He lifted some bricks which surrounded the dog but to his utter consternation it had disappeared. Momentarily Alex looked very frightened, but, when he realised it was concealed by some bricks he re-arranged them and performed his 'trick'.

I was taken aback by his response to the failure of his 'magic' and sensed his vulnerability and helplessness as his feelings of omnipotence gave way to feelings of annihilation. In subsequent sessions it became apparent that Alex identified closely with the dog. Separating the dog from the other animals, I thought, denoted an attempt to detach himself from the chaotic feelings that seemed to overwhelm him; to work through some of his feelings about isolation and separation anxiety.

The repetitive play with the dog and the animals continued for several weeks with minimal verbal communication or eye contact.

I became increasingly concerned about our lack of interaction, until I recognised that by 'holding' the situation it was becoming possible for him to experience 'the capacity to be alone' (Winnicott, 1965) in my presence. There was a subtle change in the animal play and Alex spent most of the penultimate session of the term absorbed in making a complicated connected structure for the animals. He seemed almost lost in a dream, unaware of me at times, but once or twice he acknowledged my presence by looking at me. 'There must be a place for the food', he commented, as he manipulated the bricks to make an enclosure for it. 'I'll feed them just now', (meaning later). This was the first indication of his understanding that the 'food' was a symbol. He no longer needed immediate gratification but could wait. He had internalised a memory of self interacting with a trusted figure who he knew would provide (educational) 'food' after the break. It was during this session that Alex was first able to be curious. A door banged and he looked up from his play and asked me about the noise.

Stories, reading and difficulty with symbols

It is worth remembering that children referred for educational therapy expect help with their educational 'problems'. To deny them an opportunity to accomplish tasks is to negate one of the shared aims of the intervention.

The therapist working with Alex introduced some basic work on concept formation, abstractions such as size and shape etc; counting, number bonds to ten and simple sets.

Alex was unable to cope with simple classification tasks such as sorting size and shape but this led me to realise how restricted his capacity for abstract thinking continued to be. His difficulty with symbolic thinking became apparent when I read to him. He seemed interested in the story of the Three Pigs, which Davidson (1988) suggests illustrates the precarious character of early boundaries and the fragile sense of identity. When it came to the wolf devouring one pig Alex said, 'My daddy and I don't eat pig'. Then he said he wanted to go as though the content of the story prevented any more listening. Alex seemed to have no effective basis for sublimation, Weininger (1988) and could not make use of symbols to separate his identification of self from that of father.

On several occasions Alex asked for the story but denied any memory of it, repeating that he did not eat pig. He became able to acknowledge that he found it frightening but I made the mistake of offering reassurance instead of dealing with his anxiety. He shuffled in his chair and told me he could see his father's car in the road. The following three sessions were missed but on his return Alex again asked for the story; he appeared confused about the sequence of events. The repetition of this story occasionally during the next year allowed Alex to be less overwhelmed by his fears of being devoured. The very small amount of reading we attempted together remained at a mechanical level while he continued to struggle to understand word symbols; numbers however held some meaning for him.

'Not-me', play and learning

The eager manner in which Alex entered the room towards the end of our first year's work together demonstrated the change in his self-image. I felt he now had a memory of our interaction that he had internalised and could use. Bowlby suggests that learning to tolerate separation (from mother) coincides with a developing sense of adventure, exploration of a wider environment, and discovery of self as an individual. However I remained acutely aware of his disordered thought and language process. He became enthusiastic about the educational materials I brought to the sessions, and his play with the animals became more complex, with some aggressive feelings being expressed. He began to make links for himself between home, school and the clinic. There were many indications of his curiosity about me and the room, and almost a greed for new experiences. On one occasion he rushed ahead of me and started looking through his box. 'You are in a hurry today' I said: 'I'm going to play with the animals', he replied, but just then caught sight of something on the shelf. 'What's that?' I explained it was a word game. 'I want to play it now.' I invited him to choose between the two activities; he chose the game, and enjoyed it, accepting help with words he found difficult. He also experimented with different uses of Unifix blocks and could make mistakes, accept praise, and admit to some satisfaction at completion of a task. When tackling an unfamiliar activity he was able to say 'I don't know that', without becoming upset.

Thinking

Alex made no comment when I read a story entitled *Time to Get Out of the Bath Shirley*. When we re-read it Alex said in a surprised tone, 'She doesn't listen!' On turning the page he asked if she was having a dream. 'What do you think?' I replied. He was silent for a moment and then said anxiously, 'She's going down in the water . . . she's going to go under'. He nodded when I reflected his anxious thoughts back to him.

He next chose the Dog and Bone fable but the whole idea of a reflection seemed quite beyond his comprehension. Repetition did not increase his understanding. I asked, 'I wonder who you see when you look in the mirror?' 'Daddy' was the immediate reply. I took a mirror to the next session, Alex looked at himself and smiled saying, 'It's Alex'. I said 'Yes, it's Alex smiling'. He appeared to be confirming his sense of self but his discovery was not untroubled. The precariousness of his concept of oneness was evident when he undertook some simple thinking skills tasks which required yes or no answers. Question: Can you see yourself in the mirror? Answer: 'No'. Question: What can you see? 'Answer: 'Nothing'. During this period he increased his aggressive play with a crocodile, which we compared to the wolf from the story.

Alex seems to be exploring a validation of self through Stern concepts of a core-self; self versus other and self with other.

More reading, making connections, risking more thinking

Throughout our second year Alex was in touch with his feelings. He became animated, alert and more communicative. He played imaginatively with the animals, and involved me in his play. He continued to enjoy simple repetitive number work and he was less resistant to reading and attached meaning to stories. At the end of a story about a cat that becomes fatter and fatter, hides in a cupboard, and is later found with a litter of kittens, Alex told me that the kittens 'came from the mummy's tummy'. He seemed entranced by the picture. 'She's round', he said softly, and gently traced her outline with his fingers.

I was reminded of this a few weeks later. While Alex was drawing a tummy, mine rumbled rather loudly. He said, 'that's because of all the things inside'. He drew something similar to a Christmas tree, 'that's the skeletal' (sic), he added a figure enclosed in a circle. This, he said, was the baby in my tummy. 'Oh! I've got a baby in my tummy?' he nodded. 'Is there a baby in your tummy, too?' 'I'm a boy. Boys don't have babies in their tummies, only ladies do'. After this exchange I was left feeling that Alex wanted to be a baby again but inside me.

The responses of Alex can be seen in relation to Klein's theory of the Epistemological Instinct, (1931). She said that the mother's body 'represents in the unconscious the treasure house of everything desirable'. For Alex the fat round cat and my tummy seemed to be associated with an unconscious image of an idealised mother. This conflicted with the conscious feelings that he had about his real mother's body. Her heavy smoking preoccupied Alex who once voiced his fears that his mother might die. (Many of his drawings featured smoke.)

A few sessions later Alex chose to read the fable about ants and the grasshopper. He misread this as grasshooper (sic) and laughed as he corrected his mistake. 'I wonder why he's called a grasshopper?' I asked. 'I can't think', he replied. I reflected back to him that we all find it hard to think sometimes. Alex immediately stopped reading, and instead of staying with the feeling and the task I colluded with him. This resulted in him taking over the rest of the session. He moved from one activity to another avoiding everything. He controlled me when I tried to engage him by turning away from me. Finally he shared his despair. He said, 'I'm a bit tired . . . I think . . . I'm finished . . . I can't play . . . it's too long in the clinic'.

I began the next session by suggesting that we re-read the story. Alex read 'the little ants were hard at work' I intervened, and said we had not managed to do any work last week and that I felt sad because things seemed to have gone wrong and I had not helped him. He said, 'Yes' very quietly and looked at me in a way which suggested he felt that I understood him. Then he read 'the grasshopper was not hard at work'. I said that he had reminded me of a grasshopper hopping around from one thing to another and not being able to work. He smiled and nodded before finishing the story.

This interaction illustrates the view about the 'adjustments' that take place within the mother/toddler dyad, leading to the child's recognition that his 'set-goals' may differ from those of his attachment figure (Bowlby, 1969).

Moves towards independence

Changes in Alex's behaviour could be observed, since the development of a 'verbal self' (Stern, 1985).

In the penultimate term of my work with Alex I had a greater sense of an integrated self and a relationship that was being consolidated in each new session. He became eager to show that he could do things by himself and took pleasure in his achievements. In many respects he reminded me of a much younger child who was just starting school. Our interaction changed markedly when we played word or number games, now a prominent feature of our work together. These games demonstrated spontaneity and a positive approach to tasks and an ability to anticipate the moves required to beat me, which he enjoyed.

During these activities I realised that the concepts of more or less for a child who took so long to struggle to understand the concept 'I Sum' must be inordinately difficult to master, Winnicott's (1986). There were indications that Alex was beginning to relate the value of numbers to the real world. In a story a character received a badge with six on it. Alex told me he got one when he was nine. 'I passed six, I passed seven, I passed eight and when I pass nine I'll be ten'. This was the first indication Alex was aware of the concept of time, and more importantly that he could believe in a future.

The final term: separations and ending

Alex became more able to tolerate separations, although in this, as in all other aspects of his functioning there was no clear cut progression. In the early stages he used the defensive behaviours of shutting off and forgetting, and when sessions were resumed he had 'forgotten' everything that had happened previously. In some sessions prior to a break, Alex, like many other children, spent a lot of time glueing, stapling, or sellotaping pieces of paper together.

At this time Alex folded paper over and over again with great care as though he was enfolding us as a way of holding the memory of the sessions together. Later he expressed feelings directly. When he asked me to write down my name and telephone number on a drawing, I reflected back to him his need to maintain contact. I said I would be thinking of him when our work was finished; he nodded and said, 'On Wednesdays' – the day of our sessions.

Sometimes he projected his feelings of being abandoned on to me when I discussed breaks. 'My dad's going in a plane and my mum . . . you won't see me. I'll be in Greece'. On another occasion Alex unconsciously used a symbol to express his feelings about the Christmas break. He was doing a simple sequencing task, arranging pictures to tell a story about a kite stuck in a tree. Instead of placing the cards in semantic order he chose to focus on connecting them in terms of the string attached to the kite, indicating a need for continuity. It reminded me of an umbilical cord. He once denied the existence of a calendar which we had made to help him face the break. He searched in vain and said, 'I can't think'. His anxiety appeared to have destroyed his capacity to 'know' about the calendar. I acknowledged how difficult it was to think when we are upset; after a few moments he said, 'I've got it'.

Towards the end of the work Alex did acknowledge that there would be an ending, and made direct reference to his feelings.

He asked me how to spell a word while he was labelling his drawing, and remarked, 'When someone's eleven they know how to do things'. I commented that he seemed to be ready to think about growing up and being able to manage without his sessions when he was eleven. He then looked at his calendar. 'I don't want to go, I want to see you'. I used three Unifix cubes to represent the number of sessions we had left, but Alex added all of them together. I commented on his wish to prolong the time.

The final session had a quiet feeling. He talked to me as he worked at making a sailor's hat. 'It's going to be my last day today. I'm putting lots of sellotape on my hat so I can cut it out . . . a sailor hat, look at this.' I felt he was demonstrating his ambivalence by the sticking activity, wanting to remain attached, and yet facing the reality that he was leaving, sailing away. 'I'm going to do the animals now', he said. This time he fed the animals, except the dog who was uncovered and not enclosed. I told him I thought the dog, like him, was feeling safer and could manage.

References

Barrett, M. and Trevitt, J. (in press) *Attachment Behaviour and the School Child: An Introduction to Educational Therapy*.

Bettelheim, B. and Zelan, K. (1982) *On Learning to Read: The Child's Fascination with Meaning*. London, Thames & Hudson.

Bion, W.R. (1962) 'Theory of thinking', *International Journal of Psychoanalysis*, **43**, 306–10.

Bowlby, J. (1969) Attachment and loss, *Attachment and Loss* 1, London, Hogarth Press and Institute of Psychoanalysis; New York, Basic Books.

Bowlby, J. (1973) Separation and anxiety, *Attachment and Loss* 2, London, Hogarth Press and Institute of Psychoanalysis; New York, Basic Books.

Bowlby, J. (1977) The making and breaking of affectional bonds, *British Journal of Psychiatry* **130**, 200–10 and 421–31.

Bowlby, J. (1980) Sadness and depression, *Attachment and Loss* 3, London, Hogarth Press and Institute of Psychoanalysis; New York, Basic Books.

Bowlby, J. (1988) *Secure Base*. London, Routledge & Kegan Paul.

Burningham, J. (1985) *Time to Get out of the Bath Shirley*. London, Collins Picture Lions.

Byrnes, D.A. (1984) Forgotten children in classrooms: development and characteristics, *Elementary School Journal*, Jan., 3, 271–81. Logan, Utah State University.

Caspari, I. (1974) Educational therapy, in V. Varma (ed.) *Psychotherapy Today*. London, Constable, 215–32.

Davidson, D. (1988) Playing and the growth of the imagination, in M. Sioli and M. Davis (eds) *Jungian Child Psychotherapy*. London, Karnac Books.

Lewis, J.M. and Blotchky, M.J. (1987) The withdrawn child, *Medical Aspects of Human Sexuality* **21**, 5, 94–103.

Klein, M. (1931) *The Theory of Intellectual Inhibition*. London, Hogarth Press.

Renken, B., Egeland, B., Marvinney, D. and Mangelsdorf, S. (1989) Early childhood antecedents of aggression and passive-withdrawal in early elementary school. Special issue: long term stability and change in personality, *Journal of Personality* **57**, 2, 257–81.

Rockwell, A. (1987) *The Three Bears and 15 other stories*. London, Hamish Hamilton.

Sroufe, A. (1983) Infant caregiver attachment and patterns of adaptations in pre-schoolers: the roots of maladaptation and competence, in M. Perlmutter (ed.) *Minnesota Symposium in Child Psychology* **16** Hillsdale. New Jersey: Erlbaum.

Stern, D. (1985) *The Interpersonal World of the Infant*. New York, Basic Books.

Tustin, F. (1981) *Autistic States in Children*. London, Routledge & Kegan Paul.

Weininger, O. (1988) Symbol formation, symbolic equation and the development of interests, *Children's Phantasies*. London, Karnac Books.

Weiss, R. S. (1975) *Marital Separation*. New York, Basic Books.

Winnicott, D. W. (1965) *The Maturational Processes and the Facilitating Environment*. London, Hogarth Press; Toronto, Clark, Irwin.

Winnicott, D. W. (1971) *Playing and Reality*. London, Tavistock Publications.

Winnicott, D. W. (1986) (published posthumously) *Home is Where We Start From*. London, W. W. Norton and Pelican Books.

CHAPTER 10

The Psychotherapeutic Treatment of Withdrawn Children

Francis M. J. Dale

Introduction

One of the problems one is faced with in talking about the psychotherapeutic treatment of the withdrawn child, lies in the very wide range of problems that can be expressed through the same symptoms of withdrawal. Whilst it is true to say that withdrawing from normal social and interpersonal contacts is usually (but not always) a defensive manoeuvre, this, in itself, tells us nothing about the precipitating factors, and what needs to be done therapeutically, to help bring the child back into a healthier mode of relating to self and others.

In addition to the varied causative factors, there is the added complication that the withdrawn state can mean different things to different children. Children do not invariably become withdrawn for the same reasons; it performs different functions in different situations and it may require different methods of intervention depending on how we understand the symptom.

However, whatever method of treatment intervention we may decide to employ, one of the greatest obstacles we encounter in the psychotherapeutic treatment of withdrawn children, lies in their reluctance or inability to engage with another person in a close or intimate relationship. The establishment of a close and trusting relationship between therapist and child – or any adult – for example parent or teacher, who seeks to help the child – is of course, the *sine qua non* of most psychotherapeutic treatments. The techniques which the therapist uses in overcoming the child's defensive isolation are therefore of crucial importance in making contact with these children.

Making contact with the withdrawn child

There are several factors which can have a positive or negative influence on our ability to enter into a therapeutic relationship with the child, but the most important of these, is our ability to respect the personal boundaries of the child. For example, if we are a familiar and trusted figure, or someone whose *role* makes us safe (close relative, teacher, health visitor, nurse or doctor), then the child will feel less threatened or intimidated than if we are a relatively unknown figure (although even doctors and nurses can be frightening figures as we shall see later).

In the latter case, we may need to be more circumspect in approaching the child in order to give him or her sufficient time to 'get the feel of us' and to weigh up whether we are a safe or a threatening figure.

The younger the child, the more dependent they are on their carers, the less secure in their basic relationships, the more unfamiliar the environment (for example, a child will feel less anxious if confronted by a stranger when on his or her own territory) the more anxious they will be in an unfamiliar situation and the more in need of reassurance.

Of course, the ideal situation would be to see the child at home, or in a familiar environment and in the presence of his or her parents. For various reasons this is not always practicable or even advisable and we may have to see the child in a strange and sometimes 'hostile' environment. When this is the case, it stands to reason that anything we can do to reassure the child will increase our chances of getting through to him or her and forming some kind of therapeutic alliance.

The following guidelines are not intended to be all inclusive but more to give some pointers to the kinds of factors which we need to bear in mind when working with children who are difficult to reach.

The context

This relates to the *place* in which the child is being seen; for example, is it in the child's home, school, nursery, playgroup, or in the doctor's surgery or in a hospital? Is the child being seen in a one-to-one situation or as a member of a group? Is he being seen on his own or in the presence of his parents or some other familiar figure?

Seeing the situation from the child's perspective

This relates to how *the child* defines the situation, for example as familiar, strange, exciting, interesting, dangerous or frightening.

How the child sees you

This will depend on many factors, but above all, by *how you present yourself*: by the way you dress, the physical posture you adopt, the tone of voice, facial expression and by how you respond emotionally to the child.

Communicating with the withdrawn child

There are many ways of 'communicating', of sharing or partaking in an intimate exchange with someone else (Dale, 1991). Even with babies, a large part of how we receive any communication is through the medium of language. But it is important to note that language is the *medium* and not the sum total of the communication. It is not only what we say that matters, but how we say it and the context or ambience within which it is said.

Anyone who has watched a mother interacting with her baby will know that the communication between the mother and child is mainly taking place at a non-verbal level. While the content of what the mother is saying may be meaningless from a rational point of view, one can see that the baby is being effectively communicated to and that he does feel understood.

Analysis of the interactions between mothers and babies shows that communication occurs on many levels – even within the same modality such as language. It is quite clear that the 'meaning' of the mother's communication is conveyed as much through the tone, pitch, cadence and rhythm of her words, as it is by way of the literal meaning of what she says.

As important as what she says to her child, is what she does with her body. Her verbal communications are paralleled by correspondingly intimate movements of her body which increases the emotional proximity between mother and child and their sensitivity to, and awareness of, each other's feelings.

The communication of emotional states

Many mothers will tell you – although they may not be able to rationalise it – that they know what their baby is feeling: whether he is sad, angry, puzzled, frightened, confused, hungry, uncomfortable, in pain, falling apart, contented, ecstatic or blissful. They probably can't explain how they know because this kind of 'knowing' isn't a cognitive process. It is an understanding which is conveyed *by way of impact*, by the emotional resonance that someone we are relating to has on us. While this is an unconscious process, there are ways in which we can learn to recognise when this is happening.

The first thing to understand is that in all relationships, whether we are aware of it or not, we are continually being affected by, and responding to, the emotional and mental states of the people we are relating to. The mother knows what the baby is feeling because she experiences the emotional state of the baby *as though it were her own*.

Thus, if her baby panics or experiences intense anxiety, she experiences – if only for a moment – the same emotion. On the other hand, if the baby is blissfully contented, she shares in that state too. What this shows us, is that there is a form of communication or interaction between individuals, *which exists alongside, and which is independent of, verbal communication*.

This clearly has important implications in our therapeutic work with withdrawn children, many of whom we can only understand by becoming conscious of the emotional impact they have on us.

Different types of withdrawn behaviour

Before looking at some clinical examples of psychotherapy with withdrawn children, I would like to say a little about the importance of trying to determine the meaning behind or the function of, the symptom of withdrawal.

As already mentioned above, children withdraw for different reasons. At the most extreme end of the scale we have the withdrawal of the encapsulated or confusional[1] autistic child who seems totally impervious to other people. For him or her, other people as 'people', seem just not to exist. They may have some meaning or use as 'objects', or even more disturbingly, as parts or extensions of the autistic child's personality or internal world, but they are not allowed to have an autonomous existence in relationship to the child.

At the other end of the scale, we have the child who, on the surface, may not appear to be withdrawn at all. Here, I am referring to the child who has learnt to present to the world what Winnicott calls a 'false self' (Winnicott, 1965). Most of us learn to hide or disguise some or all of our true thoughts or feelings. If we remain in control of this process, it doesn't have to become a problem, and indeed may, in the appropriate situation, be an essential part of normal socially adaptive behaviour.

However, with some children, the false self becomes so dominant that it 'takes over from' or replaces the real or 'true self'. This usually happens where the true self cannot be revealed for fear of what may happen. In this case, the child *becomes* the false self and loses touch with a more genuine and spontaneous part of its personality. In this sense, the true self could be said to have withdrawn – even though superficially the child may appear able to relate well to other people.

Between these two extremes, there are several other types of withdrawn behaviour, the meaning of which need to be assessed so that we can decide on the most effective therapeutic approach for any particular child.

Perhaps the easiest situation to deal with is when a child has become withdrawn due to some traumatic event of acute onset. Examples of this would be the death of a parent, sibling or close relative; separation from parents, illness or involvement in an accident. In these cases, the withdrawal would not be due to pathological personality development or other chronic factors; and brief, more focused therapy of a supportive nature, may be the best way to help the child to cope with his or her distress and return to a healthier mode of functioning.

As we shall see in the cases which follow, although the initial withdrawal was precipitated by a clearly defined traumatic event in the child's life, added complications have meant that these children have required more intensive and long term therapy to help them to come to terms with the 'loss' of a parent.

Case 1 – death of a parent

Richard was eight years old when he asked his doctor if he could talk to someone about his mother who had died from lung cancer two years previously after a long illness. He complained of various symptoms including migraine, depression, poor concentration and sudden and unpredictable rages in which he would lose control of himself and smash up and destroy items of furniture in the house.

When I spoke to Richard about his mother, I learnt that he had had an older sister who had been severely physically and mentally handicapped and who had died when he was two years old. It was shortly after the death of this sister that his mother contracted the cancer from which she died four years later.

In addition to all of the above, Richard's father had never been able to mourn the death of his wife and was consequently unable to help his son come to terms with his grief.

The therapy

Although on the surface, Richard was able to verbalise his thoughts, in an emotional sense, he was completely withdrawn and 'not with me' in the room. There would be long periods of silence where he would seem to sink inside himself and I would be left with a feeling of heaviness and stuckness. Frequently, he would either fall asleep or go into a kind of trance-like state so that if I spoke to him he would 'come to' shaking his head, looking confused and disorientated as though he didn't know where he was or what had been happening.

Normally, I would either interpret a child's play or what was being said, to try to build up a dialogue or way of thinking about and understanding what was happening in the child's unconscious life; but Richard was unable to play or to use language at a symbolic or metaphorical level. For me, this was particularly frustrating because I was keenly aware – by way of his emotional impact on me – of his loneliness, quiet despair and need for contact at a deep level.

What I *felt* he needed, was for someone to pick him up and hold him and to comfort him as one would with a very much younger child. Because of the danger of confusing one's own needs with those of the child or of entering into a seductive or collusive relationship, I resisted for a long time the impulse to make contact with him physically by putting my arm around his shoulder or sitting him on my lap and cuddling him. When eventually I overcame my reservations, I experienced tremendous relief as well as overwhelming feelings of sadness.

I think that 'my' relief was *his* relief projected into me; and 'my' sadness, his overwhelming grief which was too much for him to bear. Afterwards, I felt that we had established contact at a level where he felt understood, but more importantly, that he could see that the feelings which he couldn't tolerate could be experienced in a positive way by someone else.

Richard stayed in therapy with me for about a year then felt he didn't need to see me any more. Two years later, he contacted me again and we entered into another phase of therapy. In the interim, he had matured and felt more able to share at an intellectual level, some of the feelings and thoughts which previously he had had to block out.

He was now able to realise and to accept that his father had his own problems with regard to emotional issues and was unable to talk openly about his feelings. Richard was also more aware of his isolation and being 'different' from other people – especially other children at school: 'Because they haven't lost their mothers, they don't understand'. His bitterness and sense of unfairness was also more apparent: 'Why me?', 'Why do I have to be punished? – it's not fair'. The therapeutic value of Richard being able to verbalise his feelings was that they had now found a vehicle to enable them to be expressed 'outside of himself' and in relation both to me, and to a part of himself that could think about them and take a more objective stance in relation to them (the ability to be able to observe oneself objectively in this way is called 'witnessing' or 'observing ego').

Traumatic hospitalisation

Case 2

Steven was eighteen months old when he was rushed to hospital after he tripped and crashed through a glass coffee-table. He had the most horrific injuries to his upper palate and lip and had nearly bled to death. He could still remember the accident and his terror when he had to be held down while the surgeon stitched up the gaping wound to his face (such severe damage to the mouth and consequent capacity to obtain oral gratification would be very damaging to development of the personality). When he was seventeen, he became completely obsessed with the thought that he was going to die and had panic attacks in which he would feel as if he were suffocating.

He presented himself as a very intense, serious and agitated young man whose body was so full of nervous energy that he could not keep still for more than a few minutes at a time. In addition to his fear of dying, he complained about feeling 'out of place' and not being understood or accepted by fellow students at the college where he was studying.

The therapy

Steven's defence against being overwhelmed by anxiety was to deny the significance of anything which could not be explained on a purely rational basis. Whilst this protected him from the irrational and unconscious aspects of his mental life, it also left him feeling empty and impoverished.

Trying to help Steven get in touch with his feelings and unconscious anxieties was made all the more difficult not only because of his need to over intellectualise everything but also, because his feeling life had been denied for so long, he experienced *any* contact with his emotions as dangerous and persecuting. If I made any interpretation which threatened to reveal something about himself which he didn't know of, he would become extremely agitated and defensive, and dismissive, even contemptuous of me.

What I learned of Steven's family life, further reinforced the view that being in touch with one's feelings was dangerous. For some reason, Steven's mother had never successfully bonded with him as a baby. However, she was able to form a close emotional bond with his sister who had been born just before his accident. He was closer to his father but there were tensions between his parents which had resulted in a split between mother and daughter on one side and father and son on the other. Steven described his mother as distant, cold and unemotional and remarked that his father had had a breakdown at the same age as he was now, and that as a young man he also had fears of dying.

However, in spite of Steven's ambivalence regarding therapy – seeing it as much as a threat as a help, his capacity to make links between what had happened to him in hospital and his current fear of dying, and the way his family denied emotions, made it possible for him to be able to understand his anxieties both as an expression of unresolved terrors from his early childhood and pathological patterns of relating in the family.

Case 3

Malcolm suffered from a rare congenital deformity in which one half of his body – including the bones of his head – had developed asymmetrically. By the age of seven, he was having to wear a built up shoe and the bones of one whole side of his body were noticeably smaller than those of the other side. He was admitted to hospital where the long bone in his thigh was cut in half and gradually pulled apart over a period of months to encourage extra bone growth. He spent the best part of a year in hospital but although his parents visited him regularly, he felt abandoned by them and would go into blind panics and tantrums when they attempted to leave after visits.

After leaving hospital he had to wear a plaster cast which came up to his waist, couldn't go to the toilet unaided and had to be pushed around the playground and to and from the school in a pram.

Malcolm was referred for therapy at the age of fifteen because of 'difficulties in coping with life'. However, he was completely unable to explain the nature of these problems to his doctor except to say that for the past two years he had been 'preoccupied with thoughts of life and the workings of the mind' and was unable to distinguish at times between reality and fantasy. He was very conscious that his body was different from other people's and avoided situations where this might be noticed. This meant that he never joined in with his peers in gymnastics, games or any competitive sports.

The therapy

As with Steven, it proved very difficult to make contact with him at anything other than an intellectual level. The following extract from an early session is fairly typical of the confused and convoluted way his 'thinking' blocked any attempts at understanding.

Malcolm began by saying that he had these troubles.
I wondered if he could tell me about them.
He replied that he just couldn't stop thinking about world problems.
Were there any problems in particular that bothered him?
No. He just felt that he had 'this problem' which he always had to think about and that thinking about it stopped him from concentrating.
I again wondered if he could try and tell me a little more about this problem which he had to keep thinking about.
He responded by saying that there were times when he could be distracted by something which interested him but then he would realise that he hadn't been thinking about 'his problem' and wouldn't be able to remember anything and his mind would go blank and he would panic. (Dale, 1983)

After several sessions like this one *my* mind was becoming blank. I was confused, couldn't think clearly, was losing track of what was going on in the session and becoming increasingly frustrated. What I failed to realise at the time was how much I may have been experiencing in the countertransference Malcolm's own confused state of mind. It was also a very powerful attack on my thinking. When I was able to point out to him how his thinking capacity was being used in a very destructive way in order to prevent understanding and not to promote it, the underlying cause of his present difficulties – his catastrophic experience in hospital as a child – began to emerge. Little by little we were able to build up a picture of what it had been like for Malcolm to be taken away from family, friends, school – a familiar environment – and to be subjected to various traumatic surgical procedures; to have to lie on his back in traction for nearly a year. It became very clear in therapy that he had experienced the ministrations of the doctors and nurses not as helpful but as an assault or invasion on his person in which he was a passive and defenceless victim at the mercy of cruel and sadistic persecutors.

As therapy progressed, Malcolm began to get in touch – on a more conscious level – with the damaged child he was still carrying inside, so that he became increasingly able to relate to people and situations in the here and now and less in terms of his earlier experiences. (Dale, 1983)

Case 4

Michael was born with an allergy to his mother's milk. He became severely malnourished and was admitted to hospital at six weeks of age and fed on a drip for two weeks. Following this, he had to be fed on a special milk diet but was clearly very disturbed – being almost impossible to comfort and crying almost continually for the first six months of life.

He was referred to a Child Guidance clinic when he was eight because he seemed to be unhappy and isolated, and because of his outbursts of temper which were mainly directed at his brother who was only ten and a half months younger than him.

The therapy

Michael presented as a very stiff, even rigid boy, with a serious expression and a peculiarly empty, almost 'shell-like' quality to him. He was restless, had poor concentration, few friends and seemed to live in a world of his own. In exploring his early history it became apparent that the relationship between Michael and his mother had never really recovered from the traumatic separation which took place when he had to go into hospital. His mother felt that she had never been able to get as close to him as she was with his brother.

As with other cases of early infantile trauma, the damage had occurred at a time in Michael's development before he had developed a capacity to think or to process what had happened to him. His mother's absence during those two weeks meant that she was not available to 'take on board' and manage his anxiety for him. Two weeks in a baby's life is probably an eternity. By the time he returned home, his sense of trust in his mother's capacity to protect and care for him, must have been severely damaged. The birth of his brother so soon afterwards, and the experiences of seeing his brother feed successfully at his mother's breast, must have been the final blow to any attempts he may have made at rebuilding the broken relationship between himself and his mother.

An early focus in therapy therefore, was to try to heal the rift between mother and child by encouraging her to explain to Michael *as an eight year old*, what had happened and why when he was a baby. The aim of this was to create a 'benign split'[2] in Michael between the baby part of him which hadn't been able to understand or cope with what had happened to him, and the more grown up part which now could.

As a result of the support she was given, Michael's mother was able to explain how she hadn't been able to feed him, that he had nearly died, and why he had had to go to hospital. In the process, she was able to get in touch with her sadness and her sense of guilt.

The rift between Michael and his mother is certainly less apparent; they are more open and affectionate and he behaves in a less omnipotent way towards her. In addition to the family meetings, Michael was taken on in individual therapy to help him deal with the anger which is still inside him – or should I say, still inside the 'child inside him'.

Case 5

It may seem as though every child who suffers from early traumatic hospitalisation is in need of long-term psychotherapy. Jason who was six when he was referred because of nightmares shows that this isn't always the case.

In talking to the parents before seeing Jason on his own, I learned that before he was born a routine scan had shown up an abnormality in his heart. In order to save his life, Jason was operated on immediately after his birth and unfortunately, his mother was prevented from seeing him for the first week of his life. This had caused her much anger and distress. The obstetrician in charge of the case didn't believe that 'bonding between a mother was important'.

The therapy

When I saw Jason on his own, he wasn't able to tell me about his nightmares which I understood meant they were too frightening for him to remember. What he could tell me however, was that they had got worse since he had seen one of the Ghostbusters films.

In this film, the Devil, in order to become manifest on Earth, needs to take over and possess the body of a new born baby. The baby is 'stolen' and taken to a large building where it is to be sacrificed to the Devil. The mother meanwhile, is locked out of the building and is frantically trying to get in to rescue her child.

What we can see here, is a reenactment of the original trauma to Jason when *he* was 'stolen' from his mother (taken away to be operated on); when a terrifying figure tried to 'get inside his body' and harm him (the surgeon who operated on him); and when he was separated from his mother and she was prevented from seeing him.

As with Michael, an important element of Jason's therapy was to 'put the record straight'. I told Jason that I thought the nightmares he had been having were because of something which had happened to him as a baby which was very similar to what had happened to the baby in the film. He too had been taken away from his mother and had terrible things done to him and he must have thought that these people were trying to hurt or even kill him. However, the 'big boy' inside him now knew that these people – although they *had* hurt him – had actually saved his life. His job – as a big boy – was to understand this so that the 'baby inside' wouldn't have to be so frightened any more and then perhaps the nightmares would go away.

Abduction

Case 6

Mervin was seven when he was referred. His father, who was estranged from his mother, took him on holiday to Jamaica and then disappeared with him. It took the mother a whole year before she tracked her son down and managed to bring him back home to England. The father, who was mentally unstable, had locked Mervin in a shack for long periods in a remote part of the island. Mervin had been virtually isolated from human contact and when found by his mother, was ill clothed, severely malnourished and shrank away from any contact with adults.

The therapy

Like many children who can't find the words to talk about their inner feelings

– or who don't want to – Mervin was able to 'talk' to me through his drawings which were full of terrifying primaeval monsters, tearing and slashing at each other with sharp fangs and claws.

From the very first session he drew at a furious rate and with great intensity, covering page after page with very powerful and evocative images. It was evident that this was a cathartic process for him, and although at first he didn't seem to notice my presence, I felt that these drawings were only happening because there was someone there to 'witness' them.

Gradually, as I was able to draw a link between his drawings and the unconscious themes they related to, Mervin began to come out of his shell and, although still not talking to me, began to listen to what I was saying to him.

The most frequently recurring theme was that of a boy being attacked by powerful monsters. As he became more able to confront the 'monsters inside himself', the 'boy's' capacity to deal with the monsters effectively, increased. He became a 'superboy' or, more significantly, Luke Skywalker fighting Darth Vedar. In the film *Star Wars* Luke Skywalker who is the youthful hero, finds out that Darth Vedar the hugely powerful black figure with whom he is in combat, is in fact his father who has been taken over by dark forces. Given that Mervin's father was black we can see how closely the theme of the film mirrored Mervin's need to struggle with the 'Darth Vedar' father he had inside him.

It took nearly two years of once weekly therapy to bring Mervin out of his shell and for him to regain his confidence and trust in adults. Near the end of our time together, he asked me to make him 'a book' which he titled 'That's Life'. Inside he wrote a story about a monkey who:

> Had fun with his little friend.
> He has got lots of friends.
> But something strange happened.
> A monster nearly couldn't fit into the world.
> It was too big.
> It ate people one by one.
> But he can't eat everybody in the whole world,
> Because people are born everyday.
> He tried again and again but he couldn't.

The false self

As mentioned above, some children who seem well adjusted on the surface, may in fact be hiding a state of 'internal' withdrawal. These children often go unnoticed because on the surface, they are so compliant and amenable. It is only when they are frustrated or confronted in some way that one begins to get some idea of how superficial their contact with other people is. In my experience, this type of withdrawn child is extremely hard to make contact with especially if, as is often the case, their inner withdrawal is covering up deep seated anger or despair.

Case 7

Sara came to see me when she was nine years old because her teacher felt that even though she was doing well in her work, that 'something was wrong' and Sara was unhappy.

The therapy

Initially, Sara seemed pleased to be coming to see me and was able to respond to my questions or comments without too much anxiety. She communicated mainly through her drawings which were rather stereotyped depictions of girls in different kinds of costume. At first it seemed as if she was exploring what sort of girl she wanted to be when she grew up but I began to suspect that the repetitive, bland, fixed smiles on the faces of these manikins hid an inner emptiness.

Following my saying this to her, her drawings began to change. The bland smiling faces began to disappear to be replaced by sharply drawn figures in tattered clothing with angry expressions. It seemed as though the way she really saw herself was the opposite of the picture she presented to the world. From these later drawings it was evident that she saw herself as the Cinderella in her family, as the drudge who nobody cared for or noticed.

The reality of her family life supported this. She was the second child and oldest girl in a family of twelve and had to do most of the caring for the other children, including the housework, cooking and shopping. Most of the children had different fathers and her mother seemed endlessly preoccupied with the newest addition to the family at the expense of the other children.

I came to understand that the only way in which she could maintain some sense of being special and survive in her family was to withdraw into a private internal world in which she could create her ideal family. When her mother became pregnant for the thirteenth time, both her compliant exterior and ability to retreat into her secret fantasy world began to collapse.

She became increasingly contemptuous of me and rejecting and denigrating of what I said to her. Her false self began to collapse and all her anger, frustration and bitterness seemed to find a focus in me in our sessions together. Eventually she rejected me completely (not quite, because she still turned up for her therapy) becoming totally silent withdrawn and unresponsive.

She still communicated to me however through the feelings (emotional contagion[3]) she evoked in me in our sessions together. I increasingly felt she had retreated into an early infantile state, where she was shut inside herself and unable to relate to me as 'outside of her'. This seemed to mirror her mother's inability to understand her infantile needs and explained why she had become withdrawn internally. It proved impossible to contain her anxiety in once weekly therapy but the collapse of her false self allowed us to get in touch with the deprived child inside so that eventually her needs could be met in a caring foster placement.

Case 8

Patrick entered therapy because his parents found him difficult to cope with. However, apart from complaining of his persistent head banging, they were not able to substantiate this in a convincing way. A careful investigation of their own backgrounds suggested that it wasn't Patrick's behaviour that caused them difficulty but more, *what he represented to them internally*. Both of them had had very disturbed relations with their parents and both of them had been rejected – the father to be brought up by his grandparents and the mother, while living at home, being rejected by her father. What they couldn't tolerate in Patrick was that he somehow reminded them of their own rejection as children. Their response – or defence – was to reject him so that *he* became the unwanted or objectionable child and not them.

When Patrick first came to see me aged five, he was still living with his parents. Although he was an intelligent and appealing little boy, I was aware that he was holding himself back and only relating to me on the surface. I felt that he only offered people a part of himself and that the core of his personality was shut away somewhere and hidden from view.

Although work was done with Patrick's parents to help them understand why they found him so difficult to tolerate, he was eventually placed with a foster family at their request.

The therapy

The main therapeutic work with Patrick has been to provide him with the experience of being in a long term, consistent and predictable relationship where he can 'be himself' and not have to pretend to be someone or something which he isn't. Although it is important to interpret children's unconscious fantasies in a manner in which they can understand them, with some children like Patrick, the most important element in the therapeutic relationship seems to revolve around your capacity to 'be there for the child'. They don't want you there as a 'therapist' or as an adult but more as a 'real' person who can be there for them, who can think about and experience emotional and mental states which they cannot yet deal with.

Patrick is still withdrawn internally – but less so. He is more trusting and open and this shows in his increased capacity to allow people to get close to him and to touch him.

With both of these cases, we can see how the false self, while impoverishing the child's capacity to engage in genuinely fulfilling and satisfying relationships, also protected an inner part of the child from further damage. It was this 'inner', core part of the self, which had been withdrawn from making contact with others.

Withdrawal as punishment and rejection

Sometimes children use withdrawal in order to punish and reject their parents and others for some failure on their part. In the therapeutic situation however, it is *the therapist* who is made to feel punished and shut out. In the cases which follow, each child was almost totally silent throughout the entire duration of their therapy. In each of these cases, the sole means of communication was through their drawings and art work, which was both prolific and exceptional.

Case 9

Michael was referred because he was distant, moody and uncommunicative. His parents had divorced two years previously when he was eleven, and he lived with his mother who had subsequently remarried. His step father was an ambitious, rather driven man and neither parent came across as having any insight or real interest into what was troubling Michael.

The therapy

Throughout the whole of the two year period during which I saw Michael three times weekly, he never once spoke to me to engage in a dialogue. He may have once or twice said 'yes' or 'no' but in the main, he either nodded or shook his head when I interpreted to him my understanding of what he was telling me through his drawings.

His behaviour was omnipotent and controlling in the extreme. If I failed to adequately interpret his material, he would show his contempt for me in the most patronising way by 'rewarding' me with the mere whisper of a smile and an almost imperceptible shake of the head. If I was able to understand his material, I would only know I was correct because he *hadn't* treated me with contempt and disdain.

I began to understand that he needed to project into me all his feelings of impotence, rage, frustration and rejection. I was however, more than just a dustbin for him to put his 'rubbish' into. He also needed me to understand and verbalise thoughts and feelings which he couldn't 'own' yet.

The only sign that 'something was happening' both with Michael and the two cases which follow, was that his behaviour outside of therapy was changing for the better and he kept on producing material which indicated that his internal situation was gradually improving.

Case 10

Linda, if it were possible, was even more silent and withdrawn than Michael. In addition, she wouldn't look at me – hiding her face in her hair – and shrank away from any possibility of physical contact. In school, she was totally silent and the teachers tolerated this allowing other girls in the class to speak for her. She was very artistic – perhaps even gifted and had produced a poem of such quality and maturity that both teachers and pupils were amazed.

She was referred because no-one knew what to do to bring her out of herself and the school was worried about how she would cope in secondary school if she remained silent.

The therapy

In the whole of the eighteen months that I saw Linda on a once weekly basis, she only spoke to me once and that was to ask me what my birth date was. She would come into the room where I saw her, sit down with her head bowed and hair hanging down so that her face was hidden from view and immediately begin to draw. At the end of the session, she would put her things away and get up and leave without once having looked at me.

Her drawings were remarkable – both for the speed with which she executed them, and for the artistic talent she displayed. Whilst she may have been withdrawn on the outside, on the 'inside', she revealed a liveliness, versatility, curiosity and fine intelligence which were ordinarily completely hidden from view. She also displayed a very contemptuous and denigrating attitude towards me (as had Michael above) which only changed when I was able to interpret her wish to know my birth sign as a means of getting to know about me without having to have to reveal anything of herself.

Although Linda refused to talk to people, she did want to relate to them – but on her terms. She had an extraordinary knowledge of astrology, knowing by heart all of the astrological signs, their dates, symbolic representations, their compatibility with each other, the characteristics of personality associated with each sign and much else besides.

By knowing my birth sign she could almost 'do away with me' because she could metaphorically 'get inside' me without having to relate to me at all 'on the outside'. The sense of omniscience and power which this gave her was used in a very destructive way to devalue what other people had to offer. If she could get inside them and know all about them – even things they did not know about themselves – then she didn't need them, could do without them and, as it were, feed off her own internal resources.

Over a period of months it was possible to build up a picture of her internal world based almost entirely on the drawings which she produced in our sessions together. These revealed the existence of an inner life which was in total contrast to the extremely shy, withdrawn rather insipid child that she presented to the world.

Her drawings were colourful and vibrant, and full of powerful and evocative imagery mainly drawn from her extensive knowledge of fairy stories and folk tales. These were full of allusions to the themes of sexuality, romance and jealousy and revealed how preoccupied she was by her developing sexuality and the problem of giving expression to it safely.

When Linda made the transition to secondary school – although still not talking to me – she was relating to me much more openly through the medium of her drawings, which had in any case become her way of 'talking to me'. In her new school she was able to come out of herself more, establish a close circle of friends and seemed happy and well integrated.

Case 11

As with Michael and Linda, Peter, who was referred when he was seven, was a very withdrawn, silent, angry child. He had been virtually abandoned by his mother who left him to scream and cry for hours on end in his pram. He was taken into care at six months and adopted when he was one and a half (Dale, 1991).

The therapy

Peter communicated almost entirely through his drawings. He rarely if ever spoke to me, and when he did it was usually to denigrate or mock something which I had just interpreted to him. He did however, always listen very carefully to the comments I made about his drawings and these became, from the very first session, his preferred way of having a dialogue with me.

Peter's contempt for me was really an expression of the hatred and anger which he felt over his abandonment by his parents, projected on to me. It was also I think, a very primitive way of getting rid of his own sense of not being wanted, of being rubbished and deeply wounded.

All three of these children were adept at making other people experience the rejection and frustration which they couldn't own themselves. All three had found indirect ways of 'punishing' and rendering impotent anyone who tried to relate to them. Such rejection is based on sadism but a sadism not only directed against the therapist but also unconsciously against the vulnerable and dependent part of the child which the therapist is seen as representing.

It is precisely because these children can make people feel so useless and devalued that one has to resist retaliating by rejecting them in return. I often felt like giving up on Peter but knew that if I did it would be acting out on my part and not based on therapeutic considerations. The ability of the therapist to be able to bear and 'contain' (both emotionally and cognitively) such difficult emotions, gradually helps the child to be able to do this for himself.

Withdrawal as a psychotic defence

Some forms of withdrawal in children are based on either the terror of complete annihilation or disintegration, or on the fear of persecutory attacks from malevolent forces. Frequently, there is little or no 'healthy' or integrated part of the child's personality which one can relate to. In the presence of such children, one can often feel that they are 'not there' – that there is 'nobody at home'. Alternatively, people who come into contact with such children may feel that *they* are not there for the child.

Although therapy with such severely damaged children can be exceedingly difficult and drawn out, they can sometimes be rescued if one can persevere and tolerate the long periods when no apparent progress is being made.

Case 12

John, was aged three and a half when he:

> was referred because of his very demanding, possessive, and controlling behaviour – particularly towards his grandmother. His behaviour was regressive and infantile; he was still in nappies and would not use the toilet, he had screaming tantrums in which he would bite and scratch at his grandmother if she refused him anything; he had no speech, appeared oblivious to verbal instructions, and seemed to live in a world of his own.
>
> He was seen by a child psychotherapist and diagnosed as suffering from autism – a condition in which children withdraw inside themselves, become unreachable, and often exhibit endlessly repetitive, bizarre, and robotic-like movements of hands and body. (Dale, 1984a).

The therapy

> In the very first session, I had the impression that this child was not 'there' in the room with me. He was present in body but emotionally and mentally, he was absent. It soon became clear that, in order to make contact with him, to 'engage' him, *I* had to radically change the way in which I would normally interrelate with a child in therapy.
>
> Very early on I realised that the only way I could know him and communicate with him was to reach out to him with my attentiveness and to surrender (temporarily) my sense of having a separate identity. At times I had the unnerving experience of losing all sense of bodily awareness apart from my eyes just watching him. (Dale, 1984a)

The following is an extract from the third session.

> John came up to me and put his arms out for me to pick him up. He then put his arms around my neck repeatedly pressing his face and cheeks against mine before lifting his head away to look deeply into my eyes. He began stroking my face with his hands and then put his fingers into his mouth as though he were eating. I commented that he seemed to be wanting to eat me up and have me inside.

Strictly speaking, John was not withdrawn in the sense of being shut inside himself. He was more 'confused' or entangled with people so that, in Frances Tustin's words 'fragments of the "self" are felt to be dispersed and scattered, so the "self" and "not-self" are inextricably confused' (Tustin, 1981).

Therapists working with such children can only really help the child if they understand the child's experience *as though it were their own*. This is similar to empathy – but it is a state which needs to be constantly monitored and the term 'trial identification' (Casement, 1985) is perhaps more appropriate. With John for example, the only way in which I could 'understand' him, was by letting go my sense of separateness and 'letting him in'. It was only later, when I had 'separated myself out' from him that it was possible to think about what had been happening in the session.

With another patient, a boy of twelve who was a borderline schizophrenic, it was sometimes difficult even to remain in the same room as him such was the intensity of the emotions he projected into me.

Case 13

Sundip was referred because his teachers were becoming concerned at his increasingly bizarre behaviour and social isolation. Due to his hysterical reactions when anyone made an approach to him, he was mercilessly bullied and teased at school. He wrote the following comments in an exam:

> God needed a prison, so he created the Earth . . . Thunder is when God is angry with the whole of a small area and stamps his feet, rain and snow are when he is furious with a very large area . . . After such a punishment as the Earth nobody commits any more sins in Heaven . . . Life is a sentence, so I hope I die soon. (Dale, 1984b)

The therapy

From the very first meeting, Sundip regarded me with undisguised suspicion and hostility;

> Whenever I tried to engage him with an interpretation he would become quite paranoid and shout and talk in a very penetrating high pitched voice, jumping up and down and waving his arms and threatening to tell his mother all about me and my lies . . . this sort of omnipotent and controlling behaviour left me feeling as if I were constantly on a knife edge with him and that the success or failure of therapy hung literally by a thread. However, in spite of living with the constant fear that either therapy or Sundip would break down . . . some cracks in his very brittle defences began to appear. This started with Sundip repeatedly asking me 'what therapy was' and 'how it worked' and wanting to know what the percentage of successes to failures was. . . . I gradually began to realise that despite his dread of me and of what I might do to him, nothing could be worse than being where he was already. As therapy opened up the floodgates of what seemed to be a boundless reservoir of misery, I began at last to feel a faint ray of hope. (Dale, 1984b)

Both John and Sundip needed to be seen in more intensive therapy in order to contain the anxiety that coming out of their isolation caused them. In both cases, their defence was to 'not to know', to split off or deny any awareness that would reveal what it was that they couldn't confront *inside themselves*. What differentiated them from the other children we have previously discussed, was the intensity of the affect they generated in their therapist, their failure to adapt to the demands of external reality, and their inability to maintain and defend an *integrated* personality structure from being over-whelmed and fragmented by pathological processes.

Therapeutic survival

A vital consideration in any therapeutic work with disturbed children which is often given insufficient attention, is the impact which working with these children has on the therapist. This is more easy to see when working with children who are physically or verbally aggressive but can be overlooked when working with the withdrawn child who does not act out in this way.

However, as the following quotations show, the demands on the therapist's capacity to tolerate – and even survive – 'difficult to bear states' is often crucial to the successful outcome of work with such children:

> She made me knowing myself what it was like to be excluded, discarded and shut out. Suddenly I would find myself experiencing extraordinary anger which I felt to be, in part at least, a projection of her own feelings, . . . I was to be rendered useless by her attacks on my capacity to think about and understand her pain. (Boston and Szur, 1983)

and

> He had a numb, unreachable quality which the therapist found very hard to get through. . . . This brick-wall quality was very hard to penetrate and, although expressed differently, had a quality of forceful projection of unpleasant and painful feelings into the therapist. (Boston and Szur, 1983)

It seems then, that these children are so difficult to approach, not just because they have withdrawn themselves from normal contact, but because the contact they need to make with us can only be experienced through what they make us feel.

They need us to have their painful feelings, their emptiness and despair; to be able to tolerate and think about and contain these states for them until they feel safe enough to be able to do this for themselves.

Notes

(1) An encapsulated autistic, is a child who has withdrawn inside a kind of 'psychic shell' and who seems completely unreachable or available for contact; confusional autistic children, are less 'shut off' and more 'entangled' or 'confused' with their objects (i.e. those to whom they relate).

(2) A 'Benign Split' refers to a process whereby the therapist or patient is able to differentiate an observing part of the personality which is then capable of thinking without being taken over by unconscious processes.

(3) 'Emotional Contagion' refers to a primitive process where uncontained emotional states get projected into another person and experienced by them as if they were their own.

References

Boston, M. and Szur, R. (1983) (eds) *Psychotherapy with Severely Deprived Children*. London, Routledge & Kegan Paul.

Casement, P. (1985) *On Learning From the Patient*. London, Tavistock.

Dale, F. M. J. (1983) The body as bondage: work with two children with physical handicap, *Journal of Child Psychotherapy*, **9**, 1.

Dale, F. M. J. (1984a) Baby observation: some reflections on its value and application in the clinical setting. Paper presented at the Esther Bick Commemoration Day, Tavistock Clinic.

Dale, F. M. J. (1984b) The re-unification of Sundip: the bringing to-gether of split-off parts of the personality in a boy with psychotic features, *Journal of Child Psychotherapy*, **10**, 2.

Dale, F. M. J. (1991) The art of communicating with vulnerable children, in V. Varma *The Secret Life of Vulnerable Children*. London, Routledge.

Tustin, F. (1981) *Autistic States in Children*. London, Routledge & Kegan Paul.

Winnicott, D. W. (1965) *The Family and Individual Development*. London, Tavistock.

CHAPTER 11

Treating Withdrawn Children by the Use of Play

Robin Higgins

The next three chapters deal with the subject of play, and how the events and experiences in play impinge on the withdrawn child. Does play lead to further withdrawal? Or does it pull the child back into a world of social relations? In Coleridge's terms, does play involve nostalgic whimsical fantasies, indulged in for their own sake? Or does it involve imagination, a way of exploring, learning about, and transcending the world around us?

In this chapter I consider some more general aspects of play and withdrawal. In the two subsequent ones, I focus on the withdrawn child's play as this is mediated through sights (paintings, drawings, sculptures, collages) and sounds (the voice, the hands, musical instruments, concrete objects).

Withdrawal as a process and its relation to play

A snapshot of the withdrawn child is one who is reticent, shy, retiring, inhibited, a singleton or a loner, who retreats to the corner of the classroom or playground and doesn't join in. Three points need to be established from the start about this stereotype snapshot.

The first point is that the snapshot pays no attention to sequence or change. If children labelled withdrawn are observed over a period, it often transpires that the withdrawn state is not rigidly fixed. A child may move in or out of it sometimes in the course of a single hour or day. Moreover this movement in or out of withdrawal says little about what is going on in the children's minds while withdrawn. They may be in a state of reverie, or of alert inactivity. They may be preoccupied with the solution of some perplexing problem which demands all their attention. They may have retreated and be shunning the world. Snippets of play during these phases in or out of withdrawal often offer clues as to what the withdrawal is all about. Features of play can be diagnostic.

Second, withdrawn children are often not uniformly withdrawn in all situations encountered over twenty-four hours. A child who appears isolated in one class may engage in heated social exchanges in another. A sense of isolation at school may evaporate on crossing the threshold into a warm home. A child may play with grandmother and withdraws to the point of being mute with everyone else. In the eyes of the withdrawn child, some people are safe to play with and some not. There is a distribution of affection and hostility which often follows an internal logic, a transfer of symbolic meanings. Here again the patterns of play and the places and people prompting play are the only clues we may be offered in attempts to understand the nature of withdrawal.

Third, the process of withdrawal represents a final common path for an infinite number of routes. A may be withdrawn because he's introverted by nature (inheritance); B because she's been disappointed, or feels rejected; C because he's depressed; D because she's phobic; E because he's ill; F because she's found it's the best way of being cared for. And so on.

The medical literature is full of instances illustrating the useful effect play may have on many of the situations which lead a child to withdraw: in a chronic illness (Gilman and Frauman, 1987); with cancer (Walker, 1989); requiring hospitalisation (Bates and Broome, 1986; Tregloan and Oberklaid, 1987); requiring protracted procedures like a bone marrow transplant (Atkins and Paternande, 1987); involved in disasters (Sugar, 1988); involved in sex abuse (Steward *et al.*, 1986; Saucier, 1989).

Features about play then are therapeutic as well as diagnostic. Indeed the therapeutic, healing power of play can be one of the main reasons for its being so effective in diagnosis.

These three different features behind the term 'withdrawn' (the changes over time, the changes over place, the manifold reasons behind the common path presentation) need to be borne in mind when considering the impact of play on the child caught in the flux of withdrawal.

The nature of child play

Once the withdrawn child discovers play, life can start in deadly earnest. That is the way with children's play and it follows the depths to which play is embedded in our waking and sleeping experience. Think for a moment of the many applications of the word 'play'. We play the fool, or the piano; we play havoc or hooky; the wind plays on the sea; a smile plays on her face. We have foreplay and playspace. The play's the thing wherewith we catch the conscience of the king. The word for play in latin is *Ludus* from which comes our words 'ludibrious' and 'ludicrous', with the implications of mockery added to the jesting, wit and humour. Also there comes the idea of 'Homo Ludens', Man or Woman at play, a vital dimension of life (Huizinga, 1955).

How basic a role play occupies in our evolution and development can be quickly appreciated by dipping into the literature of ethology and anthropology as well as that of child psychology. (See for example the excerpts collected by Bruner *et al.*, 1976.) Here there is only space to mention its significance for exploring and mastering our environment, relating to others, cooperating and competing, defining identity and sexuality, mobilising a capacity to symbolise. All these aspects bear directly on the issue of moving in or out of the withdrawn state.

In our grown-up world of the twentieth century, we are apt to take up a somewhat distorted and patronising attitude towards play, perhaps even to lose sight of its widespread ramifications. We become preoccupied with a career, with raising a family, with finding enough money to buy the house or car or holiday we want, or the club, the school fees, the insurance, the pension. In this preoccupation, we come to think of play as frivolous, something to be confined to spare time, linked closely with leisure, relaxation, dozing in the sun. Hours of play are set against hours of work, wrapped into job packages, a cause of strikes if deemed insufficient. In work we see ourselves as responsible, weighed down with a burden, serious, frowning, dominated by the clock-tick. In play, we are light-hearted, heedless of the passage of time, caught up in a game, singing, dancing, laughing.

Not every one observes this split between work and play. Some artists, musicians, poets, inventors, mystics don't. Neither do most children. Either in a group or on their own, it's hard not to be impressed by the sheer seriousness, the ferocity, with which pre-school children will engage in what we adults call their play. No standing and staring, no frivolity here. The 'playful' activity is pursued with the intensity and commitment of any professional (from sportsman to barrister) and the idea of distinguishing this activity from work never arises. This play is hard work. Perhaps the hardest work the children will ever do. The irony arises that behind the adult tendency to split work from play, the ability to re-integrate the two turns nowadays into a considerable accomplishment and often carries highly significant implications for productivity in a firm (see Miller, 1983). Many children enjoy this accomplishment (if only for a time) without realising it and certainly without being taught. For withdrawn children, this natural accomplishment is a life-line.

Case study[1]

When Belinda first came into the reception class at five, she walked on tip-toe and would stand with one hand always touching the wall or the book-case. She froze if another child spoke to her. In the circles of activity, she was always on the fringe, drifting from one to the other. She never initiated a game and had no companions. She had been fostered at three into a family where there were four older children. The oldest was a girl and the other three a caucus of boys who always chose the TV programmes and generally hogged the limelight.

In her first term, two things happened to Belinda. She started to play with words, building them together from the little white cards she dealt herself, and she found a friend in a coloured girl, equally shy as herself, a one off in the class, and the only other drifter. The pair would come together in a corner where for a while no one noticed them. During the spring term, the games Belinda played with her friend Harmony attracted the attention of a group of older boys who tried to break up both couple and their games, but succeeded only in bringing them closer together. The games grew longer more elaborate and louder.

Harmony left at the end of the summer term, and when Belinda returned in the autumn, she was lost again in the new class. But her Peter and Jane books and a rag-doll which accompanied her now wherever she went proved more lasting than her friend. Within two weeks of the start of term, she'd established herself quietly in the new buzzing group, one of whom soon spontaneously became her 'child scivvy' and followed her about wherever she led.

Withdrawn children who cannot play

The first point about the case study is that Belinda was able to play at all. She discovered play; not every child does. Many withdrawn children are so ill at ease with themselves that they find it impossible to initiate or sustain a game on their own let alone with anyone else. An indication of a child's being withdrawn is often a mooning and moping around, a repetitive plaintive demand directed at one or both parents 'What can I do now, mum?' or 'What shall we do next, dad?' Such clinging repetitions often push the adults into states of extreme irritation, thus setting up a cycle of further withdrawals and unsatisfied dependency on the part of the child.

Many reasons may lie at the back of this difficulty in getting play started. The withdrawn child may have a dearth, a blockage, or an excess of ideas. He or she may 'adhere' to an object, apparently fearful of exploring anything else. Or there may be such a rush of ideas that there's no time to settle on any one thing long enough to develop a game.

Or there may be a gap between the capacity to handle concrete objects and the capacity to represent these symbolically. In a world of increasingly realistic toys, and increasing passive exposure to adult realistic scenes on TV and videos, this failure in symbolic representation can pose particular problems for a child struggling to relate to the outside world and to his own imagination.

Case study

Matthew was a four-year-old who clearly had an active body and mind, who scored highly on intelligence tests, and who was never short on ideas. But he had no friends and if he played at all it was only by himself. Such games as he started, quickly foundered on a problem over symbolising. Things would get constantly smashed, he and other children constantly damaged, because there was no space for playing with possibilities. He frequently complained that he wasn't big enough, or the toy wasn't 'like it should be' (i.e. like an object in the everyday adult world). In his hurry to be grown up, to act in the realistic grown-up world, the compromises and bridges which play offered were just not good enough for him.

In a chapter on children who cannot play, Loewenfeld touches on one aspect of this failure in symbolic representation when she writes of the 'suitability of the material available' to the child struggling to play. She instances a boy who is surrounded by Meccano, toy-trains, dolls, picture books and jigsaws, and who has in his mind a predominant problem concerning the nature of earth and water. The boy 'moons' about among the available toys, discarding each in turn because they are too 'definite' for the ideas he's trying to realise (Loewenfeld, 1935).

This inability to play may be deeply ingrained, stemming from the child's earliest years and often picking up a familial pattern. As parents describe their disappointment or disillusion with their child, one can sometimes detect how difficult it has been for them to play as children or as adults. Frustration at their own failure leads them to ensure (against all their conscious intentions) at their child fails too. The atmosphere at home may discourage play actively or passively. Put more strongly, in some families play, even organised play, amounts to a form of rebellion.

In other instances the withdrawn child's inability to play is not endemic but can be dated to some cataclysmic event such as a bereavement or a severe physical injury. Mahaney describes the loss and slow recovery of a capacity to play in a three-year-old who was badly burnt (Mahaney, 1990).

When faced with these inhibitions on play, we often have to make the most of fragments and slowly build out from these. Davidson describes a four-year-old whose frantic restless seemingly unplayful search for an ill-defined something slowly turned into a game where he was a caged lion who gradually became safe enough to be fed, let out and turned into a domesticated companiable dog (Davidson, 1979). The slow evolution of this game from a fragment of play was accompanied by a change from the state of being restless and lost. The evolution occurred over a period of six weeks.

Games of all forms are occasions for risks as well as enjoyment. For the withdrawn child, imaginative play is a minefield. It means engaging with self-confrontation and self-exposure. This in turn may mean looking stupid, ideas not coming up to what was expected or, which may be worse, far outrunning expectations. In play, we all risk surprising ourselves and that is never comfortable.

Case study

Luke a shy eight-year-old was not always able to contain his urine when he was under stress. This led to his being regularly teased and roughed up by the rowdies in his class and street. In turn, this led to his becoming even shyer and more distressed. One day, he found some putty his father had left around, a hose, a bucket, and a little wheel from his Leggo set. Going to the shed at the bottom of the garden where he knew he wouldn't be disturbed, he shaped this lump of putty into a tube, and joining it up with the other chosen objects, he gradually constructed an elaborate machine for perpetual motion, like the one he'd seen last summer in the Cragside courtyard. The model took days to complete. As it grew, so did his anxiety. But in the end his excitement and surprise at what he found he could control changed his whole attitude to himself. He no longer felt a humiliated failure. He stopped being bullied. He also stopped wetting himself.

Then again, the play may get out of hand. This is particularly likely when a withdrawn child starts to come to terms with the reasons for his or her withdrawal, and pressures that have been building up over the years may suddenly burst out.

Case study

Basil, aged ten, was an only child of two serious elderly civil servants, who were constantly trying to get him more interested in his school work, specially in history, maths and Latin. One rainy Sunday afternoon, Basil started to toss a soft ball at his father and pretended they were engaging as ships of the line at Trafalgar. For a while his father was delighted with this exercise in history, but soon the engagement began to grow more frantic, the French were closing in and 'looking for a lesson', and in the end, Basil (cast in the role of the rebellious French) put all his weight behind a throw, which clapped old father Nelson in the eye. Basil had mixed feelings of triumph and mortification when his father said: you really must learn not to get so involved, old boy. Secretly father and son both recognised that more than the line at Trafalgar had been breached.

Play can cover more sinister ambiguities. Winnicott describes an instance where the objects of a boy's play (pieces of string which he used first to tie things together and later to put round his sister's neck) can turn into a fetish, and the game into an addiction or perversion (Winnicott, 1971a). In the following instance, the self-styled 'play-binges' had a similarly ambiguous quality, half cossetting half damaging the player.

Case study

Everyone said Georgina could be a stunner if only she wasn't so shy. She was always falling in love and getting hurt in the process. 'I'm nature's sucker for vicious circles', she said as she went on one of her 'play-binges' after a rejection which her friends had warned her was inevitable. At sixteen, these play-binges left her spotty and overweight, and even more desperate to be loved.

Berne's book on the Games People Play has many examples of such provocative teasing and ambiguous games, in which children may often be involved or which they may instigate (Berne, 1966).

Organisation and improvisation

Not all play is of the same kind. Another point to arise from Belinda's story is the distinction between organised and improvisatory games. Most of the games they played in Belinda's school like rounders, or singing carols or learning the alphabet and tables followed clear rules. The structure was laid out, decided on before the game started, and adhered to whilst it was in progress. If you got it right, you won, were a success, given a reward. If not, you had to try again, and might find yourself no longer included in the team.

In other games the structure was less rigid, but the same criteria were around: right or wrong, success or failure, rewards or penalties and inclusion or exclusion.

In the play Belinda set up for herself, she wandered off on a different track. With her rag doll, she both set and changed her own rules and drew as much fun from changing them as from setting and adhering to them. Even with the letters, she began to discover new words that no one else used. For a while she delighted in constructing a private language which only she and her friend Harmony remotely understood.

This distinction between what's regulated and often obligatory and what's improvised, spontaneous, arbitrary and voluntary runs through the many facets of play. We shall meet it again behind the distinction which is made between art or music education and art or music therapy. Neither mode is necessarily the ideal. Some withdrawn children enjoy the anonymity which often goes with regulated play. They can hide themselves in the pack and pass unnoticed unless they drop the ball or muff the goal. Improvisation on the other hand appeals to those who need a degree of privacy to find themselves.

Reversals

A third feature about Belinda's play was how, through it, she was able to turn the tables on what had been tormenting her. From being bossed around and trod on, she started to hatch games in which she was in control, calling the tune, and treading on her one-time masters. At first in fantasy and then in fact, her play followed a pattern of reversal well recognised by anthropologists in joking roles and rituals and the festival of Misrule (Heald, 1990). This important feature of play will again crop up in the delight of purposefully 'undoing' a painting which may have taken weeks to prepare or in the equal delight of inverting musical patterns.

Playing alone in the company of another

Belinda started playing on her own, but gradually her games began to involve others. In thus relating playing alone to playing with others, she was illustrating a crucial step in reaching out to the world.

In his paper on the capacity to be alone, Winnicott speaks of those occasions when mother and infant can each be alone in the presence of the other. The infant might be asleep but the mother would be filled with its presence whilst quietly getting on with her own life. Or the mother might be asleep or otherwise preoccupied and the infant, secure in the trust between them, feels free to explore his or her own state of being (Winnicott, 1965).

Something very similar happens in constructive and imaginative play. Indeed the complementary side of being alone in the presence of another is being able to play with this other person and this means total play, body and soul play, and not playing games where in the end we are divided against the other as well as within ourself. So many of the 'games' which Berne described and which were mentioned above are apt to have this quality of fight deception and division going on behind them, one partner seeking to pin down the other, and both in the end deceiving themselves. In the play arising from the capacity to be alone in the presence of another, something very different happens. What both being alone in this way and mutual play have in common is the release from being pinned down by instinctive excitements and guilt.

Play of this character may fulfill a vital function in the treatment of withdrawn children, as is apparent in many instances Winnicott himself describes (see for example Winnicott, 1971b).

Objects and places of play

One final point which the first case study illustrated and which arises out of playing alone in the presence of another, concerns the significance objects and places may have for play. The first possessions that a child endows or animates with a special meaning are those which link him or her to this shared sense of being alone with another. The shared experience extends to a sense of being and to a sense of joint creativity. Shared experience with extensions lie at the root of the symbolic objects and media we choose to bridge the gap between fantasy and reality.

Belinda shuffled a pile of letter-cards and went with them for a random walk to find her words rather as Paul Klee took his walk with a line. She found some props to aid her in settling into roles for exploring different viewpoints (reversals again). Above all, in setting up her rag-doll and the frame of her story books, she stumbled on the part that transitional objects come to occupy in relating fantasy and reality.

These observations are well rehearsed in the literature of play. Objects like rattles, dolls and puppets are well established in many cultures as means for enshrining crucial myths and traditions. There is often an intricate and rich connection between these cult objects and transitional phenomena (Grolnick, et al., 1978).

Again the places where play was possible for Belinda changed as she entered more freely into the social life at school. Some nine months had to pass before she played openly in the place conventionally set out for this: the play-ground. Her earlier experiments in play were carried out on her own in a quiet corner she found for herself. Children in a group or on their own frequently find a hallowed spot which by itself seems to conjure up memories and fantasies and calls for games. Sometimes this hallowed spot is determined in part by choice and in part by adult decree.

Case study

Stuart aged nine, lived in a menage of elderly ladies: his mother who had married late and her three older sisters. They all had a say in Stuart's upbringing. He coped with this concentrated attention by shrinking into the corner by the window in his bedroom and drawing elaborate grotesques of harpies. He kept these productions in his secret drawer.

When the monstrous regiment were expostulating on a new arrival in the Royal family Stuart blurted out: thank God at least it's a boy. We're fed up with all these queens. He went on to regale them with the details of how Edward VI must have been poisoned by his mother. He knew he was provoking his audience and half welcomed as he half resented being told to shut up and go to his room. Once arrived there, a further series of grotesques poured the easier from his pencil.

Play themes and potential space

The crucial point about their play for children is that through it, they open up an area of potential space between themselves and the world around, between their inner fantasy and the outer reality that lies beyond. The potential has to do with trying out conclusions or possible solutions, trying out what one's made of the past or what to expect in the future. This trying out entails an exercise in imagination over which we have some control and is very close to the exercise which occurs in dreams over which we have very little control. As Jung said the unconscious can play the maddest games when the inhibitions of the conscious mind are lifted (Jung, 1935). Play may well in part grow out of dreams as we become increasingly self-conscious.

As it happens, the potential space, the activity of trying out, the exercise of imagination and dreaming may also be very close to a state of withdrawal when a child appears to be and often is, behind closed curtains and neither in or out of the world. In the next two chapters, we will consider in greater detail how this potential space and the state of withdrawal are related. Here it only remains to point out that though the themes emerging in the potential play-space of the withdrawn child are infinite, from the examples already given some of the more common types can be identified.

For Belinda herself the themes concerned relating with her peers, behind them with her foster brothers, and behind them again with her own parents and siblings, her own family from whom she had to be removed when she was three. Her play then may be read as variations on the themes of mourning, retrieving and recreating lost objects, and conjuring up new solutions.

The theme in Basil's or Stuart's play on the other hand had to do with exploring ways of venting fury whilst confined in a setting from which there was no immediate escape.

Guidelines for using play

Just as there is an infinity of themes which may unfold in play, so there is an infinity in the way of their unfolding. From the patterns of organised violence on the rugby field to the patterns of improvised violence in a jazz group, the rules for relating are defined by the particular circumstances of play, and the choices of the players.

Treatment, too, may be thought of as involving play in a particular set of circumstances and as such may warrant the formulation of guidelines even though there may be no royal road which categorically defines correct behaviour. These guide-lines take their cue from what has been said above about potential space.

The use children can make of their potential space, their play-grounds of the mind, hinges on the relation they can establish with another person, starting with the mother, and with the non-human environments of objects, sounds, patterns. If this relation is, in Winnicott's terms, 'good enough', that is if it engenders in the child a sense of both being held and released, imaginatively fed and feeding, the result is play that unfolds at the unique pace and rhythms, the unique patterns, of the player. This is the type of play that lies behind any effective treatment.

Two guidelines contribute to the effectiveness. Both depend on the asymmetric relation between therapist and withdrawn child. The first guideline suggests that the aim is for the therapist to understand and for the child to feel understood as a result; the second that this sense of being understood on the part of the child should be implicit and not spelt out. Sometimes there is nothing more counter-productive of play than feeling forceably understood. This second guideline warns therapists against the easy unloading of their understanding in the form of interpretations. Of course interpretations have a place but the tact with which they are introduced may be as important as anything they say. Mistimed, they will be nullified however clever or appropriate. The best interpretations are those that the children arrive at themselves.

Note

(1) In this and the two following chapters, to preserve confidentiality, details have been altered and in this sense fictionalised. The points exemplified however are all based on fact.

References

Atkins, D. M. and Paternande, A. F. (1987) Psychosocial preparation and follow-up for paediatric bone marrow transplant patients, *American Journal of Orthopsychiatry*, **57**, 246–52.

Bates, T. A. and Broome, M. (1986) Preparation of children for hospitalisation and surgery: a review of the literature, *Journal of Paediatric Nursing*, **1**, 230–9.

Berne, E. (1966) *Games People Play: The Psychology of Human Relationships*. London, Andre Deutsch.

Bruner, J. S., Jolly, A. and Sylva, K. (1976) *Play: Its Role in Evolution and Development*. London, Penguin.

Davidson, D. (1979) Playing and the growth of imagination, *Journal of Analytic Psychology*, **24**, 31–43.

Gilman, C. M. and Frauman, A. C. (1987) Use of play with the child with chronic illness, *ANNA Journal*, **14**, 259–61.

Grolnick, S. A., Barkin, L. and Muensterberger, W. (1978) *Between Reality and Fantasy: Transitional Objects and Phenomena*. New York and London, Jason Aronson.

Heald, S. (1990) Joking and avoidance, hostility and incest: an essay on Gisu moral categories, *Man*, **25**, 377–92.

Huizinga, J. (1955, first published in 1939) *Homo Ludens: A Study of the Play Element in Culture*. Boston, Beacon Press.

Jung, C. G. (1935) Principles of practical psychotherapy, in *Collected works*, **16**.

Loewenfeld, M. (1935) *Play in Childhood*. London, Gollancz.

Mahaney, N. B. (1990) Restoration of play in a severely burned three year old child, *Journal of Burn Care Rehabilitation*, **11**, 57–63.

Miller, E. J. (1983) Work and Creativity. Tavistock Institute of Human Relations. Occasional paper no. 6.

Saucier, M. (1989) The effects of play therapy on developmental achievements of abused children, *Paediatric Nursing*, **15**, 27–30.

Steward, M. S., Farquhar, L. C., Dicharry, D. C., Glick, D. R. and Martin, P. W. (1986) Group therapy: a treatment of choice for young victims of child abuse, *International Journal of Group Psychotherapy*, **36**, 261–77.

Sugar, M. (1988) A preschooler in a disaster, *American Journal of Psychotherapy*, **42**, 619–29.

Tregloan, L. and Oberklaid, F. (1987) The hospitalised child, *Australian Paediatric Journal*, **23**, 85–7.

Walker, C. (1986) Use of art and play therapy in paediatric oncology, *Journal of Paediatric Oncology Nursing*, **6**, 121–6.

Winnicott, D. W. (1965) *The Maturational Processes and the Facilitating Environment*. Ch. 2: The capacity to be alone. London, Hogarth.

Winnicott, D. W. (1971a) *Playing and Reality*. London, Hogarth.

Winnicott, D. W. (1971b) *Therapeutic Consultations in Child Psychiatry*. London, Hogarth.

CHAPTER 12

Treating Withdrawn Children by the Use of Art

Robin Higgins

Distinctive features of visual art as these relate to the withdrawn child

So far we have considered the effects that the general activity of play may have on bringing a child back from a state of withdrawal and the effects that a state of withdrawal may have on the nature and type of play. Often however the play takes place within the confines of a particular medium and this medium in itself is likely to influence the impact on withdrawal. Conversely certain elements in his or her withdrawal may move the child to select one medium rather than another.

So the next set of questions we have to ask are concerned with what distinguishes one creative medium from another. What are some characteristic features about painting and the visual arts that differ from the characteristic features about music-making or dancing? Any attempt to answer these questions at length would carry us far beyond the limits of this book. The trail has already been blazed by philosophers (see particularly the works of Suzanne Langer, 1982, 1959). Here I shall confine myself to a few comments which apply particularly to the withdrawn child.

In visual arts, one obvious characteristic is that the product results in a palpable object. The image may be drawn out of the air, filtered through eyes and head, but it has to be put down on a sheet of paper or into a lump of clay and it then confronts us, is outside of us, in some ways separate from us, something we can palpably destroy in the same way that we palpably created, something that we can take away with us or have taken away from us.

For withdrawn children, the sheer fact of a painting being a manifestly

166

separate creation which can be moulded, transformed, destroyed at the will of the creator is often experienced as immediately liberating. 'You mean it's mine and I can do what I want with it?' a shy ten-year-old asks incredulously. A more suspicious four-year-old doesn't stop to ask. He simply tears his drawing up as soon as he's done it, partly to conceal it from prying eyes, and perhaps even more to prove that it's his and he can do what he likes with it.

In a painting, a truant from life may succeed in putting on record an attempt to get back into life again, may capture the elusive quality of a nightmare, and for a crucial instance, grasp and come to terms with what otherwise was only dimly felt, longed for or feared. The painting puts the experience 'out there', as events which can be addressed, held in dialogue, in a type of active imagination. In doing a painting, withdrawn children can prove to themselves that an experience is encompassable and that in the very act of encompassing, they can sometimes integrate and transcend their present experience.

The palpable object has, among its central properties, colour and shape. Both of these properties are highly relevant to the release from withdrawal symptoms. The associations between colour and emotions are engrained in our language: green with envy, red with rage, purple with passion, black or blue moods, rose-coloured spectacles. Withdrawn children who take a step into playing with colour are simultaneously stepping into the exploration and play with their inhibited emotions (see Feder and Feder, 1981).

An analogous significance is attached to the other property of the visual object, namely shape or more generally form (which of course may contain colour or be determined by colour). The release of energy such as the welling up of a withdrawn child's anger can sometimes be channelled and contained in a drawing (through this sense of form) in a way it cannot be contained without it. As with music, the pattern, the gestalt, the form itself supplies an implicit support.

Withdrawal implies a breakdown in communication. The act of painting arises from an urge to communicate. Many children withdraw because they despair that their comments will be heard, understood, or taken any notice of. When they manage to assemble these comments in a drawing which someone else looks at and struggles to understand, they find themselves, perhaps for the first time, reversing an asymmetric situation. From being the ones who were confused, always struggling to keep up with what's being said and make some sense of it, always being put down when they sought clarification, withdrawn children, when they discover painting, also discover that they are now the ones who are making the statements and the rest of the world has to take notice perhaps even make an effort to comprehend. This turning of the tables is an archetypal image of childhood (see Jung and Kerenyi, 1963). We have already met it in the previous chapter. It's clearly an image that exerts a special force among children who find themselves shoved into the shadows.

Many withdrawn children may have a special problem with words. Indeed being inarticulate may have been one of the reasons for withdrawing in the first place and difficulties over 'putting it into words' can quickly escalate into vicious circles. 'What are you trying to say, dear?' a rushed and well-intentioned parent may burst out in exasperation as the six-year-old equally exasperated fetches around for the right verbal formula. Sometimes if the question is followed up by the suggestion, 'Why not try drawing it?' both parties find surprising relief.

Memories and fantasies are often more easily accessible to consciousness as images than as words (Freud pointed out that dreams are preponderantly visual) and the reasons for this difference in accessibility are especially relevant when we consider withdrawn children. An image is apt to be more intense, more focused, yet less explicit. In an image, a person is not 'named' and this relative inexplicitness may well be one way of escaping censorship. Withdrawal often reflects a heightened degree of censorship, so any means that bypass censorship and keep communications flowing must be welcome (Horowitz, 1971).

In making a palpable object, we discover we can make our own transitional object and this discovery again in itself can excite and encourage a withdrawn child. A child's paintings, drawings, sculpturings in clay or plasticine, collages etc., may be seen as an aspect of play, and read as transitional phenomena bridging unconscious with conscious, self with outside world. The productions are closely analogous to a dream, and as such are self-reflective or recursive exercises, areas for transformation, and studies in life style. In a painting, a child often captures moments of being, in a non-verbal, pre-verbal, as well as a verbal form (painting with a story).

Paintings are frequently about objects, human and non-human, about things that happen to objects including ourselves, and so about events which we can come to describe, a form of the healing fiction (see Hillman, 1983). But they can also represent more abstract elusive experiences which stand in their own right and are somehow reduced by attempts to translate them into words. 'It's a pattern' a child painter will often say when asked to explain his picture, partly in order to keep intruders at bay (they will be told if and when the moment is ripe), partly because if a painting can be explained in words, why take the trouble to paint it? Similar comments have been made of their respective media by musicians and dancers.

In this and other ways, a painting can take on magic qualities: that of a talisman or a scapegoat. Being by its nature a focal point, it in turn becomes a focus of relations, receiving and transmitting projections from child or therapist alike (see Schaverien, 1982, 1987, 1989).

Organised and improvised paintings

A distinction already encountered in play was that between organised pre-structured activities such as a formal game, and looser more self-generating activities such as active imagination or a day dream. The point was made that both forms of play may have a place in work with withdrawn children, some of whom may prefer one type of play, some the other, and many may switch from one type to the other in the course of a day or over a matter of weeks.

A similar distinction may be drawn in the visual arts. A child's paintings may be organised (perhaps in response to adult instruction) or improvisatory. The play-space of the drawing may be purposively limited to a certain topic: a drawing of the family for example with every member doing something, the so-called Kinetic Family Drawing (Burns and Kaufman, 1970); or the completion of a squiggle (Winnicott, 1971). On other occasions, children on their own volition may impose their own limits. They may take great pains to copy the world about them perhaps because they can't escape past indoctrination, perhaps because they intuitively appreciate the value of submitting themselves temporarily to a discipline of observing and recording an image along the lines of a conventional 'life-class'. The image may stem from outside, as it did for the withdrawn Winifred aged four who silently mourning a favourite cat that had died, spent a week drawing the drain-pipe on the wall outside the kitchen window where the icicles hung when the pipes froze. Or the image may arise from within, as it did for John, a withdrawn seven-year-old who couldn't rest till he'd realised the shape and atmosphere of Stonehenge where he'd spent a 'day he'd never forget', the last day he'd seen his father who'd gone missing.

Behind this distinction of organisation and improvisation lie some other related ones: art as therapy or art as education, art as a tool for other purposes (with the hint of behaviourist conditioning) or art as a self-sufficient activity eschewing any suggestions of ulterior motives.

When children say 'I can't paint' or 'I don't know what to paint' or 'I'm no good at painting' or 'what do you want me to paint?', the educationist in us will be inclined to give them a subject and a shove of encouragement; the therapist in us will feel more inclined to suggest they paint whatever they feel like, or question why guidance and assurance is needed. Neither response is right or wrong. Both are determined by context. And whilst at any one point in time, the two may be incompatible, in general the task has to do with relating these two sides of creativity (the thrust from the subject or the thrust from the medium) rather than in keeping them apart. Both sides, education and therapy, can contribute to the play with an image: visual, motor, tactile, verbal or whatever. Both have a place in relieving symptoms of withdrawal.

Case study

Kenneth, a ten-year-old with Downs syndrome had gone into what his mother called a 'brown study', most unlike his usual happy sociable self. He sat at the table for hours making marks with his pencil on a pad, pulling the sheets angrily off the pad and throwing them on the floor. Suddenly after some four days of this moroseness, his face lit up and looking over his shoulder, his mother saw that he'd stumbled on a way of 'doing a face' on paper. He went over the elements of the pattern (the two eye-circles, the nose- and mouth-lines) time and again for a week. The repetitions were entirely of his own devising and were clearly aimed at consolidating his inscape.

Should we call Kenneth's repetitions educational or therapeutic?

In treatment itself, aspects of these distinctions lie at the roots of two different approaches which have been espoused towards this product we call a painting. On the one hand, painting or sculpting may be seen as a form of symbolic speech (Naumberg, 1966, 1975) and thus closely linked with psychotherapy, in which verbal speech is the central medium. On the other hand, the visual arts are seen as ends in themselves, unlinked with, let alone subservient to any other medium. Creating the painting and all that goes into shaping it into what one wants is in itself healing (Kramer, 1971).

Jakab describes the catharsis which can sometimes be achieved by painting a picture without interpretation, comparing the exercise with that of primitive people when they seek relief by modelling their demons, or power by modelling their enemies (Jakab, 1966). With Howard, however, Jakab also reports a case of a child who became phobic after witnessing a suicide, and whose phobia was relieved when she drew the suicide scene and was thereby able to talk about the event (Jakab and Howard, 1969).

Since both approaches have proved their value in relieving symptoms of withdrawal, the guideline would seem to be: take your cue from the child, opting for one or the other as and when seems appropriate.

Painting as encounter

Winnicott's 'squiggle-game' is essentially an informal way of organising doodles, and involving a visual dialogue as a mode of encounter. Once directions are hinted at, the visual images may be talked about visually or in words. In this expansion of the non-verbal into verbal, the painting may become the basis for a story or move in and out of a play-drama.

For the therapist, a number of further communications may arise: with the child himself (his associations to the picture, life at the moment in the treatment hour, and life more generally at home and school); between child and therapist (in the transference which may appear in the paintings themselves, in the sheer offer of the painting as a creative act, or in activities which run parallel to the painting); and within the therapist (the evolving situation within and outside the frame of any particular picture).

Such dialogues with children who at the start are shut in on themselves may run some unexpected courses. Sometimes what seemed a promising beginning peters out. Nothing happens. Resistance? Or have I mis-timed the introduction of the game? More often, however, some sort of dialogue develops, however one-sided.

Case study

Anyone who knew Peter, aged six, knew they were either in the magic circle of those to whom he talked or they weren't. Most of us including me weren't. So when it came to playing squiggles, I had to rely on a dialogue through drawings. It was uphill work and I was never permitted to know whether I'd understood any particular drawing. Over the three months I saw him, he never failed an appointment and the magic circle at home increased by two, including another sibling. So something seemed to be happening.

With Samantha on the other hand, who was also mute in class, the one-way traffic worked in the opposite direction. I was treated to a non-stop monologue for four weeks in the squiggle-game, never being invited to put pen to paper and roundly abused on the one occasion when I did.

Luke a five-year-old whose mother had tried more than once to do away with herself when she was alone with him, for a long time in the squiggle-game insisted on each of our moves being closely tied to each other. He would divide the paper into two equal halves, and I would have to develop events in my half strictly *pari passu* with events he was developing in his. If he got stuck he would pick up and imitate ideas from my half, sometimes growing angry with me for the failure of his own creativity.

Other withdrawn children will come to insist on a strict alternation of turn with all the fervour of a demarcation dispute. The recognition of turns is not only a comforting rule which orientates them, but an assurance that they are being treated with some show of equality.

Then again variations may be woven on the number of improvisatory media which are introduced and blended with the original squiggle. Tina, aged eight, could only speak her mind when 'she wasn't herself', when that is she was acting a part. So before long her squiggles would be dramatised with a free flow of exhortation, *cri de coeur*, and invective, in all of which I would be so deeply involved it was quite a task for both of us to leave the theatre at the end of the session.

For withdrawn children, it is never safe to assume that what comes over in a painting is the only message that was intended. The painting is a social event, done for someone, willingly or otherwise. It's a communication in which much or little of oneself may be included, intentionally or not. There may be purposeful or unconscious deceptions of painter or viewer. What are we to make for example of events described in a family drawing? Are these what the child actually saw? What he wants us to believe he saw? What he wants to distract us into believing he saw, like a mother bird distracting intruders from the nest? And all this is further complicated by whether the painting was offered spontaneously or in response to a 'friendly' suggestion.

It is tempting for the therapist to think he's on surer ground with those paintings which reflect feelings directed at (or transferred on to) him or which evoke feelings in him. As a general guideline such a thought is justified but there are many catches. Withdrawn children will sometimes reveal their feelings quite openly. Directly or through the painting, they convey their love or hate. They 'can't wait' till the next meeting or can't abide the prospect. More often though, the feelings are ambiguous. Ninetta a timid eleven-year-old sought to captivate and subdue me by the 'gift' of a painting 'for you and your wife if you have one'. Simon, a devious mischievous silent ten-year-old, saw me and my co-worker as dangerous persecutors, waiting to pounce and put him into care. His paintings were barbed gifts designed to pin us both down and put us out of action.

In his caricatures of his pompous headmaster, along with a string of epithets that all too frequently appear in reports (selfish, indolent, careless, disinterested, a mess) Hugh, aged fourteen, sought to convey his sense of isolation, and a Hobbesian dissatisfaction over the injustices of life. By trusting me with the drawing, he was also warning me that as an adult, for a long time I was likely to be on the receiving end of feelings very like those he entertained towards the teacher. It was my privilege to be his guide, confidant and target. In similar fashion, Winifred whose painting of the frozen drain outside the window was mentioned earlier often delighted in teasing me by scribbling over the paintings she'd done in the session, seeking to undo in this and other ways the work we'd done together.

Perhaps the important thing about these paintings loaded as they are with ambiguous feelings is the opportunity they provide for reflecting basic modes of relating, basic styles of behaving. Their exposure in the present, their self-mirroring, gives withdrawn children the option of retaining, modifying or jettisoning whatever bits of themselves they choose. These experiences are part of the containing frame, from which the child can grow. The frame refers to the conditions under which the painting is done as well as to the form and content of the product.

Themes in painting

Out of an infinite number of possible themes, there is space in this chapter to cover only four which crop up fairly frequently in the paintings of withdrawn children: dreams, the body, the family and a life style.

The similarities between play, painting and dreams has already been noted. What sometimes happens in addition is that a child who has had a frightening experience in a dream decides to record it in a drawing as part of a move to encompass the fear.

Case study

Nicola's teacher–parents grew increasingly worried as they saw their daughter change from a lively sociable twelve-year-old, the hub of the class, to a recluse who in the end refused to go to school. 'Is she anorexic?' they kept asking themselves and anyone else they thought might know. It turned out that the girl was terrified of being sick. She had been ever since she watched a late TV film on exorcism. An image from this film kept cropping up in her dreams and in the end, she managed to extrude it into a painting which she called: the Great Green Splurdge. Having transformed this dream-image into a painting, Nicola was able to proceed on to some of the issues which were being covered by this 'screen' experience.

One of the first systems which is contained in, contains or is developed in any painting is the body. As the seat of sensuality or of the ego, the body has served as the kernel of visual expression from earliest times, both personal and cultural. The representation of the body directly or in metaphor, the ramifications of body imagery provide a central theme through the history of art (see for example Clark, 1956; Rawson, 1978; Lucie-Smith, 1972; Blacking, 1977).

Certain areas of the body especially those relating to sexuality and fertility have long been singled out for particular attention: the genitals, breasts, buttocks, face and hand. Fascination with these areas does not escape the attention of children, least of all withdrawn children whose withdrawal often arises from some anxiety, shame or guilt about their body and its natural functions. The body fantasies described in the psychoanalytic literature of children or adults are re-created in drawings sometimes explicitly, sometimes in a more veiled, defended fashion.

The phallus can crop up priapically in the most unexpected places. Hugo, a shy Dutch nine-year-old suddenly gave his mother one in the shape of a large Easter egg on a celebratory card he prepared for her on Mother's Day. The head or a bit of the head such as the tongue may replace the phallus symbolically as the mouth may replace the vagina. (Consider Magritte's condensations and displacements in his picture of 'Rape'.) Parts standing for other parts may decrease or increase in number.

Case study

Zachary aged five had secretly been worrying for some time about a proposed operation for an undescended testicle. He got confused when the doctor and his parents tried to explain, didn't trust them, and became convinced he was the sacrificial lamb, destined to be changed into a woman. He stopped talking to people. Fortunately when he came to see me, he drew a picture of himself in which he omitted two fingers of his right hand. When he spotted this omission himself without any comment from me, we both laughed and he put it right. Then he aired his anxieties and confusions about the forthcoming operation.

With Henrietta the parts increased rather than diminished.

Case study

Henrietta had her first epileptic attack when she was seven. The state of confusion into which she was thrown disturbed her deeply, not least because she was no longer sure she could control her limbs. They might just fly off out of the window and be lost. In a self-portrait done at this time, she sought to counteract this threatened centrifugal dispersal by multiplying her body parts after the fashion of ancient Indian goddesses. Safety in numbers she seemed to be saying. If one goes, another can always replace it.

After the body physical, the body-politic and for children that usually means the family in the first instance. The significance of different family-members may sometimes be gleaned from the sequence in which they are drawn. Who goes first and last? Who goes together? What is the distance between any pair? And between the painter and another? Hugo, the Dutch boy who gave his mother a phallus, clustered his family together on a single page. Simon, the fount of devious mischief, painted himself first as a wasp on one page and then allotted each family-member (markedly shrunk) a separate page, the better to pick them off one by one. He included as a prominent sibling his pet mouse.

The house as an extension of the self or the family is frequently given significant treatment. For Henrietta, the epileptic girl, her house like her limbs was under constant threat of being dispersed. Though she lived in a detached home, the house she drew was put in the middle of a terrace, with exactly similar houses arranged symmetrically on either side of it, anchoring it down. For Tina, who could only drop her withdrawal when she was acting a part, her house was an elaborately detached, theatrical creation set in the middle of a park, though in reality she lived on the second floor of a highrise. Other frequent variations on the house theme include: the context of the home (street, urban or rural, terrace, detached); the garden and its function; the disposition of rooms and the support walls lend to rivalries and extrusions.

In many of their family drawings, withdrawn children broach an issue which will be taken up again in the next chapter: the paradoxes and absurdities which are part of family life, as they are part of human development.

Case study

Hugh, the adolescent with a Hobbesian view of life sought to celebrate his escape from adults particularly his parents (on whom he'd come to depend like a leech) in a denigrating picture of his father as the penurious 'old guy' begging for a penny. In this lampooning of paternity, he quickly realised he was posing himself a problem over reaching and confirming his own manhood.

The route into paradox often involves some link between painting and those literary critical idioms which reflect life styles and some of which such as satire, irony, the grotesque (see for example Thomson, 1972) contain inbuilt elements of paradox. In the previous chapter, we saw how Stuart used the grotesque to articulate his stifled comments on the monstrous regiment of older women who surrounded him.

In somewhat similar vein, the theatre of the absurd crept into the narrative of Tina's over-dramatised paintings. Farce peppered the diverging series of drawings by Aziz, a restrained Kenyan Asian eleven-year-old whose induction into English society seemed for a while mainly through his addiction to comic cartoons on the television. When she finished her careful picture of the drain as a first phase of mourning, Winifred started a satirical illustrated poem on the theme of Who Killed Cock Robin as the next phase.

Withdrawn children use painting as an exploration of life-style and as a focus for cross-media expression. The root experiences of body-imagery provide a basis for the imagery of body-politic in family or school. The critical idioms and their accompanying patterns of life-style grow out of these body-experiences.

One final analogy may be mentioned: that between the paintings of these withdrawn children (especially as play and recorded dream) and the life-style of Surrealism. There is the same fascination with collage and transmodal communication; the same attempt to bridge levels of consciousness through the use of improvisatory techniques (such as squiggles); the same embrace of chance and the more tentative embrace of paradox; the same search for a release from the deadening hand of convention, text-book rules and dry restrictive super-ego voices.

References

Blacking, J. (1977) (ed.) *Anthropology of the Body*. London, New York and San Francisco, Academic Press.

Burns, R. C. and Kaufman, S. H. (1970) *Kinetic Family Drawings*. New York, Bruner/Mazel.

Clark, K. (1956) *The Nude*. London, John Murray.

Feder, E. and Feder, B. (1981) *The Expressive Arts Therapies: Art, Music, and Dance as Psychotherapy*. New Jersey, Prentice-Hall.

Hillman, J. (1983) *Healing Fiction*. New York, Station Hill.

Horowitz, M. J. (1971) The use of graphic images in psychotherapy, *American Journal of Art Therapy*, **10**, 3, 156.

Jakab, I. (1966) Coordination of verbal psychotherapy and art therapy, *Psychiatry and Art*, **2**, 95.

Jakab, I. and Howard, M. C. (1969) Art therapy with a 12-year old girl who witnessed a suicide and developed a school phobia, *Psychotherapy Psychosom*, **17**, 323.

Jung, C. G. and Kerenyi, C. (1963) *Essays on a Science of Mythology: The Myths of the Divine Child and the Divine Maiden*. New York and Evanston, Harper Torch Books (Bollingen Library).

Kramer, E. (1971) *Art as Therapy with Children*. New York, Schocken Books.

Langer, S. K. (1982, first published 1941) *Philosophy in a New Key: A Study in the Symbolism of Reason, Rite and Art*. Cambridge, Mass., Harvard University Press.

Langer, S. K. (1959) *Feeling and Form*. London, Routledge & Kegan Paul.

Lucie-Smith, E. (1972) *Eroticism in Western Art*. London, Thames & Hudson.

Naumberg, M. (1966) *Dynamically Oriented Art Therapy: Its Principles and Practice*. New York, Grune & Stratton.

Naumberg, M. (1975) Spontaneous art in education and psychotherapy, in E. Ulman and P. Dachinger *Art Therapy in Theory and Practice*. New York, Schocken Books.

Rawson, P. (1978) *The Art of Tantra*. London, Thames & Hudson.

Schaverien, J. (1982) Transference in Art Therapy, *Inscape*, September, **10**.

Schaverien, J. (1987) The scapegoat and talisman: transference in art therapy, in T. Dalley *et al. Images of Art Therapy*. London, Tavistock.

Schaverien, J. (1989) Transference and the picture, *Inscape*, Spring, **14**.

Thomson, P. (1972) *The Grotesque*, in The Critical Idiom series edited by John Jump. London, Methuen.

Winnicott, D.W. (1971) *Therapeutic Consultations in Child Psychiatry*. London, Hogarth.

CHAPTER 13

Treating Withdrawn Children by the Use of Music

Robin Higgins

The distinctive characteristics of music: its relevance to withdrawal and return

Compared with the visual arts, the product in music and music-making is much more ephemeral. Snatched out of nothing, dissolving into nothing, musical experience can of course be notated but only comes alive when we leave the written page behind. This very quality of transience, ephemerality, is in itself quite close to experiences in withdrawal when the solidity of other people and one's own self or body may be subject to questioning and doubt. But in addition, because of the infinite possibilities implicit in making something out of nothing, the medium of music provides a milieu for events which range from Dionysian frenetics (pure emotion) to Apollonian calm (pure reason). In the treatment of withdrawn children, this wide-ranging spectrum can be a rich and never-ending resource.

Case study

Walter was a retiring seven-year-old whose symptoms of withdrawal included the apparent suppression of all emotion. His voice was flat, and usually little more than a whisper. Since his earliest days at school, he was a loner. He slowly began to re-find feelings when his elder brother gave him a discarded Walkman. Walter would spend the evenings on his own locked into cassettes of heavy rock. Gradually he became knowledgeable about the different groups and the sounds they made. The first break-through was when he corrected the class know-it-all on a point of rock music, and within the space of a few minutes, became recognised as an authority. The second break-through came at the end of term, when with the aid of a sympathetic teacher, Walter gave a short Christmas concert with his skiffle group.

Hilary was another withdrawn child in the same class as Walter. Her discovery of music followed a different course. She became fascinated like Pythagoras in the details of sound and set up around her house objects that picked up different sound-qualities: rustling, beating, air passing through them like an Aeolian harp. Later she called this 'playing the house'. In her music-making, which unlike Walter's, continued as a solitary pursuit, her interest shifted to transforming the sounds she made, discovering for example that halving the length of a string doubled the frequency of the plucked note, and so bridging her studies in music to those in mathematics.

These two vignettes illustrate some distinctions we've already met in other modes of play among withdrawn children. In music, ideas can grow and be developed in solitude, with one other person, or in a group. Pieces in a highly structured state may be absorbed passively as happens with much listening like Walter's rock groups through his Walkman or they may be actively formed and transformed as Hilary found with her explorations into the origins of sound. Often the two approaches combine tight and loose structures in their active or passive treatment. The choice of approach, like the choice of solitude or group, can stem from the child or be imposed from without. In music as in art, a distinction has been raised between education and therapy.

Case study

When she was with a teacher, Sally a shy apparently conforming twelve-year-old sat down at the piano, played the notes in front of her, and followed the printed dynamic markings as accurately as she could (and indeed as she was encouraged to do). When on her own, she took snippets of the Associated Grade pieces apart and improvised her own variations on them immediately stopping if anyone entered the room where she was supposed to be practising 'properly'. She kept this secret musical life of improvisation hidden for years and only wheeled it out into the open when she joined a jazz-group in her early twenties.

As with the distinction between art education and art therapy, there may lurk behind the distinction between music education and music therapy other differences such as that between a behaviourist and a humanist approach (see Feder and Feder, 1981). But again the complementary links may warrant more attention than the differences. Music-making may indeed be used as an instrument for improving a withdrawn child's capacity to relate in a group as distinct from music-making as a medium for developing spontaneity and authenticity. Structured conditioning techniques may be applied in bringing this improvement about. Once achieved, however, a new type of improvisation may open up and this collective improvisation can sometimes reach the dynamics of the individual child's emotional and intellectual inner life with revelations that can stir and reward.

From earliest times, the experience of music has been recognised as underpinning human experience and influencing the mind (see McClain, 1984a, b). Many cultures have tapped this power in education and healing (see Blacking, 1977). Rycroft noting that none of the pioneers of the unconscious thought naturally in auditory terms speculated on the psychology which might have arisen had they done so: a psychology in which thoughts might be 'conceived of as themes, which can occur in different modes and keys, which can vary in their audibility, which can be harmonious or discordant, and which can undergo development and variation' (Rycroft, 1985). With increasing interest in the use of music in therapy, Rycroft's speculations are now being put to the test.

Music and the body

Again from earliest times a close association has always existed between music and dance. Both are concerned particularly with the unfolding of events in time, with the ebb and flow of tensions and release, and with the embodiment of ideas and feelings. In dance, the frame is movement as filtered through the body. In music, the frame is sound as filtered through selected regions of the body: the ear, voice, hand, feet, skin, muscles, endocrines. There is a constant translation from one frame into the other. Consider for a start the dance of a conductor communicating through the written score with the seated orchestra.

Case study

Shari, an African five-year-old stayed silent and morose during the singing class. She took no part in it and the teacher wondered if she was deaf. One day, this same teacher noticed the little girl dancing in a corner of the play ground and singing the song she'd refused to have anything to do with ten minutes earlier. The music it seemed made no sense to her unless it could be danced.

As we have already seen, for withdrawn children, experiences about their body can prove a crucial area in prompting and dissolving withdrawal. So the link between music and dance with its central focus on embodiment and transmodal communication, can be particularly significant in this respect. Withdrawn children are often out of tune with their bodies. They may move awkwardly, their co-ordination impaired. In these instances, music especially in the form of rhythm can act as an integrating structuring force. Moreover the sense of rhythm with its driving organising and co-ordinating qualities, can be transferred to areas of the withdrawn child's experience other than the strictly musical. The effect of such transfer along with the possibility of unrestricted repetition is often effective for all types of withdrawal but particularly those associated with physical handicap or mental retardation (Alvin, 1976). This same rhythmic structure within the music may carry over into the setting of the music-making. Many withdrawn children find it hard to resist the pull of the drum-band. Huddled in a corner against the grain of all their defences, they suddenly find their feet tapping with a Rumba or even a march. Rhythm entrains, gently locking the listener into its beat.

Rhythm

The rhythmic structures of music, then with their accompanying driving, energising and ordering forces (Gaston, 1968) often provide a welcome base for the withdrawn child's journey of return. A repetitive beat ensures a sense of continuity whose impairment lies so often at the roots of a child's withdrawal. The pleasure in sheer repetition which informs so many fairy tales and stanzaic poetry may exert a winning appeal to come back from the shadows (see Coriat, 1945). Sometimes with autistic children, the repetition from without can tune into the compulsive repetition from within and in so doing constitute the first move in dislodging the fixed state.

The various rhythms of the body underpin this power of rhythms in general to hold a child whose sense of support may be wavering. One of the simplest of such rhythms is that of the heart-beat or pulse. A comatose patient can sometimes be contacted by the simple move of quietly singing a tune in the rhythm of their pulse rate (Aldridge *et al.*, 1990).

Case study

Giles, a reticent three-year-old who resisted cuddling, always chose the same tune on which to curl up on his mother's lap before dropping off to sleep. The tune adhered to a strict metrical beat which was exactly half the pace of his own heart beat.

The heart beat may not always be experienced as regular. Hearts like anything else can be played with.

Case study

Hiram a four-year-old withdrawn to the point of autism, broadcast with the tapping of his foot a rhythm that more or less followed the pace of his pulse but was eccentric. When the teacher copied this rhythm, she found it consisted of alternating 5 and 7 beat bars. The manner in which the copying was done might have been labelled 'mirroring'. But a better term would have been 'resonating' the message the child was seeking to convey. Once he realised his rhythm was being picked up in this fashion, Hiram smiled and started to vary it. A dialogue had begun.

(For a more detailed description of musical mirroring in the treatment of autistic children see Nordoff and Robbins, 1965.)

Beating a drum can often provide an opportunity not only to express inner feelings of pent up anxieties and tensions but also as with Hiram to express a slow move from the eccentricity of erratic beats to a mergence with a steady assured regularity and to the confirmation that he has it in his control to decide when and how he merges. In this last respect, he employed the same means of keeping the environment at arm's length till he was ready to receive it as Walter with his Walkman which to begin with would be played at full blast to prove every sound in the outside world other than the selected few could be filtered out.

The heart-beat is only one among many body-rhythms which can be picked up and resonated on their own or in combination. The intake and outflow of air in breathing, the tensing and relaxing of voluntary or involuntary muscles, even the entrainment of alpha-rhythms in the brain, provide other well-recognised patterns for rhythm exchange with children whose sense of rhythmic connection may have temporarily gone awry.

Nor is there any reason to stop with rhythm as conventionally defined when, as Stockhausen among others has shown, rhythms and pitch are on the same continuum of vibrations, pitch being no more than speeded up rhythm. Examples of presenting and resonating pitch experiences with a child who feels an outcast would include the identification of a favourite tune, a favourite 'sound-scape', or the moulding of a sound into a favourite geometrical shape (square, circle, triangle) which then plays on a particular emotional set (see tapes of Soundshapes by Lawrence Ball).

Besides rhythm and pitch, other musical dimensions available for establishing 'resonance' are those which have close affinity with dance: tempo, direction (is the music moving forwards, sideways, backwards? Is it moving in a straight line, curving or meandering?), dynamics including weight and effort.

In the previous chapter, we saw what an important part a squiggle can play in aiding a withdrawn child to find his confidence, stability and identity. An analogous squiggle game can be arranged using sound instead of drawings.

Case study

Hiram repeatedly came back to exploring the drum. When he came into the class-room in the morning, he never went directly to the instrument, which he insisted the teacher keep apart on the top shelf. He would sit in his corner watching the other children arrive and as soon as they were settled to their various games, he'd ask the teacher to fetch it down for him and he'd take it to his corner and for a time would just hold it and stroke it gently. Sometimes he'd smell or lick it as though to make sure it hadn't changed. Tentatively he began to tap it, first with one finger of one hand, and then gradually increase the number of fingers till both hands were involved. Or else he might keep one hand free to beat on the floor while the other beat the drum. Sometimes it seemed all his sounds could thus be drawn from the drum; sometimes he needed an outside source as a counterpoint to orientate the drum-sound.

Towards the end of the first term, Hiram began to introduce nonsense words which he half sang to his drum rhythms. At this point another child might stop in passing and watch him as he played. By the end of the second term, several children were joining in what became known as Hiram's Band.

In the early stage of resonating, the dialogue may appear to be sequential. First the child lays down a pattern, then the adult 'copies', then the child resumes, then the adult and so on. But from the start sometimes, another form of communication evolves in which the messages are telegraphed simultaneously. Like a well-attuned duo of soloist and accompanist, or like two expert tennis-players, each harbours a strong sense of what the other's going to do before he does it. This interactive rhythm (Davis, 1982) can become a central component in dissolving withdrawals because in general, it is only safe to be genuinely separate when we have experienced being together.

Music as space-time

I have already touched on the idea of potential space and the key part this plays in all modes of play. Whenever we seek to organise a body of thought, we turn inevitably to a spatial image. Music is specially relevant here in part because of the parallels which exist between the 'spaces' of music and human development. In music, where we are engaged in an unfolding process, the spatial image is more appropriately described as space-time, but in any event, the expansion occurs in two directions: outwards in the world around us, and inwards in the texture of the music itself.

Outwards, music comes from a source, which rises from within or outside oneself. Our distance from the source without can be varied. We can get closer to or further from it and in this connection, we develop a sense of personal space in which an outside source can sometimes feel comfortably sited and sometimes intrusive. Withdrawn children are often sensitive about any such intrusion. One of the reasons they withdraw is to give themselves 'room to breathe', and that means being far enough away from threatening sounds however seemingly friendly.

Inwards, the sense of musical space arises from the layers in between silence and sound; from the layers in a single sound between the fundamental, overtones, combination tones, etc.; and from the layers in a musical pattern which like a psychic pattern has been described as having a fore-, middle-, and back- or ur-ground (see Sloboda, 1985). These layers may be conceived as static, like floors in a house, or dynamic, like a spiral (see Purce, 1974). They entail levels of perception at any one moment and of experience (memory). Each layer is a distillation of what lies above. We may reach down to the core (the ur-stuff) or up to the surface. In either movement we draw on means for linking the levels such as symbols and the translating or transcending functions.

For purposes of our work with children moving in or out of withdrawal, the interesting feature about musical space-time is the parallels it suggests with more recent models of human development, and so with those occasions which give rise to withdrawal or its resolution. A model which is gaining increasing recognition in our understanding of the earliest years in development suggests a series of successive levels or selves closely analogous to the successive layers of musical patterns described above. In these successive selves (emergent, core, subjective, verbal), the later levels sprout from, develop and coexist with the earlier. All four selves inhabit an expanding psychological space, just as the musical levels inhabit an ever changing and expanding musical space (see Stern, 1985).

Withdrawal occurs when a crisis crops up over the connection of one level with another and the closeness of the model which music can provide can sometimes in itself offer suggestions for reconnection. The way in which in a piece of music the deepest structures can be picked up, examined and put down again for something more superficial gives a withdrawn child confidence to do the same for his own deep structures.

It is along these lines that music-making can sometimes be the medium for expressing internal fantasies including obsessions and phobias. It can sometimes provide a bridge for reaching back into the unconscious just as painting provides a bridge for dreams. The medium of music becomes a transitional object both in its context and its content. This aspect of music as a medium has been particularly noted in those children who are withdrawn to the point of autism (Feder and Feder, 1981).

Music as encounter

The parallels between the hierarchical models of music and human development are not always in themselves sufficient inducement for reconnection. Another reason why these reconnecting suggestions win acceptance lies in music-making being seen by withdrawn children as coming from a world untainted by the stigma of illness (let alone psychiatric illness). As with expressive drawings, music-making is felt to be a normal integrative experience like remembering or dreaming and not a painful lapse into the humiliating position of being a patient. Truants from life have often already had their fill of being pressganged into 'cures'. It comes to them as a great relief to discover that there is no sick or well music and that, among the performers, the well are sometimes more crippled than the ill.

Music is a non-threatening way of meeting up with others. Children withdraw from social relations in part because they are embarrassed by them. They don't know how to handle them. They feel self-conscious. In the impersonal atmosphere of making music this embarrassment can often be lifted. In music the focus on the activity may divert the focus on interpersonal relations which can then be approached more indirectly.

As with the visual arts, the making of music in a group offers withdrawn children an opportunity to lay down a statement to which others have to listen, to play a part where they are implicitly accepted. Music-making can sometimes shift the whole emphasis from asymmetric relations of superior and inferior. Whether on a one-to-one or a group basis, making music implies a degree of cooperation. It is this sense of acceptance, this ceasing to feel a pariah, that can draw life-truants from their closed worlds of sanctuary or prison back into life again.

Some common themes in music-making with the withdrawn child: variation, inversion and paradox

The ephemeral nature of music is one reason why a universal form is that of theme and variation. The theme as repetition, continuity, holding, represents consolidation; variation, as movement away from the centre, represents the escalation of excitement and suspense. For withdrawn children, saddled with doubts and self-questioning, it is not hard to see why theme and variations figure so prominently in the music they make. Ultimately reaching base can never be in question. But a lot of mileage can be got from exploring all manner of routes in getting there.

Theme and variation is often a game withdrawn children have played from infancy. Every time it recurs, it picks up earlier patterns which contain clues about the origins and resolution of withdrawal.

Case study

When Hiram moved on from nonsense songs he repeatedly came back to a Beatles number which must have been around when he was an infant. He would start and end his Band with this song, and in between he would often play variations on it sometimes with the most tenuous of connections. Once when singing this number, he acted a short drama about a couple rowing and separating and it became clear that this Beatles song was playing the same role in his memory as Ach Du Liebe Augustin played in Mahler's. He always returned to this song when he was troubled even though he'd clearly located its point of origin and exorcised some of the associated pain.

Variations occur as transmutability, as putting the same foot into the changing river. They may also occur as comparisons, as something different, contrasting, the opposition which realises the definition. Our appreciation of opposites plays a fundamental part in our distinction of ourselves as separate entities, in the discovery of what is my body (and in due course of what is me) from what is not. On our capacity to relate opposites rests our capacity to define ourselves, to merge with our surrounds and to transcend our self-boundaries. Periods of withdrawal often go with a struggle to recognise and cope with opposites.

An essential move in relating opposites is the operation of inversion, which means turning something upside down, a favourite exercise of a withdrawn child as already noted. Now it happens that the world of music is full of such tricks. There are for example the inversions that switch the melody into its accompaniment (or vice versa) a favourite trick of Haydn's; there are inversions representing contrasts in pace and dynamics. There are the more formal and exact inversions of pitch, rhythm and sequence. Inverting is a perfectly respectable activity in music. So for withdrawn children whose heads may be full of fantasies about the Lord of Misrule, updated as Mick Jagger or Michael (I am bad) Jackson, the respectability of inversions in music can often bring all-round relief. The urge to turn things upside down is no longer a thought which has to be hidden and denied.

A third feature arising out of a variation is paradox, an issue whose wide ramifications can only be touched on briefly here (for a fuller review see Zaehner, 1970 and Slaate, 1968). A paradox occurs when the two sides of an opposition cannot be resolved; it is the simultaneous irresolvable presentation of two contradictions. The capacity to use words, a function of the verbal self we met earlier when discussing levels of development, presents us with one of our earliest paradoxes. For on the one hand this capacity provides us with tools of enormous creative power. On the other hand, this same capacity faces us starkly not only with a number of uncomfortable paradoxical bases on which all human experience is founded, but also with potentially severe limitations on our transmodal communications, our sixth sense of intuition.

Some of the confusions which characterise withdrawn children especially those with an intelligent curiosity, stem from an intimation of paradox at the centre of their world. They do not always find it easy (who does?) to accept these paradoxes and not attempt to resolve them.

It is a common experience among those working with families and children, that the identification and articulation of a paradox in their behaviour may sometimes suffice to bring about a move from a long-sustained impasse. Winnicott's own case studies (Winnicott, 1971) are full of examples: Robin who goes forwards by going backwards; Ashton who gets excited at the interpretation that his abstract drawings represent simultaneous acceptance and refusal. The Milan School of family therapy focused their theoretical base on defining the paradox in the family system (Palazzoli *et al.*, 1981).

Once again, it so happens that paradox is a central experience in music. Its identification can take a number of forms. There is first the idea we met at the beginning of this chapter: the weaving something out of nothing, 'snatching sounds out of the air' as Elgar said. Or in Mahler's words, the need for musical expression starts only 'where the dark emotions begin, at the other world, the world in which things are not any more separated by time and place' (Kohut, 1955). Sound as a transitional object is both there and not-there, and if there, both outside and inside me.

Case study

Hilary searched in the piano to find the sound which was all around but couldn't be seen. She was looking for the roots to all her experiments, the alchemists' stone. Peering into the belly of the piano, she fought for weeks against having to accept that there is no such magical solution or resolution. How can one be both in control and not in control of one's own destiny?

Then again, Hilary's music came to her in her dreams, from a cavern, from the deep waters. But she had no say in when or how it came and she found that deeply puzzling. It might overwhelm her suddenly or leave her waiting for weeks. She didn't know where to search for it, or how to tame it when it took her. Slowly she tried to shape it in her voice or under her hands. But it was never the same twice.

Perhaps the biggest paradox in music is that in so many different ways it creates and destroys at one and the same time.

Case study

Andrew's mother was ill. He was desperate to fashion her a song, something that would really stir her and wake her up for his fifth birthday. He wanted to find a new sound for his singing and so he secretly took one of her glass jars which he knew she valued and which he'd discovered produced a wonderful sound when struck lightly with a finger. He started to rehearse a song-dance around this jar, touching it, and responding with a line of song when it spoke, touching and responding. The excitement mounted so did the intensity of shout and blow. In the end, one blow too many nudged the vase off the edge of the table. It shattered.

Song, wrote Schneider, is a sounding sacrifice of the breath of life (Schneider, 1957).

In Conclusion

In these three chapters, I have sought to show that a number of options are open to anyone who uses play in its general or more specific modes (visual arts, music, movement) when treating a withdrawn child.

The child may play on his or her own for long hours at a stretch, openly or secretly (day-dreaming, wrapped in alert inactivity, silently thinking). Or drawings, music, a dance may be made with one other person. Or general and specific play may occur in a group: in the family, at school, in the street, or with a collection of other children chosen by themselves or by somone else.

The different forms the play takes may be graded on a spectrum which runs from the tight structure of an organised game, through the looser structures of an appointed or a suggested task (a family Kinetic drawing, a squiggle, a folk-song, a theme and variation) to spontaneously generated improvisations, the structures growing, changing, developing like the patterns in a dream.

For the withdrawn child, certain common features lie behind all these aspects of play: returning to explore a world from which one had temporarily retired; trying out different possibilities, confirming some, rejecting others; quietly moving into alliances and friendships, coping with competition and hostilities; perhaps above all, exercising a delight in creating fantasies, tossing about ideas in a symbolic, representational even abstract guise rather than the concrete unmalleable guise of everyday life.

Some of the themes that are taken up in the specific modes of play may be shaped by that particular mode. But the ease with which children can slip from one mode into another means that themes like the body or family relations can be equally easily accommodated in a painting, musor a dance, and swiftly transformed from one into another.

Behind all modes of play is the aim of creating and filling a potential space in which the solitary lonely child can find solace and authentic identity in the presence of another.

References

Aldridge, D., Gustorff, D. and Hannich, H-J. (1990) Where am I? music therapy applied to coma patients, *Journal of the Royal Society of Medicine*, **83**, 345.

Alvin, J. (1976) *Music for the Handicapped Child*. Oxford, Oxford University Press.

Blacking, J. (1977) (ed.) *Anthropology of the Body*. London, New York and San Francisco, Academic Press.

Coriat, I. H. (1945) Some aspects of the psychoanalytic interpretation of music, *Psychoanalysis Review*, **32**, 408–18.

Davis, M. (1982) *Interaction Rhythms: Periodicity in Communicative Behaviour*. New York, Human Sciences Press.

Feder, E. and Feder, B. (1981) *The Expressive Arts Therapies: Art, Music, and Dance as Psychotherapy*. New Jersey, Prentice-Hall.

Gaston, E. T. (1968) (ed.) *Music in Therapy*. New York, Macmillan.

Kohut, H. (1955) Review of Theodor Reik's 'The Haunting Melody', *Psychoanalysis Quarterly*, **24**, 134.

McClain, E. G. (1984a) *The Myth of Invariance*. New York, Nicolas-Hays Inc.

McClain, E. G. (1984b) *The Pythagorean Plato*. New York, Nicholas-Hays Inc.

Nordoff, P. and Robbins, C. (1965) *Music Therapy for Handicapped Children*. New York, Steiner Publications.

Palazzoli, M. S., Boscolo, L., Ceccin, G. and Prata, G. (1981) *Paradox and Counterparadox*. London, New York, Jason Aronson.

Purce, J. (1974) *The Mystic Spiral*. New York, Avon Books.

Rycroft, C. F. (1985) *Psychoanalysis and Beyond* p. 115. London, Hogarth.

Schneider, M. (1957) Section on primitive music, in *New Oxford History of Music. Vol. 1)*. Oxford, Oxford University Press.

Slaate, H. A. (1968) *The Pertinence of the Paradox: The Dialectics of Reason-in-existence*. New York, Humanities Press.

Sloboda, J. A. (1985) *The Musical Mind: The Cognitive Psychology of Music*. Oxford, Clarendon Press.

Stern, D. N. (1985) *The Interpersonal World of the Infant*. New York, Basic Books.

Winnicott, D. W. (1971) *Therapeutic Consultations in Child Psychiatry*. London, Hogarth.

Zaehner, R. C. (1970) *Concordant Discord*. London, Oxford University Press.

Index